Dr. Peter Mazareas and John Hupalo's book provides students, parents, and family members an excellent resource that is very thorough and easy to understand. *Plan and Finance Your Family's College Dreams* offers families the extensive (wide-ranging) information about the financial aid process and the guidance needed to establish effective savings and financing plans for a college education at any stage in the student's life.

Bernard (Bernie) Pekala, Director of Student Financial Strategies
Boston College

Two things keep parents, students, and grads from properly and responsibly managing their debt: easy access and accurate information. John Hupalo and Dr. Peter Mazareas adroitly address both at a time when rumors of a crisis loom and young borrowers and their parents need to be more educated on financing, now more than ever before.

Vince Passione, CEO and Founder
LendKey Technologies

The high cost of college and the ensuing student debt has derailed dreams for young people today and, in many cases, led to devastating consequences. That's why this book is such a worthwhile investment—it empowers families to become smart shoppers about their college choices and plot saving strategies that realistically fit their financial circumstances. I highly recommend it.

Bob Carr, Founder and President
Give Something Back Foundation

Plan and Finance Your Family's College Dreams

A PARENT'S STEP-BY-STEP GUIDE FROM PRE-K TO SENIOR YEAR

WITHDRAWN

John A. Hupalo and
Peter Mazareas, Ph.D.

 PETERSON'S®

PETERSON'S®

About Peterson's®

Peterson's®, a Nelnet company, has been your trusted educational publisher for over 50 years. It's a milestone we're quite proud of, as we continue to offer the most accurate, dependable, high-quality education content in the field, providing you with everything you need to succeed. No matter where you are on your academic or professional path, you can rely on Peterson's publications and its online information at **www.petersons.com** for the most up-to-date education exploration data, expert test-prep tools, and the highest quality career success resources—everything you need to achieve your educational goals.

For more information, contact Peterson's, 3 Columbia Circle, Albany, NY 12203-5158; 800-338-3282 Ext. 54229; or visit us online at **www.petersons.com.**

ISBN: 978-0-7689-4080-0

Printed in the United States of America

10 9 8 7 6 5 4 3 2 1   18 17 16

First Edition

Table of Contents

Foreword

Fortunately, there are only two questions that students and families have to answer when it comes to college:

- Can the student get into the school they want?

- How can we pay for it?

Those fifteen simple words sure cause a lot of anxiety for families.

College planning can be a stressful and confusing process and is particularly overwhelming for those who start—or think they start—too late. Many parents feel ill-prepared to deal with the complexities of saving for college and then successfully navigate the college admissions process. The result: Many families simply wait and defer to high school guidance counselors and begin to focus in the child's junior year. Other parents—some in panic mode—employ expensive "college coaches" or "college consultants" to help them with the college process. Either way, the die has already been cast by then, and meaningfully affecting a more positive outcome is quite difficult.

This book is designed for parents with newborns to high school seniors. The primary goal is to demystify the process by providing age-appropriate guidance and information to help you understand how to plan and save for college for children of any age. As parents, we want to increase our child's college options and ensure their success when it is time to select, apply to, and attend the college of their dreams. Starting a savings plan as early as possible contributes to the attainment of that dream by providing increased college options, while minimizing burdensome college loans for you and your child.

Here's what we believe:

- You will be significantly better off if you start planning and saving now—no matter how old your children are or what grade they are in.

Even minimal attention or small amounts of savings will compound and produce larger gains in the future.

- You can take control of the college admission process to minimize the emotional toll on you and your children. This process is not pre-ordained to be an emotionally gut-wrenching, knockdown, drag-out fight. It can actually bring your family closer together at a critical time in the life of all families: when teenagers are spreading their wings to become young adults.

- Planning and paying for college is a family affair. The decisions you make for your first child are likely to have a significant impact on the children that follow, unless, of course, you have just one child.

- The "right college fit" means selecting a school that you can afford, that is a good value, and that offers students an environment in which they can thrive and be successful—socially and academically.

THE CHALLENGE ALL FAMILIES FACE

As a parent, you don't need fancy marketing firms with focus groups to tell you that saving for college and then matching your child with the college of their dreams can be confusing and overwhelming. Why? Because it hits two of our top "hot button" emotional issues: our kids and our finances. It's the daily double of parental fragility and raises all kinds of ancillary questions—not the least of which is: Whose decision is it? Yours or your student's? We know a few things about this:

- There is no correct answer. The final decision maker varies from family to family—and sometimes it's different with each child in the family. There is no "one size fits all" model.

- Preparing for and selecting a college comes at a time when our "kids" are quickly transitioning to young adulthood and increasingly exercising their will to be free of parental control.

Choosing a college may well be a young person's first major life decision—and is likely to be the most expensive one for a decade or more to come! As parents, we want to be supportive but often struggle to determine how best to help. For many, it is also a reality that hard-earned savings are now at risk—savings often resulting from significant sacrifices made over many years. So we have a vested interest not only in wanting our children to be happy and successful but also in knowing there will be a tangible return on that investment.

Notice that we have not talked about the large elephant in the room over which none of us has control: the runaway cost of college. This book is written to provide some navigation tools to deal with issues you can control from the time your child is born through senior year in high school. This book offers concrete steps you can take to best position your children individually and your family as a whole to plan and save for college no matter what happens with the variables we can't control.

AS PARENTS, WE'VE BEEN THERE

Planning and paying for college is an innately emotional process. However, by following our guidance, you can have much more control over the process and outcomes than you may think. Understanding the cost and value of different colleges, your options to establish a consistent savings program, and how to navigate the admissions and financial aid processes early will best position your children (and your family) for personal, academic, and financial success.

Together, we have more than sixty years of professional experience planning and paying for college, including serving as an admissions interviewer for Harvard College for over thirty-six years. Nationally, we have been pioneers, innovators, and leaders in the creation of both the 529 and private credit student loan industries and have positively influenced many of the programs in place today.

With our wives, we have also successfully helped our 5 children, 2 of whom are still in college, successfully navigate the college admissions and financing process. We know firsthand, not just professionally, the real challenges and emotional issues facing both parents and children throughout the college process.

Our goal in writing this book and creating our website, www.InviteEducation. com, is to share our knowledge and experience with you. By providing straightforward information and clear guidance, we want to help you help your child achieve the best possible outcome given his or her goals, abilities, and potential. The outcome parents desire most—successful college graduates with terrific job prospects and minimal debt—can be achieved.

Good luck!

John A. Hupalo

Peter Mazareas, Ph.D.

Introduction

HOW THIS BOOK WILL HELP YOU

No matter the age of your child—newborn or teenager—this book will help you navigate the stressful and complex college financing, academic planning, and admissions process for your child. College planning is common for high school students, but for babies and young children? Yes, within reason. By establishing a systematic savings strategy now, you will help your child have more college options, avoid or minimize long-term student loan debt, and succeed at the school of their dreams.

We want to simplify the process and identify the issues for you by providing age-appropriate guidance and information to help you understand how to best:

- Save for and finance a college education.

- Prepare your child well in advance for the college admissions process.

In the end, we all desire a common outcome: a college graduate with a well-paying job and minimal or no student loan debt. That goal can be achieved with some good age-appropriate planning.

Although circumstances are completely different for every family, the issues that families deal with in saving for college, gaining admission to the right college, and paying for college are universal.

To help you develop a meaningful plan for your family, this book is divided into three parts:

- **Part 1**—Financing College
- **Part 2**—Preparing for and Applying to College
- **Part 3**—Pulling It All Together

The Appendixes include:

- A list of 529 College Savings Plans by state.
- An introduction to www.InviteEducation.com, an online, mobile accessible program that complements this book. It provides grade-by-grade guidance in even greater detail; an easy-to-use savings and college-cost financial planner; a search engine for colleges, scholarships, and 529 plans; links to important websites, and the ability to save important information and receive automated e-mail alerts for critical deadlines.

PART 1: FINANCING COLLEGE

Chapter 1: Saving for College—Start Now!

Here you'll find information about why and how to save for college:

- For younger children, establishing a consistent, disciplined savings plan—even small amounts—over a longer period of time is preferable to socking away a few more dollars each month over a shorter period. Learn about the Rule of 70, types of tax-advantaged college savings programs and investment vehicles, and how to identify which is best for your unique circumstances.
- For older children, recognize that it's never too late to start saving to defray future college expenses. A dollar saved in high school will earn interest and help defray costs later in college. Saving a dollar today yields a far more favorable result for a student than borrowing a dollar tomorrow and saddling them (or you) with future interest costs and debt repayments.

Chapter 2: 529 Plans—An Excellent College Savings Vehicle

For many families, the tax-advantaged 529 College Savings Plans provide the greatest benefits for long-term college savings. This chapter identifies the important savings issues for you to consider:

- Learn about the 10 most important benefits, including the favorable tax treatments that allow you to save now without paying tax on the earnings.
- Understand the difference between types of 529 plans: Prepaid Tuition Plans and Savings Accounts, as well as in-state and out-of-state plans. Learn about the various and different investment options and portfolios available to you.
- Find answers to 30 Commonly Asked Questions on tax benefits, setting up accounts, ownership and control, beneficiaries, investments, financial aid implications, and prepaid tuition accounts.
- Gain expert tips to create your family's college savings plan.

Chapter 3: Financial Aid Primer—The Basics

Here, you will find an overview of all you need to know about the college financial aid process. This chapter explains:

- Terms such as Cost of Attendance, Expected Family Contribution, the FAFSA® and CSS/Financial Aid PROFILE®, need- vs. merit-based aid, Federal vs. Institutional Aid Award Methodology, and more.
- Sources of financial aid and how to differentiate the types of aid available.

Chapter 4: Scholarships—Get Free Money

This chapter will help you understand the world of scholarships and grants:

- The differences among the different types of grants and scholarships.
- Third-party vs. institutional grants and scholarships.
- When to begin the search.
- How scholarships affect financial aid packages.

Chapter 5: Student Loans—Finding the Right Balance

Student loans are often a necessary evil for families to complete their financing package for a college. You'll find the following helpful information in this chapter:

- An easy-to-follow overview of the two primary types of loan programs—the government's Direct Loan Program and private lenders' programs—to help you determine how best to sensibly include student loans in your college financing plan.

- Four keys to understanding borrowing for college and the basic terms associated with student loans.

- Expert tips to create your family's loan plan.

Chapter 6: Tax Benefits for Higher Education—Tax Credits and Deductions

Here, you will find a brief overview of the most popular federal tax programs including:

- Tax credit programs, such as the American Opportunity Credit and the Lifetime Learning Credit.

- Tax deduction programs, such as the Student Loan Interest Deduction and the Tuition and Fees Deduction.

- Tax consequences of receiving a scholarship.

PART 2: PREPARING FOR AND APPLYING TO COLLEGE

Chapter 7: The College Admissions Process—Prepare, Prepare, Prepare

College admissions planning and preparation formally commences in the junior year. If you wait until then, however, you and your student will be behind and will play catch-up in the admissions process. This chapter identifies important preparation steps and admissions process issues for you to consider:

- Social Media Alert: It's time for your student to clean up his or her social media accounts.

- Important actions your freshman, sophomore, and junior should take to set the academic and extracurricular foundation to build a successful high school record that can be the ticket to the college he or she wants to attend.

- Supporting your senior as he or she prepares and submits the very best college application. How students present their story on the application, including grades, test scores, essays, accomplishments, and letters of recommendation, will make the difference in the decision: accepted, rejected, or wait-listed.

- Detailed discussion of the standardized exams. Which test(s) should be taken? How many times?

Chapter 8: The College Application—Pulling It All Together

The big drum roll to college is now underway as the college application deadlines near. We will guide you through the steps necessary for you to help your child prepare to build their college portfolio as they enter high school to ensure that you both understand what it takes for admission to the college of their dreams. If the goal is to gain admission to a highly selective school, specific strategies can be developed and decisions made as early as freshman year to best position your child. Regardless of the type of college (public or private, large or small), know the nuts and bolts of the process that is common to all schools. By understanding the admissions process, criteria, timelines, and requirements, you can make the process less stressful and increase your student's opportunity for success in the competitive admissions process. This chapter:

- Outlines the college application process, including Early Action and Early Decision options.

- Introduces the types of applications, including the Common Application, the Universal College Application, and others.

- Gives tips on writing college essays, having a successful college interview, maximizing the impact of letters of recommendation, and reconsideration strategies for wait-listed or rejected candidates.

Chapter 9: Financial Aid—The Second Application Process

Every family wants to know: "Will we qualify for financial aid?" and, if so, "how much financial aid will we get?" These are "THE" questions haunting most parents. Often, they are nearly impossible to quickly answer. The answers depend not only on your financial circumstances at time of application but also on the credentials of your student, their potential eligibility for merit-based aid, and the admissions goals and availability of financial aid funds at each particular college or university.

This chapter identifies the important financial aid issues for you to consider:

- Understand the different kinds of financial aid in the offer. Is it free money or must it be earned or repaid? Is it merit- or need-based aid?
- See the sources of aid, the key dates in the financial aid process, and key factors that colleges weigh when determining merit aid.
- Be sure to know what the Base Year is, and follow the seven steps to appeal for more financial aid to help make the college more affordable.
- Learn how your Expected Family Contribution (EFC) drives the sticker price of college for your family. What goes into it? What you can do to lower your EFC.

Chapter 10: Filing the Financial Aid Forms—It's Worth the Effort

Government programs require government forms. In this case, it's the Free Application for Financial Aid (FAFSA®). Not to be outdone, some colleges require an additional form, the CSS/Financial Aid PROFILE®, in order to qualify for their institutional aid. This chapter identifies and explains in detail the required financial aid forms and issues for you to consider:

- Step-by-step guidance to obtain and file the FAFSA® and CSS/Financial Aid PROFILE® forms—what they require, when you can access them, and when they're due.
- Ways to manage assets and your Base Year for the most favorable FAFSA® profile and best result in the financial aid process.

PART 3: PULLING IT ALL TOGETHER

Chapter 11: Financial Literacy—For High School and College

In high school, our once little kids quickly mature to become young adults and consumers of financial products. With increasing levels of sophistication, this process continues through college. This chapter focuses on three critical topics for you to introduce to your young adult:

- **Budgeting.** Tips and suggestions to help students and recent graduates understand the basic concepts of budgeting: balancing income, expenses, giving, and saving.

- **Credit Scoring.** Credit scoring modes are very important for future financial transactions, such as procuring loans, renting an apartment, and even applying for a job. Understand why an appropriate level of student loans is an opportunity for students to establish excellent habits for paying bills that will one day result in great credit scores. Know the components of the score and what drives a score up or down.

- **College Loan Refinancing.** Upon graduating from college, many students transition to a new economic reality of having a job and managing their debts. Understanding the trade-offs between lower but longer payments and how that fits into their first post-college budgets is key.

Chapter 12: Create a Family College Plan—You'll Be Glad You Did!

The theme of this chapter is "here's what you need to do." It provides detailed age- and grade-appropriate suggestions in the areas of college affordability, college admissions preparation, and financial literacy for children who are:

- Pre-schoolers through the fifth grade.

- Sixth through eighth grade.

- Each year of high school—ninth through twelfth grades.

Creating a successful college strategy and plan does not need to be cumbersome or time consuming. Your plan evolves as your child's abilities and interests become apparent and your financial circumstances change. Your family's college plan should be based on good decisions that are based on knowledge of the process and timely information, at each step along the way. This chapter provides a systematic way for you to create a plan that makes sense for you.

- Step-by-step guidance through the college application process in high school, with tips on the most important things you can do for your child in each high school grade.

- Financial guidance on how to consider the right savings strategy.

- Ways to maximize eligibility for financial aid and lower your Expected Family Contribution (EFC).

- Tips to help understand the value and true cost of a particular college, the probability of gaining admission to that college, and determining if it is the right "fit" given your child's personality and career interests.

- Age- and grade-appropriate advice on what you can do to develop your student's financial literacy and help him or her make sound college and financial decisions.

HELP YOUR CHILD PLAN, PREPARE, AND SUCCEED

This book will help you develop a clear understanding of the many elements and steps necessary to position your child for future success. For parents with younger children, come back to it as a resource as your child advances from grade to grade. For parents with high school children, follow the timely and valuable road map to navigate the stressful college admissions process. For everyone, it will help you achieve the goal of having a college graduate with a well-paying job and minimal or no debt.

PART ❶

Financing College

Chapter 1

Saving for College—Start Now!

Yes, college is expensive, and getting more so. The costs can be truly breathtaking. So . . . take a deep breath. Relax. If you begin early, a savings plan can be a simple yet effective way to help pay for college. If college is coming soon, saving something now is still preferable to borrowing later.

Consider Aesop's ancient fable about the ant and the grasshopper. In the summer, the ant stores up grains of wheat, while the grasshopper sings and dances. When winter comes, the ant is well prepared, while the grasshopper goes hungry. Today, the ant would have grain piled high in a college savings account, perhaps a Coverdell Education Savings Account, or a Section 529 savings plan, while the grasshopper's college-bound kids would need massive student loans. The moral: Try to save regularly, particularly in a tax-advantaged account.

Thanks to the effects of compound interest, saving and investing even modest sums over time can make a huge difference when the first tuition bill arrives. Using special, tax-advantaged accounts will also enhance your returns. Slowly but surely, these two strategies will maximize the amount you can save, putting the cost of most tuitions within reach.

If your student is about to enter college, you may be thinking that it's too late to start a savings plan. It's not. It may be late to cover all or even a large percentage of college expenses, but it's not too late to offset some of the burden. With at least four years of college expense ahead, whatever you save will likely reduce the amount that might need to be borrowed during the last few years of college. As illustrated in the next pages, saving a dollar today is far better than borrowing one tomorrow.

For all families, the keys to a successful savings strategy include:

- Determining how much you can save and setting up an automatic savings schedule.
- Identifying the savings vehicle and investments that work best for you—preferably those that at least keep pace with tuition inflation.
- Being disciplined about regularly socking away money and contributing some of the child's birthday or holiday gift money.
- Starting right now—there is a big cost to procrastination.

More savings means more options. It means less dependence on grants, scholarships, loans, and other solutions that put your family's future in the hands of others. It also means that cost will be less of a consideration when deciding which schools are best for your children as you will have more options to choose from.

Unlike buying a house or car in a few years' time, saving for college seems to be more complicated because there may be many years until the purchase—and the final sticker price is unknown. Are you hoping to purchase a Toyota or a Maserati? How do you set a savings goal for something when you really don't know the eventual sticker price?

Paying for college starts with a solid and systematic savings plan.

Some parents determine how much they can save for each child and set up a disciplined plan with the knowledge that these savings will be the foundation for paying for college. More money may be needed when the first bill arrives, but other sources such as financial aid, grants and scholarships, and loans will be counted on to fill the gap. Savings reduce your reliance on these hoped-for sources and will expand the list of colleges your family can afford.

Now let's focus on what you need to know:

- How the power of compound interest significantly increases your savings potential.
- Why it makes more sense to save rather than borrow.
- How to choose a savings plan that works for your family.

THE POWER OF COMPOUNDING—START SAVING TODAY

It turns out that a penny saved, invested over time, is gradually worth much more than a penny earned. Finance professionals talk about the "Rule of 70": the number of years it will take your savings to double is approximately 70 divided by the annual interest rate. For example, if you invested $100 today at 7 percent, you would have $200 in ten years (70 ÷ 7 = 10). If your money earned 10 percent, it would double in seven years.

The two important variables:

- Time (a.k.a. your Investment Horizon)

- The amount earned on your savings

You will benefit from extending your Investment Horizon as far as possible to take advantage of compounding. This is a variable within your control, so take advantage by starting your savings program today.

On the other hand, you cannot fully control the ultimate return on your investments because that depends on many factors, including the stock market, the health of the world economy, and interest rates. The best way to affect your return on investment is to select investment vehicles that produce the desired return for the risk you are willing to take. More about risk and return later in the chapter.

The benefits of compounding fade as college grows near, so it is important to begin saving as far in advance as possible. The Rule of 70 means that even minor changes in spending and saving today can have a major impact on your ability to pay for college years later. Begin with whatever you can afford—maybe $50 a month to start—to establish the good habit of disciplined savings. Nothing is more important than getting started now.

Double Your Money!!
(Using the Rule of 70)

Interest Rate/Year	Years to Double	
1.0%	70	
1.5%	46 2/3	
2.0%	35	
2.5%	28	
3.0%	23 1/3	
3.5%	20	
4.0%	**17 ½**	This is the
4.5%	**15 ½**	prime range
5.0%	**14**	for education
5.5%	**12 ¾**	savings.
6.0%	11 2/3	
6.5%	10 ¾	
7.0%	10	

What does this mean? You are highly likely to double your initial savings in the time a child goes from being a toddler to a freshman in college—as long as you start early enough and have a portfolio of investments that earn or grow at least 4 to 5 percent per year.

Now let's illustrate the power of compounding and how important it is to have as long an investment time horizon as possible.

DON'T WAIT TO SAVE

Here's the value of $1,000 compounded monthly until the child's 18th birthday AND the value if you also save an additional $100/month

Your Child's Age	Annual Return on Investment	Value at Age 18	Value if you also save $100/month
1	3%	$1,664	$28,233
	4%	$1,972	$31,121
	5%	$2,336	$34,388
3	3%	$1,567	$22,265
	4%	$1,820	$26,429
	5%	$2,114	$28,843
5	3%	$1,476	$20,527
	4%	$1,681	$22,089
	5%	$1,913	$23,824
10	3%	$1,271	$12,106
	4%	$1,376	$12,668
	5%	$1,491	$13,265
15	3%	$1,094	$4,856
	4%	$1,127	$4,945
	5%	$1,161	$5,037

At your child's first birthday, if you invested $1,000 that earns 5 percent annually, it would be worth $2,336 on the child's eighteenth birthday. If you were able to also contribute $100/month, the amount available for college would be $34,388.

But, if you waited until that child's tenth birthday to start saving, your initial $1,000 investment will only grow to $1,491. If you contribute an additional $100 per month, the total saved will be $13,265. That decade of delay reduced the amount available for college by $21,123—leaving you a bit more than a third of what you could have saved.

TIPS
• Begin as early as possible to get the greatest benefit from the power of compounding. Remember the Rule of 70!
• Whenever your son or daughter receives cash on a birthday or holiday, place a chunk in the college savings account.
• Establish a routine for saving. No matter what your current expenses are—and there will always be expenses—try to set up an automatic contribution each month or quarter, no matter how small the amount.

Save Rather Than Borrow

It's pretty simple: saving means earning interest. Borrowing means paying interest on the amount borrowed (a.k.a. the Principal), in addition to repaying the Principal in full. Anything you save and invest now means correspondingly less to borrow and repay in the future.

Assume that you **invest $10,000 today** for a 10-year period, compounded monthly:		Assume that you **borrow $10,000** and pay it back over a 10-year period:	
Interest Rate	Interest Earned	Interest Rate	Interest Paid
3%	$3,494	3%	$1,587
5%	$6,470	5%	$2,728
7%	$10,097	7%	$3,933

More than 70 percent of the undergraduate Class of 2015 left school with an average of approximately $35,000 of student loans to finance their four-year college education. Heavy student loans can burden students and families for years after graduation. It is highly likely that some of the borrowing in the past was in excess of what was truly needed to attend college (a.k.a. over borrowing). No doubt we would be reading fewer headlines about recent graduates in trouble over their student loans if there had been better decision making at the time of the original borrowing.

Keep Up with Tuition Inflation

Another reason to save: college tuition is a moving target. Because tuition continues to increase, saving may be essential just to keep up with future costs. From 1985 to 2015, Bureau of Labor Statistics data show that college tuition and fees rose 504% compared to 265% for medical care and 116% for the Consumer Price Index (CPI).

Earnings on college savings accounts are needed to prevent you from falling too far behind the increasing costs of college.

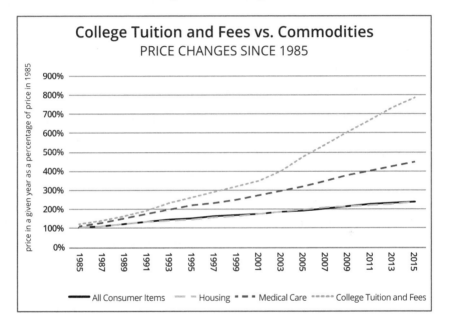

SAVINGS VEHICLES: YOUR MILEAGE MAY VARY

The decision to save is critically important, but so is where you choose to invest your savings.

Many people quickly feel intimidated when it comes to choosing a proper investment vehicle for college. They (incorrectly) think that choosing an investment is too complicated or they don't have enough money to invest or they're not sophisticated enough. So they choose to do nothing and regret it later. Let's start by understanding a fundamental concept about investing: Acceptable Risk and Expected Return.

Understand the Concept of Risk and Return Before Making Any College Investment Decision

To evaluate how your plan for college savings will unfold, you need to consider how much risk you are willing to take to make a return that at least keeps pace with rising college costs.

Risk evaluation is one key concept to consider—specifically the Risk of Principal Loss: how likely you are to lose some or all of your savings? This risk is found in two elements of savings:

1. **The Risk Profile of the Investment:** What is the Risk of Principal Loss of the specific investment vehicle you are considering? No guesswork here. The providers of these investments are required to provide historical return information and risk measures to investors.

2. **Your Risk Profile:** How much Risk of Principal Loss are you willing to accept? How will you feel if the investment doesn't work out, and you lose some or all of the principal you invested?

Generally, the greater Risk of Principal Loss, the greater the return on the investment should be. Investors want to be compensated for taking risk so they demand a higher interest rate or expectation that the investment will grow in value faster than less risky investments. For example, savings accounts have almost no Risk of Principal Loss and return less to investors who own bond funds. As we will discuss later, bond funds generally have less Risk of Principal Loss than stock funds so their expected return is expected to be less. The Risk of Principal Loss is greater in stock funds than the other investments so the expected return is greater.

Some aggressive investors are comfortable risking their entire savings with the hope of making a killing. The most conservative investors want to ensure there is no Risk of Principal Loss and accept much lower gains on their investment. Those in the middle accept varying degrees of Risk of Principal Loss in return for larger potential gains. Many investors prefer to diversify risk by assembling a balanced and diversified portfolio of investments that include a mix of conservative and more aggressive investments.

Everyone's Risk Profile is different and there is no generic right answer. One litmus test: do you go to sleep worrying about losing your principal? If so, your personal Risk Profile is misaligned with the Risk Profile of your investments. You should consider selling the riskiest and reinvesting in more conservative, less risky investments. At least you will sleep better at night.

Understanding that there is a trade-off between risk and reward (a.k.a. Return on Your Investment) sets the stage to focus on the different types of savings and investments used to generate returns to pay for college. Investment returns are the fundamental result of one or more of the following:

- Interest received from savings accounts, CDs, or bonds.

- Dividends received from stocks or mutual funds.

- The gain (or loss) on the investment—that is the difference between the price you paid for the security (a stock, bond, CD, and so on) and the price it is sold (a.k.a. Capital Appreciation or Loss).

The sum of interest, dividends, and Capital Appreciation or Loss at the time you cash out of the investments, less state and federal taxes paid, determines its return and is the measure of success of the investment in your college savings plan. The goal is to ensure that your Return on Investment exceeds the college inflation rate.

Let's Get Going: Time to Choose Investments and a Savings Vehicle

There are two issues to address when setting up a college savings account for your child:

1. What investments will you make to save for college?

2. Should those investments be held in a bank or brokerage account, a trust, or a 529 account and should they be held in your name or your child's name?

How to Hold College Savings Assets

Be sure to know that when setting up a college savings account, future eligibility for financial aid may be affected by how you establish the ownership of the account. The financial aid methodology treats parent- vs. student-owned savings differently:

- Student-Owned Account—A savings account that is in the students name.
- Account Owner—the person who is legally the owner of the account and controls changes and distributions, usually the parent.

As discussed next, it may be very beneficial when applying for financial aid to ensure that the Account Owner is the parent, not the student. The current formulas used to calculate financial aid consider in whose name the investments for college savings are held. Twenty percent of savings held in a student's name (except in a 529 account) are considered to be available to pay for his or her college each year. If those same assets are held in the parents' names, only 5.64 percent of the assets are considered to be available to pay for college. In most cases, it is advantageous, for financial aid reasons, to hold college savings assets in the parents' names.

Having said that, some families use gifts under the Uniform Gifts to Minors Act (UGMA) or Uniform Transfers to Minors Act (UTMA) or establish Trusts to shelter assets from estate taxes. Both of these vehicles accomplish the goal of removing college assets from the parental estate. These strategies, particularly UGMA and UTMA accounts, were more widely used prior to the creation of 529 Plans in the late 1990s.

Gifts Under the Uniform Gifts to Minors Act (UGMA) or Uniform Transfers to Minors Act (UTMA)

Most states allow adults to make gifts of cash and securities to minors without the creation of a trust. These gifts offer tax advantages because the minor recipient is usually in a much lower tax bracket. Plus, under the UGMA and UTMA, a portion of the investment income on any asset is tax-free, and some is taxed at the child's lower tax rate. An adult custodian manages the account on behalf of the minor until the minor reaches legal age and then has complete legal control of the account and all funds therein. The downside, however, is that for financial aid purposes, these funds will be considered a student asset and will be assessed at 20 percent vs. 5.64 percent if they are in the parents' names or in a student's 529 account.

If a legal trust structure is of interest to you, use the following discussion as a basis for consultation with your accountant, lawyer, or financial planner who will help you properly create the trust that works best for your circumstances and goals.

Trust

A trust is a legally binding agreement in which the grantor (the person establishing the trust) conveys an ownership interest to a beneficiary. Some families prefer to remove the assets from the family's estate for tax purposes and usually establish one of the following:

- Section 2503 (c) Minor's Trust, is an irrevocable Trust agreement, in which a Trustee is appointed to act on behalf of a minor child—including managing the investments and making payments from the account. At age 21, the child receives any amounts remaining in the Trust and controls all funds.

- A Crummey Trust permits the periodic withdrawal of assets by the beneficiary and multiple beneficiaries; it does not require final distributions at age 21.

Families generally use trusts as part of their larger estate and tax plan: assets conveyed to beneficiaries via a trust are no longer part of the grantor's taxable estate. A significant advantage of a trust is moving assets out of the parents' taxable estate while maintaining control of the education trust through the trustee, who is appointed by the parents. Disadvantages of a trust include the additional costs of an attorney, accountant, and trustee. Earnings are also taxed at a substantially higher rate than ordinary income tax.

Happily, families now have other cost-effective ways to contribute to their children's education without incurring double taxation, including making gifts under UGMA/UTMA or contributing to Coverdell Education Savings Accounts or a 529 Plan.

Most families find that 529 Plans, discussed in detail in Chapter 2, or UGMA/UTMA structures meet their goals without enlisting the help of a lawyer, accountant, and trustee to administer a Trust. In addition, 529 Plans can own trusts so existing trust funds can be transferred into a 529 Plan to avoid taxation.

What Investments Can Be Purchased?

There aren't any restrictions on which investments can be used to fund college, but some very aggressive, illiquid investments are not appropriate for a college savings account.

There is a spectrum of suitable products to save for college ranging from very conservative (Passbook Savings Accounts, Certificates of Deposit, and Government Bonds) to more aggressive (stocks, mutual funds). Usually, more conservative investments produce less of a Return on Investment and more aggressive investments assume more risk and are expected to reward investors with a greater expected return.

Try to avoid a common investment trap: paralysis by analysis. Do enough research and perhaps consult with a financial advisor to get comfortable with your plan and make the first investment. It does not have to be permanent or "the very best"—it just needs to be made. If you're unsure of what to do, open a conservative account as a temporary investment until you formulate a more permanent plan. You can change the savings plan, account type, and investments in the future, but for your sake, remember the Rule of 70 and do something now as there is a true financial cost of waiting.

When choosing a savings vehicle, you should consider:

- The initial amount of your first investment and how much you plan to contribute periodically because some types of investments have minimums for first investments. Others have no minimums if you establish an automatic plan.

- The risk elements we previously discussed: Your Risk Profile and the Investment Risk Profile, specifically the projected Return on Investment vs. its risk.

- The tax implications of the investment. As we will see next, some investments can be free of taxation and increase your savings rather than be used to pay taxes.

- The time horizon for the investment.

What Are My Investment Choices?

One of your first and most important decisions is whether you should invest in a taxable or a tax-advantaged investment vehicle. The latter permits you to defer or pay no taxes if withdrawals are used for college. A 529 Plan, a Coverdell Education Savings Account, and U.S. Savings Bonds are tax-advantaged vehicles. A comparison chart of these three investment options is presented at the end of this chapter.

If you have a brokerage account, your Financial Advisor will be a great resource and can recommend a savings strategy that is appropriate for you. If you do not have a Financial Advisor, no problem. You may want to start with a simple savings account and then consider other alternatives as your savings grow and you become more comfortable with the options to increase your Return on Investment.

Let's begin with some of the more conservative, least risky savings options. These accounts are easy to open and can start you on your way to saving quickly. The downside: the returns on these investments are significantly lower than other options and are very likely to pay you substantially less interest than the rate of college inflation.

Here is a brief overview of some of the most conservative savings options that you can easily find at any bank or credit union:

Passbook Savings Accounts

These accounts with a bank or credit union offer low but compound interest. Compound interest is favorable because, unlike simple interest, interest is calculated daily (or sometimes monthly or quarterly) so you earn interest on the interest. Simple interest merely pays out one interest payment based on the amount you invest and is less than compound interest. Conservative investors like Passbook Savings Accounts for two primary reasons: they are safe and liquid. There is virtually no Risk of Principal Loss, i.e., they offer maximum safety—mostly derived from federal insurance guaranteeing zero Risk of Principal Loss for most accounts. Passbook Savings Accounts are also highly liquid, meaning that you can withdraw principal immediately upon demand. Be careful though. Returns on these accounts are unlikely to keep pace with college tuition inflation. Why? For the very reasons conservative investors prefer them: there is little, if any, Risk of Principal Loss, and they are highly liquid—good for security but a serious drag on your Return on Investment.

Certificates of Deposit

A Certificate of Deposit (CD) is issued by a bank or credit union to a depositor (you). The CD guarantees you a certain amount of interest on the investment to a specified date (a.k.a. the Maturity Date). Typically, CDs are purchased with fixed maturity dates of three months, six months, one year, or five years (a.k.a. the Term of the CD). They generally pay interest rates greater than Passbook Savings Accounts, usually at a fixed rate with more interest paid for longer-term maturities. The downside: higher interest rates are offered because the issuing bank may charge the holder a substantial penalty to redeem the CD before its Maturity Date. Also, check to see if the CD is insured. Some higher yielding CDs are offered without insurance, which means that you are taking a risk that the issuing bank will remain solvent until the CD is due. While not a huge risk, it can be avoided with insurance from the Federal Deposit Insurance Corporation for CDs issued by banks or from the National Credit Union Administration for CDs issued by credit unions. The CDs will come with the insurance attached so you need not do anything other than check to see that the paperwork says the CD is FDIC or NCUA insured.

If you are a first-time saver or are evaluating other college savings options, parking your initial investment in a Passbook Savings Account at your local bank or credit union or purchasing a short-term CD is a great way to get started. One downside is that your return on investment will be reduced because you will have to pay taxes on your earnings. Although these accounts permit you to start quickly and easily, their low return is highly unlikely to keep pace with the college inflation rate. Most 529 Plans offer similar conservative, risk-free vehicles that grow tax-free. If you choose a low-risk, low-return bank savings, or 529 Plan savings vehicle, you can begin saving with these types of accounts and later transfer them into other, higher yielding investments.

The reverse strategy may also help when a student is in high school. As college approaches, you can protect your college savings by moving some or all of them from higher yielding, but riskier, investments to investments like these to ensure that your savings will not be eroded before college begins. Don't forget to factor in the tax consequences to your Return on Investment if you move money from a tax-exempt vehicle to a taxable one. As we'll see later, many 529 Plans have options called Age-Based Portfolios that automatically reallocate assets to safer investments as your student nears college age.

Passbook Savings Accounts and CDs are among the safest investment options but are unlikely to keep pace with college inflation rates. For this reason, many families may initially invest in one of these and then shift into one or more types of higher yielding investments such as stock and/or bond mutual funds, which are more likely to meet or exceed the rate of college cost increases.

INVESTMENT CHOICES: CASH ACCOUNTS, DEBT, EQUITY, OR SOME OF EACH?

For those who have brokerage accounts or use financial advisors to plan to pay for college, there are four primary investment choices that are most appropriate for college savings accounts:

1. Cash Accounts, such as money market accounts, are often used to hold funds before payment of college expenses or prior to making a longer-term investment. The significant advantage of these accounts is that you can get your money back at any time (a.k.a. Highly Liquid), and the Risk of Principal Loss is practically zero. The downside is that cash accounts are the lowest yielding investment options for the very reason conservative investors like them: they are Highly Liquid and safe.

2. Debt (a.k.a. Bonds): an I.O.U. from the issuer to you in which the issuer takes your money in return for a promise to pay a certain amount of interest (a.k.a. the Coupon Rate) to the Maturity Date.

3. Equities (a.k.a. Stock) are ownership interests in a company. When you purchase a stock, you own a piece of that company and your return is linked to the economic success of the company. Some stocks pay dividends, while others don't. An investor's total return on an equity is the combination of dividends received plus the capital appreciation on the investment.

4. Mutual funds and stock Exchange Traded Funds (ETFs) consist of a portfolio of individual stocks or bonds. One advantage of mutual funds is that the risks associated with owning a single stock is diminished by the diversification of owning a small piece of many stocks. Mutual Funds and ETFs are designed to be less risky than investing in individual stocks.

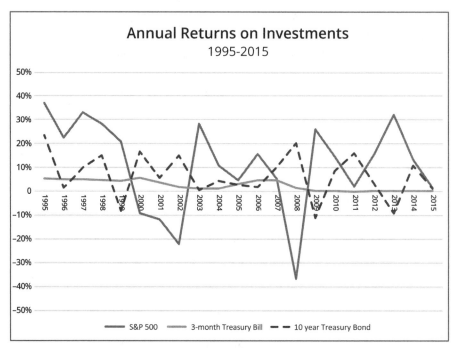

Source: Federal Reserve Bank, St. Louis. Compiled by Aswath Damodarian, Ph.D., Professor of Finance; NYU Stern School of Business, January 6, 2016.

This is not a comprehensive book on how to invest in stocks and bonds, but we want to highlight some of the basic concepts and investment options to get you comfortable. It isn't rocket science, but since it involves money and your child's future, it's helpful for you to understand some of the general investment options available to you.

Bonds

Investing in bonds is considered a conservative strategy for those with a low Risk Profile. Independent rating services such as Moody's Investors Service and Standard and Poor's, among others, provide a scale of ratings to help investors judge the relative Risk of Principal Loss in bonds. Investors of college savings should stick to those rated Single-A or higher (a.k.a. Investment Grade bonds). One significant disadvantage of investing in bonds is that the amount you earn on the investment is likely to be less than the increase in cost of college over time. Returns on bonds may not keep pace with inflation, let alone college tuition. This doesn't mean that you should not have bonds in your college investment portfolio. Bonds are appropriate for low risk-takers who want to add a safety component to a broader, diverse portfolio. Just be aware that the return on investment-grade bonds will likely lag the college inflation rate—maybe by a lot. Bonds are offered by municipalities (state and local governmental entities) and the federal government, as well as corporations. Some are subject to taxation, others are not.

- **Qualified U.S. Savings Bonds (Series EE/E).** Though the interest rate paid to you by the government may be low, education savings bonds are considered the safest of investments because of the Government-backed guaranteed payments of interest and principal. In addition, certain education savings bonds permit you to receive all or a portion of the interest tax-free when you are paying tuition or fees at a qualified educational institution. For more information about qualifying for the Education Tax Exclusion, visit the U.S. Treasury Direct site at: www.treasurydirect.gov/indiv/planning/plan_education.htm.

- **Treasury Bonds and Notes (a.k.a. Treasuries).** Like U.S. Savings Bonds, debt issued by the U.S. Treasury is considered to be the safest investment vehicle. The full faith and credit of the United States makes these the lowest yielding, but safest, debt investment. Treasuries are subject to federal tax. To increase your return on the investment, The U.S. Treasury advises that purchasing Treasuries in a child's name alone or with a parent as the beneficiary would result in the income being attributable to the child—and presumably taxed at the child's lower rate. For more information, visit https://www.treasurydirect.gov/indiv/planning/plan_education.htm.

- **Tax-Free Bonds.** Municipalities or other governmental entities offer Municipal Bonds that pay interest that is tax-free—sometimes free of all local, state, and federal taxes. In exchange for the tax-free benefit, the Coupon Rate is lower than for taxable bonds. Investors count on the municipality to pay interest and principal when due. We know that not all cities and towns are in great financial shape, so choosing bonds that will not default is very important. The risk that an issuer will not repay interest when due or principal at maturity is known as Credit Risk. Be sure to check the bond ratings and stick to investment-grade bonds. Don't be fooled: an investment-grade rating is not a guarantee that the issuer will make timely interest and ultimate principal payments. It is a third-party's evaluation of the credit.

- **Taxable Bonds.** This debt is issued by a government or corporation with interest payments that are subject to income tax. They share the same general characteristics of Treasury and Municipal Bonds: they pay interest over time at a stated rate (the Coupon Rate) and principal at maturity and are subject to Credit Risk. Although the Coupon Rate on an investment-grade corporate bond is higher than Municipal and Treasury Bonds, the after-tax earnings may still lag college inflation.

- **Bond Mutual Funds.** This is a portfolio of bonds assembled by a professional manager who then sells shares of the fund to investors. Bond Funds come in all sizes and shapes. Some focus narrowly on tax-exempt municipal bonds to benefit investors in a particular state. Others are broadly constructed, i.e., an investment-grade corporate bond fund or a global bond fund. Be sure to understand the risk level associated with the various Bond Funds.

Stocks

Investing in equities is a more aggressive strategy because there is a greater expected Risk of Principal Loss. The share price changes frequently during the course of the day as investors from around the world buy and sell the securities. Stocks expose investors to Risk of Principal Loss but also afford opportunities to earn returns that will keep pace or exceed the college inflation rate, making equities a staple in college savings accounts. Look for stocks that pay regular dividends to boost your earnings and reinvest the dividends to increase your holdings.

There are a few different ways to incorporate equities into your college savings plan.

- **Individual Stocks.** Purchasing individual stocks for a college fund is generally not recommended. Putting all of your eggs in one basket by picking one or a small number of stocks—no matter how well known or large a company may be—is a highly risky strategy. It could be great if you happen to guess right and disastrous if you don't. The less risky strategy is to diversify the risk of owning individual stocks by purchasing a stock mutual fund—a single investment that combines many underlying equities into one instrument.

- **Stock Mutual Funds.** Like a bond fund, a stock mutual fund is simply a collection of stocks. Professional portfolio managers invest the fund's assets under management in many companies, producing a diversified, less risky investment than purchasing individual stocks. There are literally thousands of mutual funds, from portfolios of stocks very concentrated in one sector of the U.S. economy to global funds that buy international equities. Mutual funds that are purchased and sold are done so at the end of each trading day based on the Fund's closing Net Asset Value. Mutual Funds charge fees for investing in the funds, so be aware if there are front-end or back-end fees. Fees are generally higher for mutual fund investments when compared to stock purchases, in part to incent investors to keep the investment for longer periods of time and not to frequently trade them.

Index Funds

An index fund is basically a mutual fund constructed to exactly track the performance of a broad market index, such as the S&P 500, by purchasing all of the stocks in the index and then offering Index Fund shares to individual investors. The benefit to investors: a low fee structure, access to a very diversified portfolio of stock, and many fund choices.

Exchange Traded Funds (ETFs)

Although similar in design to mutual funds, ETFs can be immediately bought and sold during the trading day like a stock as opposed to a mutual fund whose price is set at the close of the stock market each trading day.

Investments Other Than Stocks and Bonds

For the record, your college savings account can include any asset that is available to the investing public, including, but not limited to:

- Commodities such as gold, silver, etc.

- Currencies such as the yen, euro, etc.

- Real estate such as residential or commercial properties.

- Alternative investments such as hedge funds.

Most of these options expose investors to very different risks than do stocks and bonds and may be an appropriate diversification opportunity for sophisticated investors with large portfolios. However, for the most part, investments like these are not suitable for the large majority of investors saving for college.

Finally, there are other financial services products, which have other primary purposes but can be used to pay for college.

IRA Accounts

These general retirement accounts allow you to make annual contributions, which grow tax-free within your account. In a Traditional IRA, your contributions are tax-deductible, but distributions are taxed; in a Roth IRA, contributions are taxed, but distributions are tax-free. You can begin taking distributions from either at age 59½, with early withdrawal penalties for funds taken out before then. Though not exclusively focused on promoting education, these accounts have one feature than makes them desirable for this purpose: early withdrawal penalties are waived when funds are used for qualified higher education expenses. It's hard to be a big fan of withdrawing money from your retirement account to pay for college. After all, you've been sacrificing to build your nest egg so you could be comfortable in retirement. Why undo years of good planning and sacrifice when you're likely approaching your retirement age? Remember the Rule of 70. You are likely to have a limited number of doubles left in your investment horizon, so preserving and adding to principal should be a primary goal of retirement accounts. Take advantage of all the time you have left to double your money.

Insurance Products

Insurance companies offer a number of products that may be applicable to your college savings program.

- **Annuities.** When you buy an annuity, you make a lump sum payment or a series of payments to the insurance company over a number of years. In return, when you retire or at some point in the future, you receive a fixed amount for a proscribed number of years.

    - **Benefit of annuities for college savings:** Annuities are currently excluded from your assets when filing for financial aid, and the issuers offer a guarantee on earnings while federal taxes are deferred.

- ◆ **The issue with annuities:** Insurance companies often charge hefty fees, including initial commissions, high annual fees, and surrender charges, if you reclaim your money before the term. There may also be other restrictions.

- **Permanent/Whole Life Insurance.** Although you need to pay premiums to maintain what is, essentially, a loan that charges interest, insurance policies allow tax-deferred growth and are excluded from your financial aid assets. Although excluded from financial aid consideration, the cost may not equal the benefit as premiums are costly and broker commissions could be as high as 7 percent.

Now that we've identified the range of primary types of investments for your college savings accounts, let's spend a moment exploring the vehicles that may be used to house these investments. The U.S. Congress has generously established two significant tax-advantaged programs that are excellent savings vehicles for college. With these programs you pay no taxes at all if used for college expenses.

Coverdell Education Saving Account

If your modified adjusted gross income is less than $110,000 ($220,000 if you file jointly), you are eligible to set up a Coverdell at your local bank or credit union. Coverdell ESAs allow you to make nondeductible contributions, up to $2000/year, to pay for both qualified college and K–12 expenses, with wide investment discretion. Withdrawals are tax-free at the federal level as long as they are used for a Qualified Education Expense. They may also be subject to state taxes and may be subject to restrictions based on your income and your child's age. For more details, visit http://www.irs.gov/publications/p970/ch07.html.

529 Plans

The Congress empowered states to set up these tax-advantaged college savings plans, which have become the most popular college savings programs. Currently, there are more than 100 different 529 Plans to choose from. Chapter 2 describes these plans in detail.

The following chart compares three tax-advantaged programs available to help you save and pay for college:

	529 Plans	Coverdell / ESA	Savings Bonds
How Counted Against Financial Aid	Counted as asset of parent if owner is parent or dependent student.	Counted as asset of parent if owner is parent or dependent student.	Counted as asset of bond owner.
Federal Income Tax	Nondeductible contributions, tax-free withdrawals.	Nondeductible contributions, tax-free withdrawals. Also for K–12 qualified educational expenses.	Tax-deferred for federal, tax-free for state. Certain post-1989 EE and I bonds redeemed tax-free for qualified educational expenses.
Federal Estate Tax	Value excluded from donor's estate gross; partial inclusion if donor dies during five-year election period.	Value excluded from donor's estate gross.	Value included in owner's estate gross.
Income Restrictions	None	Modified Adjusted Gross Income must be less than $110K for individuals and $220K for married joint filers.	Interest exclusion phases out for incomes between $112.05K and $142.05K for joint filers or $74.7K and $89.7K for single filers.
Time/Age Restrictions	Only if imposed by specific program	Contributions to beneficiary up to 18; use of account by beneficiary up to age 30.	Purchaser must be 24.
Maximum Investment	Depends on the specific program; many in excess of $400,000 per beneficiary.	$2K per beneficiary per year.	$10K face value per type of bond, per owner, per year.
Ability to Change Beneficiary	YES, to another member of beneficiary's family.	YES, to another member of beneficiary's family.	Not applicable.

Chapter 1 Takeaways

Saving for college is very important for children of any age. Start now.

- Saving is the first and most important step in preparing for college costs. Start early, even if you start with as little as $25 a week.

- Establish a systematic savings schedule via automatic electronic bank debits or payroll deduction to make it easy for you to contribute and watch your savings grow.

- Remember the Rule of 70: 70 divided by the interest rate is the number of years it will take for your savings to double.

- Saving for college shares the general principles and best practices of any savings or investment strategy:

  - Understand Risk—Your Risk Profile and Risk Profile of the Investment

  - Know the relative trade-off between risk and reward. You should earn more return for taking on greater investment risk. It is necessary to take on some risk if you want your investments to at least keep pace with college tuition.

  - Understand the "Rule of 70" —the number of years it will take your savings to double—and the importance of compound interest.

  - Know that the returns from many conservative investments, such as savings accounts and bonds, have not kept pace with rising tuition costs.

- Know that there are many investment options available that may meet your personal investment criteria and needs. Pick one or several that work best for your family's circumstances.

- Thanks to Congress, there are special tax-advantaged college savings vehicles available to you. You should consider these tax-advantaged programs as part of your college savings strategy.

- Get started! Once you select your investment vehicles, establish a systematic savings schedule by electronically debiting money from your payroll check or bank account into your college investment account and watch your money grow.

Chapter 2

529 Plans—An Excellent College Savings Vehicle

Many Congressional and tax experts view Section 529 as one of the most generous tax provisions ever passed by Congress for the benefit of American families.

Created by Congress in 1996, 529 Plans combine tax-free incentives with a host of unique features and benefits designed to encourage families at all income levels to save for college-related expenses.

Does this sound like an exaggeration or too good to be true? Take a look at the following benefits and decide for yourself. The scope of the unique benefits available within 529 Plans make them an outstanding option for saving for college. You should seriously consider utilizing a 529 Plan for your children, grandchildren, nieces, and nephews—or even yourself.

Ten of the Many Benefits of Section 529 Plans

1. Tax-deferred growth: Interest, dividends, and capital gains accumulate free of federal taxes.

2. Tax-free distributions when the proceeds are used for qualified higher education expenses at over 7,000 schools in the United States and abroad.

3. Special estate and gift tax treatment, with five year accelerated gifting.

4. Continued ownership and control for account owners, including the ability to change beneficiaries to extended family members without penalty.

5. Professional financial management of investments by states, in partnership with leading financial services firms.

6. Very high maximum contribution and account balance limits.

7. No income limits restricting who can invest.

8. No age restrictions on beneficiary or contributor.

9. No required distributions in most programs.

10. Protection of savings from bankruptcy for account owner against creditors.

In addition to the previous benefits, 529 Plans are treated favorably for financial aid purposes. 529 assets are treated just as savings accounts, mutual funds, or other financial assets are for purposes of financial aid calculations. One myth that is occasionally promulgated by the media and some ill-informed financial advisors is that 529s—more so than other savings assets—will reduce the amount of financial aid you might otherwise qualify for. This is simply not true, so disregard this if you have read or heard it from either the media or uninformed advisors (see additional details and explanation in the following Q & A section).

THE UNIQUENESS OF SECTION 529

In a preamble to its proposed regulations, the IRS commented on the unprecedented advantages of qualified state tuition programs (QSTP):

> "In addition, the estate planning and gift tax treatment of contributions to a QSTP and interest in a QSTP is generally different from the treatment that would otherwise apply under generally applicable estate and gift tax principles."

As you can see from the preamble, the benefits of these plans go beyond tax-free investing and withdrawals. There are no income limits, full control for account owners, special estate planning and gifting options, very high contribution limits, and a host of other features that make 529 Plans one of the best ways to save for college. However, despite the many benefits of 529 Plans, most Americans, and even many financial advisors, are not familiar with and do not understand the many benefits and the flexibility available in 529 Plans. As explained in detail later in this chapter, there are two types of 529 Plans:

1. **Prepaid tuition plans**—the first generation of 529 Plans

2. **College savings/investment plans**—the more recent and most popular plans

Each type of 529 Plan provides different benefits and features. Both plans, however, are designed with one overriding goal: to provide you with a tax-advantaged incentive for you to save for college.

Appendix A lists the 529 Plans by state and program. The chart also indicates the types of plans that are available in your state and whether there is an in-state tax deduction benefit.

COLLEGE FINANCING CRISIS IN THE 1980s AND 529 PLANS

In the mid-1980s, American families were faced with a college financing crisis. Tuition costs were skyrocketing while federal and institutional financial aid was being drastically reduced. According to the General Accounting Office (since 2004 known as the Government Accountability Office), from 1981 to 1995 average household incomes increased 82 percent while average public college tuitions rose by 234 percent. Low federal loan-dollar caps on student loans during that period exacerbated the crisis. Not unlike today, American families were overwhelmed by the cost and needed help saving and paying for college.

Establishment of Prepaid Tuition Savings Programs

In response to this crisis, state legislatures stepped in and created tax-advantaged college savings programs, primarily in the form of state-run, prepaid tuition programs. Though beneficial to all income levels, these programs were principally designed for middle-class families facing a double-edged sword: just enough income to be ineligible for financial aid but not enough income to pay for college without taking on considerable debt. A secondary goal was to help all families plan more effectively by giving them the tools to make sound decisions about college selection, costs, and loans.

IRS Challenge Prompted Congress to Act

In 1986, Michigan established the nation's first prepaid tuition program and created the Michigan Education Trust (MET) to oversee it. This innovative program gave Michigan families the opportunity to lock in future tuition at current prices for Michigan public colleges and universities. Other states created similar public college savings programs: Florida and Wyoming in 1988, and Ohio, Alabama, Alaska, Kentucky, Louisiana, Pennsylvania, and Massachusetts thereafter. Massachusetts' program, the UPlan, was the first to include both public and private colleges.

The Internal Revenue Service issued a controversial ruling that placed a damper on these efforts, however. In IRS Letter Ruling 8825027, the IRS said that Michigan's MET did not qualify as "a tax-exempt state instrumentality" and would have to pay taxes on its earnings from investments. The MET was forced to stop issuing new prepaid contracts as it had to pay income taxes on the investment earnings of the Trust, thereby substantially exposing the state to unfunded liabilities of future tuition growth and tax payments.

In 1990, Michigan filed suit against the IRS, demanding a refund of taxes paid on the grounds that the MET was, indeed, a state instrumentality and should be tax exempt. In an effort to mobilize public and political support, a small group of officials from the above-mentioned states formed the College Savings Plans Network (CSPN). They filed an amicus brief on Michigan's behalf and began lobbying Congress for legislative relief.

In 1994, Michigan won the case (*Michigan v. United States*, 40 F.3d 817, (6th Cir. 1994)). Meanwhile, the CSPN members, working with the National Association of State Treasurers (NAST), successfully lobbied Congress to create Internal Revenue Code Section 529 to clarify the law and prevent further court battles.

SECTION 529 BECOMES LAW IN 1996

In 1996, Senators Mitch McConnell (R-KY) and Bob Graham (D-FL) successfully cosponsored an amendment to the Small Business Protection Act creating Section 529. President Clinton signed the bill into law. In addition to providing tax-deferred treatment of existing prepaid tuition and savings programs, the law created a new and flexible savings/investment option that could be used at over 7,000 accredited institutions receiving federal loan funds. It was the first of a series of 529 college savings bills passed by Congress over the next twenty years.

In 1997, through the Tax Payer Relief Act, Congress expanded the benefits of Section 529, adding room and board and mandatory fees to the list of qualified education expenses. It also provided a number of special estate and gift tax features for Section 529 Plan participants, all designed to encourage American families to save for college.

As more states launched Section 529 Plans, Congressional support grew. Members of Congress recognized that encouraging families to save through Section 529 Plans was sound public policy and in the national interest. In the Economic Growth and Tax Relief Reconciliation Act (EGTRRA) of 2001, Congress improved Section 529 by making distributions tax-free if used to pay for college. Prior to that, earnings had been tax-deferred so that taxes would be due at time of distribution. Now, 529 Plans provided a powerful vehicle for families to save for college without paying taxes on the earnings or the distributions for qualified educational expenses.

These tax-free benefits, like other provisions in EGTRRA, had sunset provisions and would expire in a few years. CSPN, NAST, and a newly formed industry association of plan managers, called the College Savings Foundation (CSF), successfully lobbied Congress to pass tax-free permanence for 529 Plans. Both the House and Senate bills had numerous cosponsors and deep bipartisan support. President Bush signed the legislation into law in 2006.

THE COLLEGE-FINANCING CRISIS CONTINUES

It is not surprising that congressional support for Section 529 Plans grew dramatically during the early to mid-2000s as the college-financing crisis deepened.

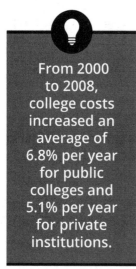

From 2000 to 2008, college costs increased an average of 6.8% per year for public colleges and 5.1% per year for private institutions.

At the same time, the percentage of tuition covered by federal loans decreased because caps on the amount students could borrow under the federal loan programs remained unchanged. To make up the shortfall, students and families took on unprecedented levels of private student loans offered by colleges, banks, and other financial institutions. Total student loan debt exploded from $15 billion in 1999 to $86 billion in 2007. The total amount of annual student loan debt has continued to increase to more than $100 billion in 2015. Total student loans outstanding now exceed 1.3 trillion dollars.

Faced with an ever-worsening college financing crisis and encouraged by favorable federal legislation and widespread bipartisan support, all fifty states had established 529 Plans by 2006. In response to widespread demands for portability and choice, 529 Plans have since evolved from state-specific prepaid tuition plans to broader college savings plans with a variety of investment choices and options. These range from static and age-based portfolios of diversified funds to FDIC-insured savings accounts.

Today, forty-nine states, the District of Columbia, and a college consortium offer over 105 savings and prepaid plans. Wyoming is the only state that does not offer a 529 Plan, having ended offering its plan in 2006. Ninety-two are savings plans, and thirteen are prepaid programs. The Private College 529 Plan consists of a consortium of private colleges from across the nation participating in a single prepaid tuition plan.

> Chapter 5 has a more detailed discussion of federal and private loan programs.

Section 529 Plans: A Legislative and Regulatory Timeline

1996: Congress creates Internal Revenue Code Section 529, using the Small Business Protection Act

1997: Congress passes the Taxpayer Relief Act, enhancing Section 529

2001: Congress passes EGTRRA, ensuring 529 accounts remain tax-free through 2010

2001: IRS allows annual investment change

2005: Bankruptcy Act protects 529 assets

2006: DOE changes financial aid treatment of 529 Plans

2006: Pension Protection Act makes Section 529 tax treatment permanent, thereby eliminating the 2010 expiration of tax-free treatment.

2014: ABLE (Achieving a Better Life Experience) legislation passed, providing 529-ABLE accounts for the benefit of the disabled

2015: Congress passes HR529/S335; as part of HR2029, it included a number of improvements to the rules for 529 Plans: reimbursements for computers and lifting the in-state residency restriction for ABLE 529A accounts to all state programs

More than twenty years after the passage of Sec 529, there remains a great deal of confusion, misunderstanding, and false myths about the scope of the true benefits of 529 Plans. However, as more American families and advisors understand the full range and true benefit of using a 529 Plan, it is expected that participation and contribution rates in 529 Plans will grow dramatically.

As the following chart illustrates, the amounts saved in 529 Savings Plans and Prepaid Programs have increased steadily from less than $15 billion in 2001 to more than $244 billion. This amount is invested in over 12.6 million separate accounts as of September 30, 2015. Of this total amount, $221 billion in 11.4 million accounts are invested in 529 Savings Plans. Prepaid Tuition Programs have $23 billion invested in 1.2 million accounts. The average 529 account size continues to grow, reaching an all-time high of $20,934 as of June 30, 2015.

Yet despite the terrific benefits of 529 Plans, participation and awareness rates are relatively low. In comparison to total investment in 529 Plans, American families saving for college have invested approximately $611 billion in other investment vehicles. The majority of these non-529 investment dollars are in taxable accounts. If you are investing for college in a taxable account, the taxes you pay on your earnings erodes your investment return and reduces the total potential savings amount. You may want to consider establishing a 529 account and reallocating these taxable investments into the 529 Plan to legally avoid paying the IRS and keeping the tax savings in your account.

GROWTH IN 529 SAVINGS AND PREPAID PLANS 2001–2014

Growth in 529 Assets ($Billions), 2001–2Q 2014

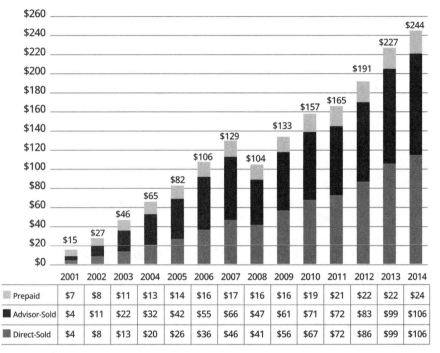

	2001	2002	2003	2004	2005	2006	2007	2008	2009	2010	2011	2012	2013	2014
Prepaid	$7	$8	$11	$13	$14	$16	$17	$16	$16	$19	$21	$22	$22	$24
Advisor-Sold	$4	$11	$22	$32	$42	$55	$66	$47	$61	$71	$72	$83	$99	$106
Direct-Sold	$4	$8	$13	$20	$26	$36	$46	$41	$56	$67	$72	$86	$99	$106

Source: Strategic Insight. Paul Curley

SECTION 529 PLANS TODAY

As mentioned earlier, there are two types of 529 programs: prepaid tuition programs and saving plans. Both offer tax-free growth and tax-free withdrawals if used for higher education expenses. Some states offer both.

- Prepaid Tuition Programs allow you to pay for future college tuition at a locked-in price. The tag line for many of these programs is "Tomorrow's Tuition at Today's Prices." Purchasers of prepaid tuition plans do not have the risk that their investment will not keep pace with college costs because a certain percentage of the future tuition is purchased. You, as buyer, have passed the risk of cost increases to the seller (a state or the consortium).

- Savings plans permit you to save and invest for over 7,000 postsecondary education institutions in a variety of traditional investment vehicles. Unlike prepaid programs, the return on your investment (the earnings) is subject to market and economic volatility. As the investor, you accept the risk that your investments return less than the increasing cost of education or may not be enough to pay when you need the money. For example, if there is a sudden drop in the stock market, as there was in 2009, at the time you need the money, your account will decline accordingly. The result might be that you no longer have the amount you need to pay for college. More optimistically, you also benefit if the return on the investment exceeds the increasing cost of college or if the stock market rallies and leaves you with more money than you need to pay for college.

Types of Section 529 Plans Compared	
Prepaid Tuition Plan	**Savings Account**
You purchase tuition credits or certificates for a beneficiary. You can purchase via a lump sum or on an installment plan.	You make contributions to an account invested for a beneficiary in investment vehicles overseen by states that partner with the nation's leading financial service firms. A broad range of investment choices is available to suit your goals and tolerance for risk.
You receive a "defined benefit"—future college tuition at a price locked in when you sign up for the plan.	Your annual contribution may be defined, but the future benefit is not. The amount you ultimately receive depends on how much you save and how well your investments perform over time.
The tuition credits of certificates may only be used at colleges enrolled in the specific program you bought. In many states, the benefits may be limited to in-state public institutions. There are also two prepaid tuition programs that include participating private colleges.	Savings plan proceeds can be used at over 7,000 accredited schools, including schools in other countries.
May cover only tuition and mandatory fees.	In addition to tuition and fees, you may be able to use savings for room and board, supplies, and other education-related expenses.

Prepaid Tuition Programs

Thirteen states and a college consortium currently offer Prepaid Tuition Programs, which permit purchasers to contract for up to 100 percent of future tuition at today's rates, regardless of the age of the child. For example, if the tuition at a hypothetical in-state college is $10,000 today, a Prepaid Tuition Program would permit you to pay approximately $10,000 today with a guarantee that when your child reaches college age, you have one year of college tuition fully paid for—no matter what the cost is at that time. In effect, you have completely eliminated tuition inflation and have taken the guess-work out of how much you need to save over the coming years to meet tuition costs. Of course, you may not have $10,000 currently available. Perhaps you have saved $2,500. You could purchase a certificate for one-quarter of future tuition today. In subsequent years, you have the option of purchasing additional portions of future tuition—at the prices then in effect.

Some of the drawbacks to Prepaid Tuition Programs include the following:

- A Prepaid Tuition Program does not guarantee admission to any of the participating schools in the program you purchase.

- As the name implies, Prepaid Tuition Programs only cover the cost of Tuition. Costs for room and board, travel, and other costs of attendance must be covered separately.

- Your student's options for attending a college would be limited to those participating in the plan. Realistically, this likely means state schools or a limited number of private schools if you participate in one of the two private college plans.

- If your child does not attend a participating college, you will not receive the full tuition benefit. Many states offer refunds and 529 transfer options at different payout levels. You should check with the program to determine to whom the benefits can be transferred or how to receive a refund. Ask if there are any related penalties or restrictions.

In recent years, due to financial issues and actuarial projections regarding potential funding liabilities and the need for the prepaid program's investment return to match the growth of actual tuition growth, some states are limiting new investments and or are increasing the price of a prepaid contract.

Several state programs have agreements with some private colleges in their states. Check your state's prepaid tuition program to determine if private institutions are included and the nature of the tuition benefits offered.

There are two programs that offer full prepaid tuition benefits for private colleges and universities:

1. The **Massachusetts UPlan** has 79 participating colleges, of which 52 are private colleges and 27 are public colleges. The UPlan is open to non-Massachusetts residents. The UPlan was created prior to the enactment of Section 529 and is underwritten by Massachusetts State Bonds. Although there are unique features including "locking in future tuition at today's prices" and certain tax advantages, it does not have all the benefits of a 529 Plan.

2. The **Private College 529 Plan** is a national program consisting of approximately 270 private schools from around the country and is available to families no matter where they live. Like other prepaid tuition programs, this plan allows investors to purchase some or all of future tuition at today's prices at the selected participating college.

TIP

If you decide to use a Prepaid Tuition Program, consider also saving in a 529 College Savings Plan in order to pay for the additional costs of attendance, such as room and board and books, that the Prepaid Tuition Plan does not cover.

---

529 College Savings Plans

College savings plans are the most popular 529 option. As mentioned before, there are ninety-two college savings plans available from which you can choose. Almost all states offer one savings plan, and some offer several different savings plans, which accounts for the ninety-two.

As you will see next, savings plans offer more flexibility, cover more college costs, and offer more college choice than do prepaid plans.

College Savings Plans: Where They Can Be Used and What They Cover

Section 529 savings plans cover most expenses at most postsecondary institutions.

Eligible Educational Institutions

- Public and private colleges and universities nationwide and some international colleges, including certificate training programs; two-year, four-year, and community colleges; and graduate schools.
- Some undergraduate and graduate schools abroad.
- More than 7,000 institutions are eligible to use 529 Plans. In fact, any school that awards federal financial aid qualifies. Check the list of eligible institutions by visiting the U.S. Department of Education's website at https://fafsa.ed.gov/FAFSA/app/schoolSearch and enter the school code to determine if the school your student is interested in is listed as an eligible institution for 529 purposes.

Qualified Higher Education Expenses

- Tuition and mandatory fees.
- Book, supplies, and equipment (including computer and Internet service) required for enrollment or attendance.
- Room and board for students enrolled at least half time, but limited to either the allowance determined for financial aid purposes OR the actual amount charged if the student lives on campus.
- Expenses for special needs services incurred by a special needs beneficiary at an eligible educational institution.

Who's Who in a 529 Plan

A typical 529 Plan involves a number of participants. Here, briefly, are the key players and their roles:

- **State Agencies**—Oversee all aspects of managing the plan, including selecting the investment providers and program managers. Several states manage their own investments and programs internally.

- **Account Owner**—The person who establishes, contributes to, and controls the account (usually a parent or grandparent) can be a student as well.

- **Beneficiary**—The future student for whom the account is established: in many cases a child, but beneficiaries may be adults, extended family members, or even unrelated individuals.

- **Successor Participant/Owner**—A person designated to take control of the account by the Account Owner if the original participant dies or is incapacitated or at any other time the Account Owner determines.

- **Program Manager**—A financial service company retained by the state to manage investments, market them, and perform administrative duties. Some states serve as program manager and manage their own state plan.

Why Section 529 Savings Plans Are Viewed as the Best Savings Option for Many Families

> Many financial experts view Section 529 Plans as the best strategy for college savings because of the ownership, tax benefits, and ability to re-designate beneficiaries in the future.

Section 529 savings plans, unlike other education or retirement tax-advantaged plans, impose no income limits and have very significant total income limits. Many plans permit contributions in excess of $400,000. You can make annual contributions in excess of what is usually permitted under gift tax laws. Most plans do not have a maximum account balance, making it possible for Section 529 accounts to grow substantially beyond the contribution limit and the full cost of college. In most programs, if funds remain after the beneficiary has graduated from college, the account owner may change the beneficiary to another family member without penalty. This means, for instance, that a parent may establish a 529 account for a child, who then completes college and still has a balance in the 529 account. The account owner may then decide to switch beneficiaries to another child, a grandchild, or any other family member. This is powerful way to save for college and pass monies on to future generations with the earnings and distributions free from taxation.

This favorable federal treatment is available to any person of any age investing in any state's Section 529 Plan. Though each state has its own Section 529 Plan, federal law does not require you to choose your state's program. Instead, state-sponsored Section 529 Plans compete nationwide for your savings, each offering different investment portfolios, options, and fee schedules. As an investor, you may weigh the costs and benefits of each plan and purchase the one that meets your criteria. You may also roll one plan into another without tax consequences if you determine in the future that another plan is better suited to your needs.

TIP

Always check your state's Section 529 Plan before making an investment in a 529 Plan. Many states provide favorable state tax benefits that make their program the best alternative for in-state residents.

In addition to favorable treatment at the federal level, Section 529 Plans enjoy additional state tax advantages.

State Tax Benefits

- States conform to the federal tax rule and do not tax qualified distributions.

- Thirty-three states (plus the District of Columbia) provide tax deductions or credits for contributions to in-state Section 529 programs. See Appendix A for a list of states offering an in-state tax deduction.

- Some states offer additional benefits, such as matching grants and special in-state financial aid treatment.

- Six states provide tax deductions for their residents for contributions to any Section 529 Plan, in- or out-of-state.

  - ◆ Arizona
  - ◆ Kansas
  - ◆ Maine
  - ◆ Missouri
  - ◆ Montana
  - ◆ Pennsylvania

Three Additional Reasons to Save Using a 529 Plan

Reason 1: You can change your mind and always control the money.

For those parents and grandparents who are worried about losing control of the money set aside for college, 529 Plans offer an important reassurance: the donor maintains control of the account. Usually, under federal law, a gift is not entitled to favorable tax treatment if the donor retains substantial control over it. Section 529 Plans are a special case. Contributions are treated as a gift and are removed from your gross estate for tax purposes, but you can still alter or take back your gift at any time.

Though treated as a gift for estate tax purposes, a Section 529 Plan lets you do the following:

- Change the beneficiary to another extended family member, including other children, nieces, nephews, grandkids and their spouses, and even yourself or your spouse.

- Control how the account is invested, changing investment options twice a year or when you change the beneficiary.

- Direct how distributions are used and who receives them.

- Revoke your gift entirely and use the money as you see fit. If 529 monies are not used for qualified educational expenses, the distribution would be subject to income tax on the earnings portion only as well as a 10 percent penalty on those earnings.

Reason 2: You can contribute up to five years of tax-free gifts to a 529 Plan in a single year without incurring a gift tax or using up any of your lifetime exemption.

Under the IRS Code, taxes are imposed on transfers of wealth other than to a spouse or charities through an Estate tax, Gift tax, and/or Generation-skipping tax. Currently, the lifetime exemption is $5.43 million per individual and $10.86 million for a married couple. Under current tax law, you are permitted to gift up to $14,000 per year to another person for any reason without having to pay a gift tax or a generation-skipping tax (GST). This limit is sometimes referred to as the "annual exclusion amount." With a 529 Plan, however, you are able to make a lump-sum contribution equal to five years of annual exclusion gifts to a beneficiary in a single year. This means that you can give up to $70,000 (if you are single) or $140,000 (as a married couple) at once, per beneficiary, without having to pay gift or estate taxes.

There is one catch: if you elect to make a lump sum contribution of multiple years of annual exclusion amounts, you must comply with the "Add Back Rule." In our example, where you made a lump sum contribution equal to five years of annual exclusion amounts, the Add Back Rule stipulates that you must survive into the fifth year in order to have the entire amount excluded from your estate. If you survive only three years, for example, two years will be subject to the Add Back Rule, which means that the last two years of contributions would be considered as part of your estate. Note that the money stays in the 529 account and is not affected whatsoever. Just the technical IRS accounting of the gift exclusion in your estate is affected.

Additional contributions can be made at any time, but you would use some of your lifetime exclusion. If Congress increases the annual exclusion amount, you can contribute up to that amount without using up your lifetime exclusion.

After five years, additional accelerated gifts can be made again without incurring a gift tax or using up your lifetime exclusion.

Reason 3: Section 529 Plans are simpler and more cost-effective than trusts.

Setting up a trust for a child or grandchild can accomplish many worthy goals, but it may not offer all the tax advantages and flexibility of a 529 Plan. There are also legal fees, taxes, and administrative costs involved in establishing and maintaining a trust.

In many states, if you already have a trust, the trust can be the owner of a 529 Plan and receive the same tax-advantaged benefits as an individual owner. Unlike personal income tax rates, trust tax rates are compressed, and a well-funded trust could end up paying 55 percent in annual income taxes.

Trusts can own and invest in a 529 Plan and avoid taxation.

TIP
If you have money already set aside in taxable investments or a trust, consider investing the money into a 529 account. Why pay trust taxes to the IRS when you can let that money compound tax-free until it needs to be used for college?

FINDING THE RIGHT 529 PLAN FOR YOU

With over a hundred 529 Plans scattered among the states and more than 1,500 investment options, selecting the right combination sounds daunting. It doesn't need to be. If you have an account at www.InviteEducation.com, use the Section 529 Plan Comparison Tool to evaluate your options. You will quickly see if there are in-state tax benefits as well as the investment options and other features that may appeal to you.

If you don't have an account, take these four simple steps and become an investor in a 529 Plan:

Step 1: Choose a Plan: Prepaid or Savings.

Step 2: Choose an In-State or Out-of-State Plan.

Step 3: Choose to Purchase Directly from a State or Through a Financial Advisor.

Step 4: Choose Among the Many Investment Options That May Be Best for Your Investment Style.

Step 1: Choose the Type of Plan—Prepaid or Savings

As we discussed, many states offer separate 529 Savings Plans and Prepaid Tuition Programs.

Your first decision is whether to select a Prepaid Program (if your state offers one) or a Savings Plan. As previously described, Prepaid Programs offer certainty, but they limit your college choices and may only pay for college tuition and mandatory fees in participating schools. You will need additional monies for room and board and other college expenses. Savings plans offer the potential of a higher return on your investment, can be used at virtually every college in the country, and cover more expenses. But their flexibility comes with a degree of risk that the earnings may not keep pace with college costs or they lose value right at the time you incur the college costs.

TIP

Consider choice of colleges as well as financial goals when weighing the risks and benefits of prepaid tuition and savings plans. For some families having both a prepaid and savings plan is a good strategy to lock-in tuition while also saving for other costs.

Remember, Prepaid Plans:

- Permit you to lock in the price of tomorrow's tuition today by purchasing a certificate representing some or all of a college's future tuition.

- Are generally used at in-state public schools in which the plan is purchased. A consortium of more than 270 private colleges and the state of Massachusetts also offer private prepaid plans, which may be of interest to you.

- Lock in only the cost of mandatory fees and tuition—there will be other expenses, such as room and board, in the future.

- Include some penalties if you do not use them for their intended purpose and do not guaranty admission to a participating college.

You do not have to buy all of the tuition at once. Some plans offer several options to meet your needs, including a lump-sum purchase or an installment plan. Alternatively, you can save from year to year in a Passbook Savings Account or another temporary savings vehicle and then buy another percentage of the tuition next year.

A Prepaid Program may be a great option for one or more of your children if they are likely to attend an in-state school or one of the colleges in the private college plan. The primary benefit is that you will be guaranteed to keep pace with tuition inflation: there's no chance your savings will fall behind or that stock market dips will erode your investment as college approaches. Depending on whether a state's legislature guarantees its prepaid program, there may be a level of risk and potential for unfunded liabilities. It's best to check with your state's prepaid plan for funding details.

For the previous reasons, purchasing a Prepaid Program buys *you* peace of mind and simplicity.

529 Savings Plans do not lock in future tuition but are worthy of investigation because they offer college savers many important benefits, including more college choice and higher potential returns.

So what should you consider when choosing a 529 Savings Plan?

- Is an in-state or an out-of-state plan best for you?
- What are the Plan's features?
- What do you know about the Plan's performance?
- What are the fees?
- Do you need to purchase through a broker or directly from the state?

Step 2: Choose an In-State or Out-of-State Plan

If your state is one of the thirty-three states that offer tax deductions or credits to residents who choose an in-state plan, the deduction may tip the scale in that state's favor. If, however, you live in one of six states that offer a tax deduction for enrolling in any state's 529 Plan, you are free to consider other factors beyond the tax deduction.

Even if your state gives you a tax break for staying in-state, it may make more sense to choose an out-of-state plan with lower fees, better performance, and/or more flexible rules. Such other features may matter more than the plan's tax treatment. In every case, it makes sense to consider your in-state plan, but that does not necessarily mean it is the best option.

TIP
When deciding between in-state and out-of-state plans, don't automatically choose your own state's plan. Weigh investment choices, rules, performance, and fees against the value of the in-state tax deduction.

If your state does not have an income tax or in-state tax deduction, research and select another state's plan that best meets your needs, as there is no tax advantage for you to enroll in your state's plan. See Appendix A for each state's tax treatment.

In many cases, particularly in states that offer in-state tax benefits, the state plan may be most advantageous for investors. But don't automatically enroll in your state's plan without considering other options. Similarly, don't enroll in a plan solely because your financial advisor or broker recommended it. Ask the advisor for a comparison of a few plans and related fees and expenses or do a little research and comparison-shopping on your own so you will be better able to make an informed decision about which plans offer the most benefits and the lowest fees.

Comparing Plan Features: Not All Programs Are the Same

Each state's 529 Plan is different, depending on the specific state legislation enacted, the agency that manages it, and the financial firm that serves as program and investment manager. Some plans are designed to provide more flexibility than others. Although most have investment options similar to those described below, portfolio composition and fees may vary according to the state or the selected investment manager. Important features such as maximum contribution limits, maximum account balances, designating who gets taxed and receives a nonqualified distribution for tax reasons (the owner or the beneficiary), and other benefits differ from state to state.

Just as plans vary widely, no two investors are exactly alike. Choosing the right plan is heavily dependent on your family's needs and goals. By researching different plans, you can find a Section 529 Plan that is a good fit. If you already have a Section 529 Plan and are unhappy with it, you can look for a different plan and easily roll over your existing plan into it—federal income tax free. Below are some of the issues to consider when selecting or changing a 529 Plan.

Fees and Expenses

States often charge fees to cover to the administrative costs of providing a Section 529 Plan. There may be an annual program management fee (i.e., a flat fee) or a percentage of assets fee (i.e., a fee of 0.25% multiplied by the assets invested in the plan per year). Some states charge both.

In addition, the fund companies that manage the assets usually have an "expense ratio"—an annual fee for the mutual funds in your portfolio. It can range from less than one-tenth of one percent to over 2 percent. Such fees can have a considerable impact on what you actually earn.

Brokers and financial advisors also have fees. Depending on the 529 Plan, these fees are either paid out of the expense ratio charged by the mutual fund company, or, if you purchase a Plan through a broker or advisor, there may be an additional fee known as a "load," which can be up to 5.75 percent of the amounted invested.

TIP

Beware of the fees and expenses a plan charges, as these can significantly diminish your investment returns over time.

The good news is that all 529 program fees, whether direct or advisor-sold, continue to decrease as states use their contracting processes with Program Managers to successfully lower the fees charged to the consumer. Nonetheless, spend the time to understand a Plan's expenses and overall fees.

Step 3: Will You Buy Directly from a State or Use a Financial Advisor?

There are two ways you can open a 529 account—from a state's direct purchase program ("direct-sold") or through a financial advisor ("advisor-sold"). Most states permit out-of-state residents to participate in their state's direct purchase program. Thirty-two states offer thirty-five advisor-sold plans, which are marketed nationally but can only be purchased through a financial advisor.

There are advantages to both approaches. Direct plans often have lower costs, as there are no advisory fees, and overall expenses are often lower. Advisor-sold plans tend to be more expensive and may involve paying fees to the advisor and to the fund companies that sell, manage, and market the program.

If you feel comfortable managing your own investments, a direct-sold plan might be more cost-effective. If you need help managing investments or if you already have a trusted financial advisor, an advisor-sold plan is a good choice.

TIP

Buying direct can help you avoid some fees, but it also requires you to devote time and effort to selecting and managing your Section 529 investments yourself. You may prefer to pay fees to a financial advisor if you have one, if you are not comfortable investing your money, and if you need help deciding which plan best fits into your overall financial goals.

Step 4: Choose Among the Many Investment Options That May Be Best for Your Investment Style.

Section 529 Plans offer a broad array of investment options to match your goals and tolerance for risk, as discussed in Chapter 1. Choices range from diversified age-based portfolios to conservative stable value funds and FDIC-insured Certificate of Deposits to riskier individual mutual funds. Age-based portfolios are used by the majority of account holders and are the core offering of 529 Plans.

Investment Options for Section 529 Plans

Age–Based Investment Portfolios

Age-based portfolios are the preferred choice of most Section 529 investors. Similar to retirement age driven funds, these diversified portfolios are designed to reduce market risk as the beneficiary gets closer to college age. The investor indicates a desired level of risk, and, over time, the portfolio's asset allocation automatically changes from more aggressive to more conservative. Assets are gradually shifted from equities into fixed-income securities and cash. This strategy reduces the likelihood that a stock market correction will wipe out or diminish your college savings when it is time to use those funds.

Static Portfolios

With a static portfolio, the investor can select from several investment styles, including conservative, moderate, and aggressive. Unlike age-based investments, static portfolio allocations do not change as the beneficiary approaches college age and therefore are riskier than age-based investments.

Individual Mutual Funds

Many plans allow an investor to select from a list of individual mutual funds, which may include domestic and international equity funds, index and ETF funds, fixed-income funds, and specialty funds. The funds offered differ from plan to plan and may be riskier than age-based investments.

Stable Value or Principle-Protected Funds

For the conservative investor, many plans offer "stable value" or "principal-protected" funds aimed at protecting the amount invested. These options are designed for those who willingly sacrifice return to avoid market volatility and risk. These funds do not hold equities and consist of fixed-income securities only. They are not FDIC insured, however.

FDIC-Insured Options: Savings Accounts and Certificates of Deposit

For the highest degree of safety, thirteen state plans offer federally guaranteed investment options that protect the principal amount invested. These options rely on a certificate of deposit or savings account, insured by the FDIC and the National Credit Union Administration (NCUA). Investors who choose this approach sacrifice return for safety, as interest rates on savings accounts and CDs tend to be low.

Most plans use age-based portfolios as their core offering; however, each plan's age-based portfolios is different. If you are seeking other approaches, such as a stable value and principal protection investment option, you need to select a program that includes them. Ideally, a Section 529 Savings Plan will offer a menu of twenty to thirty solid performers across all asset classes, including large-, mid-, and small-cap mutual funds; bond funds; stable value funds; and cash.

TIP

Choose a plan with a range of investment options that meet your specific investment goals and tolerance for risk.

Account Maximums and Minimums

Section 529 has generous limits on account balances, allowing you to contribute seven years of higher education expenses—four years of undergraduate and three years of graduate school—for each beneficiary. Each state sets its own contribution limit, and these vary from $235,000 to over $452,000. Some programs have no account balance limits, and balances can grow to any amount, even in excess of $1 million. Others have limits and require a distribution if the limit is exceeded. So, depending on your estate planning needs, time horizon, and funding strategy, it is best to understand these limits.

Most plans have minimums on initial and additional investment amounts. Many allow you to invest as little as $25 for your initial and follow-up investments, provided you set up an automatic investment plan. Some programs also allow you to set up an automatic bank account withdrawal or paycheck deduction without any initial contribution at all.

TIP

Setting up a systematic savings strategy via automatic bank debits or payroll deductions and contributing regularly can help make it easy to save. Data show that those with an automatic savings plan do save and accumulate substantially more than those without an automatic savings plan.

Gifting Programs

Now that you have established a 529 Savings Plan, consider boosting the amount you are saving by using one of the various "Gift Plans" to increase your 529 savings.

Utilizing a 529-gifting program for your child is a smart and efficient way to allow family members and friends to contribute directly to your child's 529 Plan. How many times are you asked by family and friends "what present should I buy or what does she need?" Other times, gift-givers generously buy an expensive toy or other gift that is discarded in short order. Why not suggest a "gift for college" in lieu of a toy or cash? Whether for birthdays, holidays, or special occasions, you can make it easy and rewarding for friends and family to regularly contribute small or large amounts into your child's account.

The 529 industry has responded to consumer demands for such programs and offers online gifting platforms and downloadable gift certificates. These programs make it easy and comfortable for parents to suggest contributions from family and friends toward their children's college savings.

Online Gifting Programs

Non-State-Affiliated Plans

These are privately run, for-profit gifting programs that are not affiliated with a specific state program and enable you to make gifts to virtually all 529 Plans.

Online gifting programs bring much needed technology to 529 Plans. Now grandparents and other relatives can give the gift of college through one of these gifting programs. Families and businesses are spread all over the country. Gift cards make it convenient with their centralized places to give and the ability to track gifts.

Some other unique features offered by Non-State-Affiliated Programs include:

- Expanded payment options, from PayPal to credit cards.
- Sharing of profiles and promoting gifts on social media and e-mail.

- Using gift cards at the retailers we frequent day to day—these companies now make saving for college easy for everyone involved.

Two things to consider if using a Non-State-Affiliated Program: reputation and cost.

First, is the program reputable? Social media and Google searches make it pretty easy to seek out information on companies, including reviews or consumer complaints. Answering a few basic questions could go a long way: Has the company been covered in the media? Is the press favorable or unfavorable? How long has the company been doing this business?

Second, are there hidden fees ? Non-State-Affiliated Programs offer convenient innovations that often come with some sort of fee or service charge. Fees in these programs range from a flat charge to a percentage of the gift. Know and understand these fees, and weigh them against the convenience.

Online Gifting Plans Offered by States

Many state plans allow account holders to invite family and friends to make a contribution through their secure websites, including printable coupons, customized gift cards, and certificates. Gift givers also have the option to mail in a contribution or call directly.

All gifting plans are designed to make it as easy as possible for family and friends to contribute to a child's higher education. These programs provide the relevant 529-account information and eliminate administrative steps and the worry of wondering if the check or cash gift was properly deposited into the college account.

Some programs let you create a customized gifting page and profile for your child or beneficiary. Account holders can sign up for the gifting service and create the online gifting page. Some programs offer online gifting certificates and e-mail notices. In many programs, contributors need to provide only the beneficiary's name and date of birth, but some require the beneficiary's social security number.

529 Credit Card Rebate Programs

Similar to gifting programs, there are a variety of 529 credit card rebate programs that you can utilize to help grow your savings. Much like frequent flyer or money-back credit card programs, the user receives a credit or rebate for each dollar spent via a credit card. Some of these credit card programs are 529-plan-specific, offered through a particular state program that limits rebates into their specific programs only. There are other 529 credit card programs, however, that enable you to direct your rebate to the 529 College Savings Plan of your choice. Consider enrolling in one of these credit card programs and deposit your cash rebates into your college savings account. Grandparents, family members, and friends can also enroll in these credit card programs and contribute to your child's 529 college savings account.

TIP
Establish a 529 Gifting Program and use social media and online services to invite family and friends to contribute. Select a gifting program or credit card rebate program that best meets your needs and get started—it's an easy way to help you meet your college savings goals.

The Achieving a Better Life Experience Act—ABLE 529A

For parents of students with disabilities, saving in a 529A account may be a wise choice to supplement a 529 Savings Account to cover additional expenses beyond what is defined as "qualified educational expenses" under a 529 Plan. The 529A is meant to help people with disabilities, as defined under Social Security rules, and will allow tax-free distributions for certain expenses for the disabled beneficiary, including housing, transportation, health and wellness, education, and more. ABLE 529 Accounts are not the same as 529 Savings accounts in terms of the rules and regulations. Over forty states have enacted their own versions of the ABLE Act, and many are in the process of setting up state ABLE programs, which will offer 529A accounts and conform to the federal law.

In order to be eligible for an ABLE account, the beneficiary must be someone who had a disability that occurred before he or she turned 26. Account holders can take tax-free distributions, provided they are for the beneficiary's qualified disability expenses. One of the biggest benefits of the ABLE account is that the money held there is exempt from the $2,000 limit on personal assets for individuals who wish to qualify for public benefits. Generally, a disabled person with more than that amount is ineligible for Medicaid and Supplemental Security Income benefits.

So, depending on the nature of your child's disability, you may want to establish a 529A account as well as a traditional 529 account. You should investigate whether a 529A account may be appropriate for your situation and whether it makes sense to have one as part of your college savings plan.

For more information on the ABLE 529A plans, contact your state 529 Plan or state Treasurer's Office.

To learn more about ABLE, visit https://www.autismspeaks.org/advocacy/federal/able.

CONSTRUCTING YOUR FAMILY'S SAVINGS PLAN

Accurately predicting college costs years in advance is a nearly impossible task. Historically, college costs have risen substantially more than the inflation rate. Will your child attend a two- or four-year college? In-state or out? Public or private? Will your child live at home, in a dorm, or independently off-campus? Add to these variables the potential increases in tuition and uncertainties about investment returns, and the task of creating an accurate savings goal becomes even more challenging.

> Your college savings plan should be organic, systematic, and dynamic—adapting to changing financial information, circumstances, and goals.

Still, it is possible to make general estimates of possible costs. As your children's college options become clearer, you will be able to gauge how much money you will require for the school they may consider applying to, and you can refine your savings plan accordingly.

Using various college search and financial calculators, you can determine the impact of a variety of factors on college costs and devise a practical savings plan. You can:

- Select specific colleges to see the current and projected future costs based on inflation rates you choose.

- Select a college type (4-year, in-state, public; 4-year, out-of-state, public; 4-year private; or community college) if you're not sure of a specific college to see the school's current and projected future costs based on inflation rates.

- Input your current and expected savings amounts and projected return on the investments to see how much you will have saved as each of your children enters college.

- Perform scenario testing, and see how affordable a particular college or type of college may be for your family based on the projected costs and savings.

- Estimate your Expected Family Contribution (EFC) to see if you might qualify for financial aid at the selected college or type of college.

- Determine your student's admission probability to selected schools based on their grade point average and standardized test scores, and use that information as you develop your saving plan.

Once you have determined how much you will need to pay for college, select the type of savings vehicle, establish a savings strategy, and begin regular weekly or monthly deposits into your college savings account through payroll deductions or electronically from your checking account.

Our goal in this chapter is to educate and make you aware of the various savings options available to finance college and encourage you to develop a savings strategy. Start early, even if you start with as little as $25 a week. Saving is the first and most important step in preparing for your children's college education and related costs.

TIP

Revisit and update your plan at least annually to refine your financial targets, assumptions, and college goals.

SECTION 529 PLANS: COMMONLY ASKED QUESTIONS

To help you better understand 529 Plans, here are some commonly asked questions and answers, organized into the following categories:

- Tax Benefits

- Setting Up the Account

- Ownership and Control

- Beneficiary

- Investment

- Financial Aid

- Prepaid Tuition Plans

Tax Benefits

What are the federal and state tax benefits?

Under Internal Revenue Code (IRC) Section 529, earnings in a 529 Plan grow tax-deferred and are tax-free when used for qualified higher education expenses. Similarly, almost every state exempts earnings and withdrawals for state income tax purposes if used to pay qualified higher education expenses. Earnings not used for qualified higher educational expenses, known as "non-qualified withdrawals," may be subject to federal income taxation and a 10 percent federal penalty tax on the earnings portion only, as well as state income taxation.

Is there a state income tax deduction if I contribute to a 529 Plan?

Thirty-three states offer residents a tax deduction on personal income tax returns for contributions made to their in-state programs. In addition, six states provide tax deductions for contributions to any state's 529 Plan. Check your state's tax rules to determine both the size of the deduction and the rules that apply to investing in a 529 Plan.

What are "qualified higher education expenses" for tax-exempt purposes?

As defined by the IRC, qualified higher education expenses include tuition, fees, room, board, books, supplies, computers, and equipment required for enrollment in or attendance at an eligible educational institution. Eligible institutions include two-year and four-year public and private universities, graduate and professional programs, and even some vocational programs, as well as colleges in other countries. A list of eligible institutions can be found at www.fafsa.ed.gov. Room and board expenses are also eligible for students enrolled half time or more, based on the published amount charged by the institution. Qualified higher education expenses include expenses of a special-needs beneficiary that are necessary in connection with his or her enrollment or attendance at an eligible educational institution.

If I contribute to a 529 Plan, can I also claim an American Opportunity Tax Credit, or AOTC (Hope Scholarship), or Lifetime Learning Credit?

The beneficiary or the beneficiary's parent may claim an AOTC or Lifetime Learning Credit for qualified tuition and related expenses, provided other eligibility requirements are met. But the same expenses cannot be used to justify a tax-free distribution from a qualified tuition program. Be mindful when determining the amount of a 529 distribution so as not to double dip and jeopardize your ability to fully take advantage of the available tax credits.

What other estate planning and gifting tax benefits does Section 529 offer?

An individual may contribute up to $14,000 annually ($28,000 for married couples filing jointly) without paying gift taxes or filing a gift tax return (assuming no other gifts are made to the beneficiary in the same year). You also may accelerate up to five years' worth of the annual exclusion amount and reduce the value of your estate by contributing up to $70,000 ($140,000 for married couples filing jointly) per beneficiary. This amount is subject to "add-back" in the event of the participant's death within five years and assumes you made no other gifts to the beneficiary during this period.

Can a trust invest in a 529 Plan and receive tax-free withdrawals?

Yes, any trust can own a 529 Plan and avoid paying up to a 55 percent income tax rate on earnings if the funds are used to pay for qualified higher education expenses.

Setting Up the Account

How do I open a 529 Plan?

There are two ways to open up an account. 529 Plans are available directly through states known as "Direct-sold" or through financial advisers known as "Advisor-sold ." "Direct-sold" are offered without sales commissions. For those who would like professional advice, contact your financial advisor as many states offer "Advisor-sold" programs that offer professional investment advice and service with standard sales commissions applying.

Can anyone open a 529 account? What about grandparents, aunts, and uncles?

Any U.S. citizen or resident alien of legal age can open a 529 account. Grandparents, other relatives, and family friends can all be account owners. In most states, a trust, corporation, nonprofit, or government entity can also open an account.

Are there age or income limitations for participating in a 529 Plan?

No. In most states, there are no age or income limits for the contributor, account owner, or beneficiary. The account owner, however, has to be of legal age to open an account.

Who can contribute to an account?

Anyone can make a contribution to an account for any beneficiary regardless of whether this person is a family member or not. There are 529 gifting websites that enable people to make a gift to 529 accounts to any beneficiary for any reason.

Ownership and Control

Who owns and controls funds in a 529 account?

The individual who opens a 529 account, not the beneficiary, is the owner and retains full control of money in the account. The owner can change the beneficiary, roll over the funds to another state's 529 Plan, or withdraw funds at any time for any purpose. Withdrawals not made for qualified higher education expenses carry a 10 percent federal penalty on the earnings portion only, unless the child receives a full scholarship, becomes disabled, or passes away. Many states permit the owner to designate who would receive the nonqualified distribution.

Why is a 529 Plan a unique estate-planning tool?

For estate tax purposes, funds invested in a 529 Plan leave your estate but do not leave your control. This feature does not exist anywhere else in the Internal Revenue Code and is a powerful benefit compared to "normal" gift and estate tax laws.

Beneficiary

Who can be the beneficiary of my 529 Plan?

Any legal U.S. resident can be the beneficiary of a 529 Plan. You can even open an account with yourself as the beneficiary to help with your own higher education expenses. There are no age or family relationship limits on 529 Plan beneficiaries.

Can a beneficiary have more than one 529 Plan account?

Yes, provided that the combined total of all accounts for the same beneficiary in the same state does not exceed that state's maximum contribution limit. (The beneficiary could get around the limit by having more than one account owned by different account owners under different state plans.)

Can I change my 529 Plan's beneficiary?

Yes, a change in beneficiaries is permitted and can be accomplished without federal income tax or penalty provided that the new beneficiary is a qualified member of the current beneficiary's extended family.

For purposes of changing beneficiaries on a 529 Plan, the IRC defines a "qualified family member" as one of the following (in relation to the current beneficiary):

- Son or daughter or descendant of son or daughter
- Stepson or stepdaughter
- Brother, sister, stepbrother, stepsister
- Mother or father or parent of mother or father
- Stepmother or stepfather
- Son or daughter of brother or sister
- Brother or sister of mother or father
- Spouse of any individual listed above
- First cousin of beneficiary
- Brother-in-law, sister-in-law, son-in-law, daughter-in-law, father-in-law, mother-in-law

Can my plan beneficiary attend college anywhere in the United States?

Yes. Withdrawals can be used at over 7,000 eligible institutions in this country and around the world. Eligible institutions include two-year and four-year public and private universities, graduate and professional programs, and even some vocational programs. A list of eligible institutions can be found at www.fafsa.ed.gov.

What if the beneficiary of my account decides not to go to college?

You have several options if the beneficiary decides not to go to college:

- Change the beneficiary to another member of the beneficiary's family.
- Defer use of your savings and leave contributions invested in the account.

> ◆ Make a nonqualified distribution to yourself or others. Earnings withdrawn (but not contribution amounts) would be subject to state and federal tax at the recipient's tax rate plus a 10 percent federal tax penalty.

A change in beneficiary to a person who is not a qualified family member is treated as a non-qualified withdrawal.

How can I change the beneficiary on an account?

To change the beneficiary, contact your 529 Plan to determine the requirements of your plan and obtain the necessary forms. As long as the new and old beneficiaries are among the qualified family members listed above, there will not be a taxable event or liability. Changing the beneficiary to a nonfamily member may trigger a taxable event, which could also include a penalty, gift tax, or both.

Investment

Once an account is established, who directs how it is invested?

The account owner does. 529 Plans offer multiple investment options for the account owner to choose from after opening the account.

What are the most common investment options offered by Section 529 savings plans?

The most common investment option is an age-based portfolio of diversified investment vehicles. This strategy is age-appropriate and risk-adjusted. As the beneficiary approaches college, the investment mix is automatically rebalanced and becomes more conservative. Other portfolio options include all-equity, balanced, and conservative-fixed portfolios. In addition, there are individual mutual funds, fixed income funds, and stable value funds as well as guaranteed or principal-protected options. FDIC-insured options include savings accounts and CDs.

Can you change investment options once you have opened an account?

Yes. You may change your selection for all or any portion of the funds already invested in a particular investment twice per calendar year or upon a change of the beneficiary. In addition, each time a new contribution is made to any account, the investor can select a different investment option for the new contribution.

Can I transfer my UGMA/UTMA account into a 529 Plan?

Yes, provided that certain requirements are met. Since 529 Plan accounts can accept only cash contributions, assets in UGMA/UTMA accounts must be liquidated. A 529 account receiving cash from UGMA/UTMA liquidations will be subject to restrictions, since all withdrawals from UGMA/UTMA accounts must be made for the benefit of the beneficiary, and the beneficiary will assume control of the assets upon reaching the age of majority. Once the funds from UGMA/UTMA accounts are in a 529 account, the same rules will apply to qualified and nonqualified distributions from the 529.

Can I roll over my existing Coverdell Education Savings Account (Education IRA) into a 529 Plan?

Yes, and without a tax penalty. Because taking a distribution from your Coverdell account to invest in a 529 Plan is considered a qualified withdrawal, it is not a taxable event for federal tax purposes. Assets in a Coverdell account must be liquidated to accomplish the transfer as 529 accounts only accept cash contributions.

Financial Aid

How does a 529 Plan affect federal financial aid eligibility?

529 Plan assets are treated just as savings accounts, mutual funds, or other financial assets are for purposes of financial aid calculations. A 529 account owned by a parent for a dependent student is reported on the Free Application for Federal Student Aid (FAFSA®) as a parental asset. Parental assets are assessed at a maximum 5.64 percent rate in determining the student's Expected Family Contribution (EFC). Any assets that you or the beneficiary owns affect your eligibility for need-based financial aid. In fact, 529 assets are treated more favorably than many other savings vehicles, such as custodial accounts, Coverdell accounts, and other assets. If

assets are in the name of the student, 20 percent of the value of the assets is considered in determining the EFC. If a student owns a 529 account, it is assessed at a rate of 5.64 percent as opposed to 20 percent.

Will a 529 qualified distribution be considered part of "base-year income" for federal financial aid purposes?

No, it will not be considered income if the account is owned by the student or parent. A qualified distribution from a 529 Plan that's owned by the parent or student to pay this year's qualified college expenses will not be part of the base-year income that reduces the following year's financial aid eligibility. It will have no impact whatsoever. However, if the account is owned by a grandparent or someone else other than the parent and student, the amount of the distribution will be considered as income to the student and will have an impact on financial aid eligibility. Therefore, it is recommended that a non-parent or student 529 account distribution be made in the student's senior year when it will not be used in the prior base year and will have no impact on the student's financial aid eligibility.

Prepaid Tuition Programs

Do I have to be a resident of a state to enroll in a Prepaid Tuition Program?

In most states, either the account owner or the beneficiary must be a resident of the state that administers the plan at the time of enrollment. Prepaid Tuition Program rules and policies vary from state to state, so you would need to check the specific requirements of a state to determine your eligibility.

Am I limited to in-state colleges if I enroll in a state prepaid plan?

Prepaid Tuition Program benefits are generally designed to be used at in-state public schools. Several programs permit their use at private colleges as well as out-of-state public and private colleges and universities. Check the plan details for the prepaid plan in your state as well as those plans that permit private and out-of-state use.

What if I have a Prepaid Tuition Program, but my child decides not to attend the in-state college?

Many states offer refund and transfer options at different payout levels. You should check with the program to determine to whom the benefits can be transferred or how to receive a refund.

Can a prepaid tuition account be rolled over to another 529 program, and can I change the beneficiary?

Each state permits rollovers and changes of beneficiaries to a qualified family member, as previously described. Rules vary so it is important to determine whether other requirements apply.

Do 529 savings or prepaid admission plans guarantee college admission for my child?

No. Your child will still be required to meet entry requirements as determined by individual colleges or universities.

If I have a special needs (disabled) child, can I save in a 529 Plan? Are there special provisions for people with disability?

Yes you can. In 2014, Congress created a new type of 529 account called ABLE 529A accounts for the supplemental costs of the special needs of disabled students. Run by the states, qualified ABLE 529 Programs will allow families to enjoy tax-free growth and allow assets to avoid disqualifying the beneficiary from state or federal aid. Earnings from the ABLE 529A account will be tax free if used for qualifying expense. Several states are offering ABLE accounts. Please note the rules and regulations are different from the traditional 529 Plans, so check with the appropriate state ABLE 529A plan for more information.

Chapter 2 Takeaways

- Tax-advantaged savings plans, particularly 529 Plans, let you save large amounts for higher education and permit tax-free compounding and distributions.

- 529 Plans offer gift and estate tax benefits while still letting you to retain control over your funds—a unique feature not found elsewhere in the Internal Revenue Code.

- Remember 529 Plans are treated the same as other assets such as bank savings accounts, bonds, or mutual funds for financial aid calculations.

- 529 Plans come in a variety of shapes and sizes—prepaid tuition programs, savings plans, in-state and out-of-state, direct, and advisor-sold. They have different investment options, management options, tax benefits, and fees.

- Trusts can own a 529 Plan, whether an existing trust or a new trust.

- Other tax-advantaged and taxable investment vehicles can play a role in saving for college.

- Develop a budget and savings strategy that is flexible and dynamic. You should periodically revisit your plan as your college goals and your finances evolve.

Chapter 3

Financial Aid Primer—The Basics

Saving may be the best way to pay for college, but sometimes it's just not enough. Do not despair. There are many strategies for filling the gap between how much you have and how much you need.

Ideally, you would step into a time machine, go back a few decades, and, armed with perfect knowledge of the future, make different choices. You could spend less, save more, and invest in a small, little-known company called "Google".

In the absence of time travel, unfortunately, you will have to turn to more practical solutions. The first one to consider should be financial aid.

The following is an introduction to key terms and an overview of the financial aid process. Chapter 9: The Financial Aid Process provides additional details and strategies for managing the process.

INTRODUCTION TO FINANCIAL AID: MAKE SURE YOUR "AID" IS ACTUALLY AID

"Financial aid" refers to any grant, scholarship, loan, or paid employment offered to help a student meet college expenses. It is important to recognize that not all financial aid is the same: "free money" (a grant or scholarship) does not need to be repaid; other aid needs to be repaid (loans) or earned (work-study).

Recent data indicate that 85 percent of undergraduate students received financial aid in pursuit of their first bachelor's degree. However, guaranteed federal student loans are included in the majority of these financial aid packages. Federal loans, like all other loans, must be repaid with interest. There's no such thing as a free lunch when borrowing money from a bank or the federal government.

In our way of looking at the world, it is misleading to categorize loans as financial aid. But the reality is that the federal government has issued more than $1.3 trillion in college loans and requires colleges to present federal loans as financial aid to students. Mind boggling, but true.

Students seeking need-based financial aid from the federal government or their college are required to file some forms to be considered for aid. Chapter 10: Filing the Financial Aid Forms will walk you through the process of filling out the forms. Applying for financial aid is, in effect, the second application process for college. At the conclusion of the process, students receive a Financial Aid Award Letter. The simplest way to classify funding on a Financial Aid Award Letter is as follows:

- **Grants and scholarships:** Because there is no need to repay, this "free" money is the most highly sought through the financial-aid process. Grants are awarded after considering a family's financial need, while scholarships and other merit-based awards are given for sports, academic achievement, or other outstanding student qualities.

- **Work-Study:** Money is earned for working at jobs typically available on campus as assigned by the program. Students earn paychecks as hours are completed, normally not exceeding 20 hours per week.

- **Loans:** Federal Direct Loans need to be repaid but are considered a form of financial aid due to the government subsidy.

When looking at financial aid for the first time, you might imagine yourself trying to learn a new language full of acronyms and abbreviations that, without explanation, can be confusing. Following are explanations of some of the most important terms.

Cost of Attendance (COA). The Cost of Attendance represents all costs, including tuition, room, board, books, transportation, mandatory fees, and miscellaneous expenses. This number also represents the maximum amount of financial aid that could potentially be paid to the account, including student loans, to cover the balance.

Expected Family Contribution (EFC). The EFC is the amount of money a family would be expected to have available to cover college costs for a single academic year. This number is initially calculated by the Free Application for Federal Student Aid (FAFSA®) using the financial information provided by the family. The FAFSA® permits students to select colleges to receive this information. Upon receipt of FAFSA® data, each school gets to work creating financial aid award letters for new students as well as returning students. The EFC is used by each school to calculate financial aid eligibility using governmental and institutional award policies and methodologies. This can include eligibility for Federal Pell Grants and subsidized Direct Loans, and it may also include state or institutionally backed grants. Generally, the lower the EFC, the more likely a student will be eligible for need-based financial aid, whereas the higher the EFC, the less financial aid will be available.

Federal vs. Institutional Award Methodology. The Federal Methodology is a formula used to determine aid eligibility for all federal financial aid programs including Pell Grants, Federal Direct Loans, Federal Work Study, and many state scholarship programs—all based on the information provided in the FAFSA®. Institutional Methodology is a formula established by the College Board and modified by many colleges for the purpose of allocating their own institutional financial aid based on information filed on the CSS/Financial Aid PROFILE® (or a specific college's required form). To be clear, the CSS/Financial Aid PROFILE® is in addition to the FAFSA® and is required by many private colleges and a few state schools.

Financial Need. Ultimately, colleges determine a student's financial need after reviewing eligibility for all funding sources and proceed to award additional available funding to students with the highest need. For example, a student receiving a full athletic scholarship may have little financial need, but a student qualifying for a Pell Grant may still have a sizable bill to cover.

Financial aid offices follow required federal policies and regulations as well as their own institution policies to ensure that students are treated in a fair and equitable manner.

Before taking another step, realize that in any language, deadlines are deadlines. If you miss a financial aid deadline—even by a day—you may be disqualified from being considered for aid. See Chapter 9 for details about these deadlines.

Where Does Financial Aid Come From?

The financial aid stork delivers aid from several sources:

- **Federal Government.** The Federal Government is by far the largest supplier of student financial aid through the U.S. Department of Education and the Federal Student Aid Program (FSA) . These programs are designed to provide aid to all students without regard to family income level, with many grant programs specifically designed to assist lower-income students. It is important to understand that the formula used to calculate financial need is largely driven by family income. Most financial aid is distributed through the Pell Grant Program (for low-income families) and the student and parent loan programs for all families regardless of income level. For more information about loans, see Chapter 5.

- **Colleges and Universities.** Colleges provide "Institutional Aid" based on merit and/or need. Some also have their own institutional loan programs as well.

- **States.** Many states offer grants to resident students attending college within the state, otherwise known as "in-state" grant programs. These state programs are part of a state budget. Some states allocate portions of property taxes or lottery revenues to fund scholarships and grants for in-state residents. Some programs are merit-based, linked to a student's academic performance on tests or in high school based on grade point average. Others are need-based, often requiring the student to be a full-time resident for one year or more before qualifying for this grant to attend an in-state school.

- **State and Regional Tuition Discounts.** Certain states may offer tuition reciprocity with neighboring states, where students may attend a qualified out-of-state institution but still receive discounted in-state tuition. Programs like the Academic Common Market, The Midwest Student Exchange, or the Western Undergraduate Exchange may offer this opportunity to a limited number of students each year and require additional application processing. The Maine Public College System now offers in-state tuition prices to any student from the New England region attending a public college in Maine.

- **Third-Party Scholarships.** Local civic organizations, employers, and large national interest groups offer scholarships to college-bound students. Unlike Institutional Aid that can only be used at the college making the award, these scholarships and grants are portable and can most often be used at whichever college or university the student attends. These scholarships are awarded after an application process used by the sponsor.

More About Scholarships and Grants

As detailed in Chapter 4: Scholarships—Get Free Money, many grants and scholarships are one-time awards that result from contests (essays) or an affiliation to a particular group that sponsors the award. Most are not automatically renewed in subsequent years. In recent years, the application process has been modernized so that students may apply for many different scholarships after searching online. It's critical to stay organized and follow up to meet all eligibility requirements.

Unfortunately, as explained in more detail in Chapter 4, a student's financial aid package may be reduced by the amount of a third-party scholarship. This sounds counter-intuitive: why would a scholarship reduce the amount of financial-aid a student receives? For purposes of the arcane world of financial aid terms, the scholarship is considered a "resource," and the schools reduce the amount of the financial aid package dollar for dollar because the scholarship is considered as available money to pay for tuition.

There is growing recognition among policy makers and others that it is unfair to penalize industrious students and families who are seeking creative ways to fund their Expected Family Contribution. Trade associations and individuals have begun to lobby Congress to change regulations that allow colleges to reduce financial aid by the amount of the scholarship. The higher education community in general will likely prefer to keep the current treatment in place as a means of stretching scarce financial aid dollars to more students.

What Kind of Financial Aid Might the Stork Deliver?

Let's begin with a fundamental point: The two types of financial aid awards are need-based aid and merit-based aid.

Need-Based Aid

If your student does not receive merit aid or if partial merit aid does not entirely fill the gap, do not give up. There is potential for need-based financial aid acquired through the FAFSA® and accompanying financial aid methodologies employed by colleges and universities.

Need-based aid is awarded after reviewing family assets and income as disclosed on the FAFSA® and/or the CSS/Financial Aid PROFILE® (see Chapter 9). Objective policy regarding each school's financial aid process must be used to fairly treat each student and consider the student's overall funding, including scholarships from third parties, when finally calculating financial need.

TIP

Apply for need-based aid by filing your FAFSA® as soon as possible regardless of your income or financial status. Even those with high family incomes are eligible for federal student loans, which require families to apply for need-based aid. It is one way to keep all of your college financing options open.

Know that college financial aid offices work hard to provide funding for all students but face predictable budgetary constraints due to overwhelming demand. As a result, they carefully consider the "big picture" when awarding monies directly from the school's budget. Before awarding a large amount of merit-based scholarship money to a student, the school may want to first determine if the student would qualify for substantial need-based aid from federal and state sources. This is one reason to file the FAFSA® early—to make it easy for the school to determine eligibility for aid from all sources, thereby maximizing the award to a student.

See Chapter 10 for details about the forms required to be considered for need-based financial aid.

Merit-Based Aid

Merit aid is usually awarded by the college based on the student's academic performance or special skills, talents, or other attributes. Colleges use merit aid to round out the incoming freshman class. Athletic scholarships are a familiar type of merit aid award; other forms are sometimes less apparent.

Perhaps the college needs an oboe player, an actress, a debate champion, or a student from Alaska to balance their class. An academically qualified candidate who happens to meet a specific need of the college may be the fortunate recipient of unexpected merit aid. Many merit-based awards are granted for each of the student's four years and do not require the recipient to do anything more than maintain good academic standing or a specified minimum Grade Point Average (GPA) while in school.

Institutional merit aid (merit aid provided by colleges) may be awarded to students without the student filing an application for financial aid. Institutional scholarships and grants may be awarded based on a wide range of qualifications, talents, or interests not always related to need. Talent in any one of many areas—music, visual arts, volunteer activity, and others—is sometimes enough to qualify a student. Scholarships may be awarded for the following:

- Academic major or interests
- Artistic talents
- Club or other extracurricular activity
- Community service
- Leadership
- Musical ability
- Place of residence geography
- Religion, race, or ethnicity
- Sports
- Winning games and contests organized by sponsors

High school seniors or juniors seeking merit-based aid often rely on their academic performance, awards, leadership, community service, or special talents to get a scholarship or grant.

A strong history of performance, in class or in extracurricular activities, is important when seeking merit-based aid—not to mention when seeking admission in general. The most selective schools choose from the most accomplished achievers. Less selective colleges accept good all-around students who may not have placed an emphasis on classwork, didn't "get it," or didn't focus academically until it was too late for one reason or another.

Like their more selective brethren, practically all of these colleges provide some type of merit-based aid to recruit and assemble a great, academically strong and diversified class of students.

After three years of high school, your prospective college freshman will have a track record of academic performance, test scores, participation in extracurricular and community activities, and perhaps some awards and demonstration of leadership. Your student's mission (with your help and from others such as their guidance counselor) is to package and present this record in the best possible light to the colleges for admission as well as consideration for merit aid.

Colleges rely on a number of factors when making their judgment on who should receive merit-based aid:

- **Course load.** A full course load per semester is ideal. Taking honors and Advanced Placement® (AP®) courses is particularly helpful and may be required for the most selective colleges.

- **Grades.** Strong grades matter, though colleges often view good grades in challenging, advanced courses more favorably than outstanding grades in easier, lower-level courses. Grades that improve throughout high school are advantageous.

- **Academic strength and reputation of your student's high school.** Admissions officers know the relative rigor of the high schools very well and often adjust students' grade point averages based on the reputation of the high school. Many large colleges have quantified the process of adjusting high school grades in order to evaluate candidates on an apples-to-apples basis.

- **Test scores.** You have a choice: pick the standardized test (ACT® or SAT®) on which your student scored the highest. Taking the test more than once is recommended. Some state and national scholarship providers base their scholarships solely on the result of certain standardized tests.

- **Participation in community service and extracurricular activities.** Demonstrating leadership, passion, and commitment in a few activities is more highly sought than simply listing a long list of activities.

YOUR FINANCIAL AID PACKAGE

When packaging need-based awards, colleges may provide students with a combination of institutional and federal aid. The following are three of the most frequently used federal aid programs:

- Federal Pell Grants, for the most financially needy students

- Federal Student Loans

- Federal Work-Study

Federal Pell Grants

The Federal Pell Grant is usually awarded to undergraduates who have a high degree of unmet financial need. Students whose families have a total income of up to $50,000 may be eligible for the need-based funding, though most Pell Grant money goes to students with a total family income below $20,000.

Pell Grants may be awarded to undergraduate students annually in amounts determined by Congress. Pell Grant are free money—they do not have to be repaid. In recent years, Pell Grant maximums have increased slightly from year to year. The Pell Grant program provides aid to more than 9 million students annually, making it the largest grant program. For the 2015–16 award year (July 1, 2015 through June 30, 2016), the maximum award amount was $5,775. For academic year 2016–17, the maximum Pell Grant will increase to at least $5,815. The amount of a student's Pell award may change annually based upon the FAFSA® submission for the next academic year.

Be sure to continue filing the FAFSA® each year and recognize that Pell may be subject to change based on (a) your family's changing financial circumstances (i.e., income, number of children in college, or other factors) each year and (b) the maximum award amount as determined by Congress.

Federal Student Loans

Federal student loans are also included in the need-based financial aid package. Chapter 5 details these programs. For now, here are the relevant points for the government's largest loan program, the Federal Direct Loan Program:

- Every student, regardless of family income level, is eligible for some type of federal student loan (as long as a FAFSA® is filed).

- The Department of Education (DoE) is your lender, and payments are made to the DoE through one of its student loan collection vendors.

- The amount that can be borrowed is capped based on the student's school year:

    - Freshman cap: $5,500

    - Sophomore cap: $6,500

    - Junior cap: $7,500

    - Senior cap: $7,500

Remember that even though the college packages these federal student loans as aid, it is not "free money" like a grant or scholarship. Don't be fooled. Loans, even those made by the federal government, must be repaid with interest. It is true that the Direct Loan program includes provisions for some or all of the loan to be forgiven; however, that is generally only granted to provide relief in difficult times or if one pursues a public service career and meets certain guidelines. At the time the loan is made, it is expected that it will be repaid. Loans can become a lifetime burden, and even personal bankruptcy will usually not discharge them.

Chapter 5 discusses the Federal Student and Parent Loan programs in greater detail.

Federal Work-Study Program

The Federal Work-Study (FWS) program helps students pay for college by providing jobs at participating institutions. It is not "free money" either because it must be earned. In 2012–13, more than 3,000 schools participated in the Work-Study program enabling more than 9 million students nationwide to earn almost $1 billion total toward college costs.

Work-Study monies are awarded first to students with the highest need. However, once the semester begins, some students may not be able to commit to their work-study hours or otherwise don't show up. This may make more work-study funding available to another student who was originally rejected due to less financial need. The bottom line: always check with your school regarding Federal Work-Study. If a student does not initially receive an FWS award at the beginning of the school year, some money may be allocated later in the year. Some students identify jobs through their professors or other campus administrator and then successfully petition the financial aid office for the job.

COLLEGE DISCRETION IN ADJUSTING THE AID PACKAGE

Colleges have some discretion in the adjustment of a financial aid package given changes in a student's eligibility. An important example cited by surprised parents is when a student qualifies for a merit-based scholarship *after* he or she was formally awarded need-based funding. Once the school determines the student is eligible for additional funding from a scholarship, his or her financial need may actually reduce, causing a reduction in need-based aid, leaving no net gain in the their total financial aid.

The school's policy may follow a dollar-for-dollar swap where the student's original funding is reduced by exactly the amount of the new scholarship. Other schools may reduce the amount of your student's loan, which is to your benefit. That means replacing loan dollars that you must pay back with scholarship dollars that you don't pay back. Other colleges may apply the scholarship award toward the next semester.

You should contact your college's financial aid office directly to ask what its policy on outside scholarships is and how your student's aid package will be adjusted.

For a more detailed discussion on "negotiating" adjustments in financial aid packages, please see Chapter 9.

EDUCATION BENEFITS FOR MEMBERS OF THE MILITARY

The U.S. military provides a free education to students accepted into one of its five service academies:

- United States Military Academy in West Point, New York.

- United States Naval Academy in Annapolis, Maryland.

- United States Coast Guard Academy in New London, Connecticut.

- United States Merchant Marine Academy in Kings Point, New York.

- United States Air Force Academy in Colorado Springs, Colorado.

Veterans, actively serving members of the military, and survivors may be eligible for a panoply of valuable education aid for use at nonmilitary educational institutions.

Select Education Benefits for the Military

Reserve Officers' Training Corps (ROTC) scholarships: These full or partial scholarships are awarded to college students on the basis of merit, not financial need. Recipients must agree to a period of active military service after graduation. This obligation varies, depending on the scholarship contract, and can range from four to eight years of service, some in active duty and some in the reserves.

Iraq and Afghanistan Service Grants: Students who do not meet the financial need requirements for federal financial aid can still receive aid if a parent or guardian died as a result of the 9/11 attacks or the wars in Iraq and Afghanistan. The award maximum reflects the maximum Pell Grant award for the current academic year.

Department of Veterans Affairs Education Benefits:

- The Post-9/11 GI Bill provides up to 36 months of education benefits for both degree and non-degree programs.

- Degree-granting institutions participating in the Post-9/11 GI Bill's Yellow Ribbon Program agree to provide additional funds for a student's education, not counted toward the student's total GI Bill entitlement.

- The **Montgomery GI Bill**®, the **Reserve Educational Assistance Program**, and the **Survivors' and Dependents' Educational Assistance Program** may also offer benefits.

- The **Service-Members Civil Relief Act** limits the amount of interest that can be charged for a student loan while military personnel are on active duty.

- The following organizations offer financial assistance for education to veterans:
  - American Legion
  - AMVETS
  - Disabled American Veterans
  - Paralyzed Veterans of America
  - Veterans of Foreign Wars

Chapter 3 Takeaways

- "Financial Aid" refers to any loan, grant, scholarship, or paid employment offered to help a student meet his or her college expenses. Some aid is "free money" that doesn't need to be repaid.

- It is important to understand that unless you are determined to have high financial need, a good portion of financial aid will likely not be free money. Rather, the majority of "aid" will be in the form of loans that must be repaid with interest.

- Aid is usually based on need or merit. Need, for purposes of federal financial aid, is determined through the FAFSA®. The amount of need-based aid you receive is based on your EFC. Merit-based aid may take the form of academic excellence, but notable talent in sports, the arts, and other areas may also be sufficient.

- To receive Institutional Aid from a college, you may need to provide further documentation, e.g., the College Scholarship Service Profile (CSS/Financial Aid PROFILE®), or another form provided by the college. Colleges may ask more questions than the federal government, but they may also be more generous.

- Know the FAFSA® and CSS/Financial Aid PROFILE® deadlines for each college.

- Applications for need-based financial aid must be resubmitted annually for a student to continue to receive aid.

- If you do not receive sufficient aid, consider "value colleges." These are high-quality public and private institutions that have a lower Cost of Attendance relative to their peers, making them more affordable, perhaps even without financial assistance.

- The military offers a wide range of educational benefits for college students, actively serving members of the military, survivors, and veterans.

Chapter 4

Scholarships—Get Free Money

To help defray the cost of college, many students seek out "free" money from third-party scholarship providers. Some industrious students have been known to pay for their entire college experience by piecing together scholarships from third parties. Other students seek scholarships as one part of their overall strategy for paying college—a terrific way to reduce the amount of potential debt they may incur.

Unfortunately, there is a dark cloud around this silver college-financing lining: the Federal Government's rules on financial aid eligibility require schools to reduce the amount of need-based aid financial aid it awards a student by the amount of the third-party scholarship. More on this later.

OUTSIDE OR THIRD-PARTY SCHOLARSHIP PROVIDERS

An outside or third-party scholarship is a scholarship awarded by an organization other than the government or your college—such as the parent's employer, a high school, a foundation, or a community organization.

Remember that receiving an outside, or private, scholarship can actually reduce the amount of financial aid from your college. However, that doesn't mean you'll have to pay a bigger share of your college costs. It just means that the scholarship dollars replace financial-aid-package dollars because scholarship money is required by the federal government to be viewed as a resource available to pay for college.

Many people erroneously believe that if their child is not a star athlete or top student, he or she has no chance of receiving a scholarship or grant. Or, perhaps you are a higher-income family so you think there is no way a college will offer you merit aid. Not so.

Every year, there are over 2 million scholarships—worth billions of dollars—awarded nationwide by colleges and other organizations for a host of reasons. Grants and scholarships come from a variety of sources, some unexpected. Sponsors can include the following:

- Your local high school, church, synagogue, and community organizations
- Your employer
- Your state government
- The Federal Government
- Colleges
- Foundations and not-for-profit groups
- Large corporations
- Private trusts and scholarship endowments

TIP

Do not pay to enter scholarship or grant contests. There are plenty of free resources to help you identify free-money opportunities. Don't pay a consultant to identify scholarship opportunities for your family.

Your Student Can Start Well Before Senior Year

Some organizations run contests of all kinds for students in a range of grades, some as early as elementary school. These contests offer cash prizes for a variety of activities or interests, including, but not limited to:

- Completing an environmental project.
- Building robots.
- Creating art works.

- Writing essays.

- Being entrepreneurs.

- Winning spelling bees and geography, oratory, haiku, or math competitions.

The lists go on and on. Google even runs its "Doodle 4 Google" competition in which winners in five grade groups (K–3, 4–5, 6–7, 8–9, and 10–12) and their schools are awarded cash and other prizes.

Searching for scholarships and grants for children under 13 can be tricky because of various federal privacy laws. Online databases that typically match an older student's interests with scholarship providers must first obtain "verifiable parental consent" for searches for children under 13. Look around. Websites are able to provide lists of opportunities for students under age 13.

Some organizations provide grants and scholarships for students to attend college in the future—not just next year. It's worthwhile for high school sophomores and juniors to explore scholarships and grants.

You Can't Win If You Don't Play: How to Find Scholarships and Grants

The old-fashioned ways still work:

- Ask guidance counselors and college advisors for lists of scholarships and grants—especially annual local grants given out by the high school or local individuals or community groups.

- Look in a book. There are many excellent scholarship search books that detail organizations offering the free money as well as their selection criteria.

And so does technology:

- Use scholarship search engines that include a wide range of scholarships and grants to identify opportunities for your child. Find out about the funding they offer and the application requirements. Search using a variety of criteria—type of award (scholarship, loan, prize, etc.), geographic area, subject matter, ethnicity, religion, citizenship, military service, and more. You may also flag and save these for each of your children and receive automated e-mail reminders when deadlines are approaching.

- Many states also have agencies that provide web-based services.

It's an exciting time to search for scholarships as more and more are being offered each year, but competition is high. Today, students are winning scholarships for utilizing social media; self-producing creative content; building portfolios of art, music, or film; and finding new ways to engage their communities to make a difference.

Effect of Outside Scholarships on a Financial Aid Package

One of the major and unpleasant surprises for students who are awarded outside scholarships is that their financial aid package is reduced by the amount of the outside scholarship. Why, you may ask? Because this is a federal rule, so that schools often do not have a choice in the matter. If all the aid you receive—outside scholarships, financial aid from your college, and government grants and loans—ends up being $300 or more above your calculated need, the Federal Government requires your college to reduce the amount of need-based financial aid it awards you.

Likewise, if a third-party scholarship is for one year only, the amount of need-based aid for which your student may be eligible may increase in a future year, as this would be a change in financial circumstances that could result in more need-based aid.

NOTE: OUTSIDE SCHOLARSHIPS MUST BE REPORTED.

If your student receives an outside scholarship, be sure that he or she notifies the college's financial aid office. If this is not done, your family may be required to pay back all or part of your need-based financial aid package to the school or government.

Know the College's Policy

Winning a scholarship is an exciting reward for students who have worked hard to develop their talents and achieve success. However, in all the excitement, it's important to realize how the scholarship fits into the big picture regarding total financial aid funding. Contact the financial aid office—preferably before your student applies for a scholarship—so you know how the award will be treated. Some colleges may have their policy clearly cited on their website.

You should contact your college's financial aid office directly to ask what its policy on outside scholarships is and how your student's aid package will be adjusted.

Chapter 4 Takeaways

- Third-party scholarships can effectively round out your student's strategy for paying for college.

- Grants and scholarships may be available based on geography, religious affiliation, or other characteristics. Identify them by asking guidance counselors and using books and/or the Internet.

- If you receive need-based financial aid, the amount of aid will likely be reduced by the amount of third-party scholarships received. However unpleasant this may be, be sure to report a third-party scholarship to the financial aid office or you may be required to repay all of the need-based aid you receive.

- Third-party scholarships may be limited to one year. Be sure to re-apply if possible, and consider how this part of your funding strategy will be replaced if it is not renewed in future years.

- You should contact your college's financial aid office directly to ask what its policy on outside scholarships is and how your student's aid package will be adjusted—preferably before winning the scholarships.

Chapter 5

Student Loans—Finding the Right Balance

Student loans are sometimes called a "devil's bargain" or "Faustian pact." According to legend, Faust was the ambitious scholar who made a deal with the devil—unlimited knowledge and power for a period of time in exchange for his immortal soul. Faust spent the ensuing years in pursuit of worldly pleasures, i.e., partying, and, in the end, was damned for eternity. This story may seem like nonfiction for the millions of people now paying off student loans decades after receiving the "easy money." It seemed simple then: Attend school now; figure out how to pay later. The key is to make good financial and college decisions to turn this Faustian pact into a good return on the investment.

Not all loans for college are bad. If used properly—as a last resort to fill in a manageable gap between savings, sources of free money, and the cost of college—responsible student and parent loans can make the difference between attending and not attending the dream college. Student loan debt paid on time may also help you establish a good credit history—easing the path to becoming a more mature financial consumer by establishing a strong credit score early on.

In this chapter, you will find the following:

- Background and context to understand college loans and their unique vocabulary.

- In-depth discussion of federal loan program options for

    - Undergraduate and graduate students.

    - Parents.

- Details about how private credit loan programs work.

- A guide to creating your family's loan plan.

As college approaches, it is important to take stock of your finances. How far can your savings go? How much financial aid is your student likely to receive? Can you afford the schools your child desires? After adding up all available resources, you may reach the unhappy conclusion that you have fallen short. You are not alone. Thousands of other families nationwide are in the same predicament. It is the reason that borrowing for college now exceeds $110 billion a year.

No single financing solution is right for every family.

Borrowing, in moderation, can indeed be an excellent strategy for bridging a financial gap and spreading out college costs over time. The key is to borrow as little as possible.

Save Money Over Time by Borrowing Less Initially

The College Board reported that in 2013–14, the average bachelor's degree recipient borrowed $26,900 to finance a four-year education. Assuming the money was borrowed from the federal government's Direct Loan Program at 4.66 percent for ten years, the following chart shows that for every $10,000 borrowed, the monthly payment is $104 greater in each month of the 120-month repayment period, an additional $1,253 per year or $12,529 over the life of the loan.

Amount Borrowed	Monthly Payment
$16,900	$176
$26,900	$280
$36,900	$384

SOME BACKGROUND INFORMATION

There are two primary sources of funds for families needing to borrow money for college:

- Federal Loans

- Private Credit Loans

These programs are very different in fundamental ways:

	Federal Loans	Private Loans
LENDER	Department of Education	Banks, Finance Companies, States, Universities
APPLICATION	FAFSA®	Each is different
CREDIT TEST	Only PLUS loans	YES
BORROWER	Student or Parent	Usually Parent and Student
ORIGINATION FEE	1.068%—Direct Loan 4.272%—Parent & Grad Plus	Often none

The Origination Fee for federal loans noted above is effective until October 1, 2016, and is subject to change. Please check www.studentaid.ed.gov for current interest rate, fees, and terms for the federal student loan programs.

Many families do well with federal student loans, which are relatively easy to get, offer flexible repayment options, and can include subsidies. For some families, private loans may offer lower rates or other advantages. We'll help you evaluate which may be the better option for your family.

Four Keys to Successful Borrowing

1. Borrow as little as possible.

2. Pay interest while the student is in school.

3. Keep total borrowing in check and avoid excessive debt. Only take what's needed with any eye toward the monthly payments after graduation and the likely amount the student will earn.

4. Consider federal loans before private loans, as they often (not always) provide the most flexible repayment options, favorable terms, and best interest rates.

THE GOOD, THE BAD, AND THE UGLY OF COLLEGE LOANS

Let's take a look at the good, the bad, and the ugly of college loans and ensure that you understand the options, the pitfalls, and the benefits of using credit to finance college. It is also critically important that your student—no matter their age or grade—fully understands that student loans, as the name implies, puts them on the hook for repayment of the loans.

First, let's understand some of the terms and concepts you will encounter:

Dependent vs. Independent Student: If you claim your student on your tax return, he or she is a dependent student. Why does this matter? Federal loan programs permit independent students to borrow more, but to be considered an independent student, one must be in graduate school, over the age of 24, or meet a number of other personal requirements as outlined in the FAFSA®. If determined to be a dependent student, financial aid eligibility will hinge entirely on the family household income, requiring parents to update the FAFSA® annually. An independent student is determined to be financially separate from their parent's household and is no longer required to document parental income directly on the FAFSA®.

Grace Period: For Direct Loans and many private credit loans, the period up to six months after graduation is the Grace Period. Loan principal repayments are not required during this time, but be careful, as this is not a free lunch. During the Grace Period, principal payments are not required, but interest accrues on the loan.

Capitalized Interest: This is the amount of interest that accrues on a loan but is not paid when it's due and is instead added to the balance of the loan. When possible, students should not capitalize interest as it significantly adds to the total amount of principal that needs to be repaid and total amount of interest paid over the life of the loan. Borrowers who capitalize interest will owe more at the time they begin to make payments on the loan than they initially borrowed. This is a source of great confusion: how can I owe more than I originally borrowed? By capitalizing rather than paying the interest while in school.

Co-Signer (a.k.a. Co-Borrower or Co-Maker): This is a second person who signs up for the loan making themselves equally responsible for the payment of principal and interest on the loan. If a payment is missed, both the primary obligor and the co-signer will be reported as delinquent to the credit reporting agencies.

Federal Loans: Students attending college at least half-time are eligible for Federal Direct Student Loans made by the federal government, including:

- Direct Subsidized Loans
- Direct Unsubsidized Loans
- Federal Direct PLUS
- GradPLUS
- Federal Direct Consolidation Loan

Private Loans: These loans are made by private lenders, such as banks, finance companies, or state-based agencies. They do not enjoy the benefits of the Federal Direct Loan Program.

Loan terms: How will interest be charged? Will it be a fixed rate for the life of the loan or a variable rate that rises or falls according to a benchmark index or interest rate? It is vital to know what the interest rate is now and whether it will change over time. Another important question: How much time will you have to repay the loan? Each loan provider needs to tell you (a) how many monthly payments will need to be made, (b) the amount of each monthly payment, and (c) the amount you are paying in interest and principal.

Non-dischargeable Debt: Some debts can be "discharged" or cancelled, meaning that the borrower can be released from having to repay the debt. Most student loans are non-dischargeable: they are not eligible for this treatment. Borrowers must repay their loans even if they drop out or can't find a job after graduation. Unlike other borrowing, such as credit card debt, student loans will usually not be reduced or eliminated even by filing for personal bankruptcy. There are, however, certain circumstances (see next page) in which a student loan may be discharged or forgiven.

Subsidized Loans: Lower income students with demonstrated financial need in the Federal Direct program are eligible for in-school interest payments. The U.S. Department of Education pays the interest that would normally accrue during the in-school payment deferment, helping to reduce total loan interest for when the student begins repayment.

Unsubsidized Loans (a.k.a. Unsub Loans): Students are responsible for paying interest on the loan as it is due or they may capitalize the interest (i.e., not pay when it's due but rather add it to the principal balance of the loan). To minimize debt, it is far preferable to pay the interest each month rather than capitalizing it and increasing the total amount owed on the loan. Students are not required to demonstrate financial need to be eligible for a Direct Unsubsidized Loan.

Deferment: Borrowers meeting one of the following conditions may apply via their student loan servicer for a deferment (temporary suspension of interest or principal payments). Interest continues to accrue and may be capitalized for Unsub and PLUS loan borrowers. Under the subsidized loan programs, the federal government may pay the interest for borrowers who are:

- Enrolled at least half-time.
- Enrolled in an approved graduate fellowship or approved rehab training program for the disabled.
- In a period of unemployment, unable to find full-time employment, or experiencing economic hardship (including Peace Corp service) for up to three years.
- On active military duty or during a period thirteen months following qualifying active-duty military service or until the borrower returns to at least half-time study.

Forbearance: Borrowers under the federal loan programs having trouble making scheduled payments may apply to the servicer to stop or reduce the amount of scheduled payments for up to twelve months. There are two types of forbearance:

1. Discretionary: This type may be approved by the lender for reasons of financial hardship or illness.

2. Mandatory: Lenders are required to grant forbearances if:

    - Borrowers who meet specific criteria are enrolled in a medical or dental internship or residency program.
    - The total amount owed each month is 20 percent or more of gross monthly income. (There may be additional conditions, so check with the lender.)

- The borrower is:

  - Serving in a national service position as a result of receiving a national service award.
  - Performing teaching service that qualifies for teacher loan forgiveness.
  - A member of a National Guard unit activated by a governor and not eligible for a military deferment.
  - Qualified for a partial repayment under U.S. Department of Defense Student Loan Repayment Program.

TIP

Remember that, most times, deferments and forbearances provide only TEMPORARY relief from payments and may result in adding the missed payments to the principal. Deferments and forbearances are terrific programs for those with temporary needs but should only be used in emergency situations.

General Categories of Loan Programs

There are three general categories of loans used to finance college, based on who the primary obligor is on the note:

- **Student loans:** The student is the only obligor. For dependent undergraduate students, student loans come almost exclusively from the federal government.

- **Parent loans:** It's your debt. You are the only obligor just as if you took a loan to purchase a car or a mortgage to buy a house. The student has no obligation to pay any part of this debt. You may borrow from a number of sources, including the federal government's PLUS Loan Program or from private lenders.

- **Co-signed loans:** Multiple borrowers (primary obligor and co-signer), usually a parent and the student, are jointly liable for repayment. If one can't repay, the other is responsible. If neither pays, you both ruin your credit with an unsightly loan default.

The goal for parents and students is to be informed and smart consumers of loans. You should understand the different types of education loans and terms available, take on only as much debt as needed and not a penny more, and pay it off on the most favorable terms possible. This chapter will help you get started down the right path.

FEDERAL LOAN PROGRAM OPTIONS

Loans for Undergraduate Students

During the administration of President Lyndon Baines Johnson, the federal government established the Guaranteed Student Loan Program (GSLP) under Title IV of the Higher Education Act of 1965. Using a model created in the states, the government recognized that banks would not lend money to students who did not have jobs and would be unable to begin repaying the loan for many years. To solve this problem, a public-private partnership was developed in which:

- Banks made loans to students.
- The government guaranteed the loans. If a borrower did not repay, the lender did not lose money.
- Lenders received a guaranteed rate of return on the loan.
- The amount a student could borrow was capped.

Since 1965, the U.S. Congress has periodically reauthorized the Higher Education Act and has fundamentally changed the original program. In 1965, the Congress visualized a private-public partnership in which the government would provide federal subsidies and/or guarantees of loan repayment to the private-sector lenders who would make the loans.

The GSLP evolved into the Federal Family Education Loan Program (FFELP), which was replaced by the Federal Direct Loan Program with the passage of the Health

Care and Education Reconciliation Act of 2010. Banks lost their spot as lenders. The Department of Education is now the exclusive lender, thereby negating the need for a loan guarantor. In effect, the guarantor and the beneficiary for the Direct Loan Program is the U.S. taxpayer who loses money when loans are not repaid. However, the government does make a profit from the Direct Loan Program—a source of much political debate on both sides of the aisle.

In 2015, Congress ended and then reinstated the Perkins Loan Program, a campus-based loan program for students with exceptional financial need. Perkins Loans are subsidized, need-based federal loans available to undergraduate and graduate students. Undergraduates may borrow up to $5,500 a year, for a maximum total of $27,500. The fixed interest rate of 5 percent is lower than rates available in the private sector. Perkins Loans also have an extended Grace Period of nine months and provide opportunities for borrowers to have some or all of their loans canceled if they take jobs in certain public service occupations. The amount of loan cancellation depends on the amount of time the student graduate is employed in the particular occupation. However, not all schools participate in the Perkins Loan program, so you should consult with the financial aid offices of the schools your student is considering if a Perkins loan might be a component of your financing plan. Funds are limited, and not everyone who qualifies for a Perkins Loan will receive one.

For the 2014–15 academic year, the federal government provided approximately $96 billion for student borrowing through its various loan programs. Sixty percent of undergraduates borrowed under the FDSLP, each borrowing, on average, $4,800 in that year. Based on the FAFSA®'s need determination, some borrowers will be eligible for subsidized loans; others will not and will receive Unsubsidized Loans. Some borrowers whose need exceeds the annual caps for federal subsidized loans may receive both a subsidized and unsubsidized loan for the same academic year. If the student qualifies, the government will pay the interest on the loan while the student is in school. The student's obligation to repay the loan begins six months after "separating" from the college. Separating means either graduating or dropping out before graduation. If the student does not qualify for a subsidized loan, the student is responsible for all interest payments while in school and during the Grace Period.

Although colleges package Direct Loans as financial aid, they are not "free." They need to be repaid. For many—if not all—undergraduates, the FDSLP is a very good deal that offers a unique combination of low rates and the most borrower-friendly terms.

If the FDSLP has the lowest interest rates and the most borrower-friendly terms, why doesn't everyone use the program?

- For some families with excellent credit and the ability to have parent co-signers, lower interest rates may be found in the private credit student loan market.

- Some higher income families do not want to file the FAFSA® form required to receive a Direct Loan.

- The maximum amount undergraduates may borrow under the FDSLP is capped based on year of study. If a Direct Loan will not cover unmet need, families may need to access the private credit loan market. Rather than have loans from two separate lenders for each year (and potentially for each student in the house), some families opt to streamline the borrowing with one private lender.

TIP

Subsidized or unsubsidized, federal student loans are an attractive option, because they often offer flexible repayment options and because the government, unlike private lenders, does not require an established credit history.

Loans for Parents (a.k.a. Parental Loans)

Parents have the choice of federal or private loans. In the 2014–15 school year, the federal government lent approximately $10.5 billion to parents under the PLUS program, while private lenders lent roughly $10 billion. Federal loans generally offer more flexible repayment options and more favorable terms than do private loans.

Direct PLUS Loans

Direct PLUS Loans from the federal government are available to parents of eligible students. The PLUS loan is available to parents without an adverse credit history. According to regulations for the program, adverse credit history exists if a borrower has had:

- Accounts 90 days or more delinquent at the time of application.

- Within the last five years, a:
  - Bankruptcy discharge.
  - Voluntary surrender of property to avoid repossession.
  - Repossession of collateral within the past five years.
  - Foreclosure.
  - Wage garnishments.
  - Tax lien.
- A lease or contract terminated by default.
- Charge-off/write-off of federal student loans.
- An unpaid collection account.
- A foreclosure procedure started.
- A conveyance of real property to avoid foreclosure (deed in lieu of foreclosure).

The current PLUS loan interest rate of 6.84 percent is higher than rates on Federal Direct Student Loans and potentially higher than private-sector interest rates. Parents with excellent credit may find lower interest rate repayment options with some private loans. However, PLUS loans are more flexible than are the private-sector loans.

The following charts provide information and detail on the various Federal Loan Programs. As you will see, there are several different loan and repayment options available to you.

Federal Student Loan Programs Compared

Program	Borrower	Rate	Term	Fee	Annual Max	Eligibility Requirement	Lender
Direct Subsidized & Unsubsidized	Undergraduates	4.29% fixed*	10 years	1.068%	For dependent freshmen, $5,500, with no more than $3,500 subsidized, rising to $7,500/$5,500 for seniors	Financial Need	U.S. Department of Education
Direct Unsubsidized	Graduate students	5.84% fixed*	10 years	1.068%	Same as Direct Subsidized	All Students Eligible	U.S. Department of Education
Direct PLUS	Graduate students or parents of undergraduate	6.84% fixed*	10 years	4.272%	Cost of attendance (determined by school) minus any other financial aid	No adverse credit. Borrowers with adverse credit may qualify if they (a) find an endorser or (b) provide documentation of extenuating circumstances to Dept. of Education.	U.S. Department of Education

*Rates change annually on July 1.

Repayment Options for Federal Loans

Repayment Plan	Eligible Loans	Repayment Period	Other Requirements
Standard	Direct Loans (Subsidized and Unsubsidized). All PLUS loans	10 years	$50/month minimum monthly payment
Graduated	Direct Loans (Subsidized and Unsubsidized). All PLUS loans	10 years	Payments are lower at first, then increase, usually every two years.
Extended	Direct Loans (Subsidized and Unsubsidized). All PLUS loans.	25 years	Payments may be fixed or graduated. Borrowers must have more than $30K in loans.
Income-Based Repayment (IBR)	Direct Loans (Subsidized and Unsubsidized). PLUS loans made to students. Direct Consolidation Loans (not including loans to parents)	25 years	Maximum monthly payments will be 15 percent of discretionary income, which is defined as the difference between your adjusted gross income and 150 percent of the poverty guideline for your family size and state of residence. Monthly payments will be lower than a 10-year loan term, but interest costs may be higher. IBR loan term is up to 25 years, with any remaining loan balance at end of term forgiven. This would be considered a taxable event under IRS regulations.
Pay As You Earn	Direct Loans (Subsidized and Unsubsidized). PLUS loans made to students. Direct Consolidation Loans (not including loans to parents).	20 years	Maximum monthly payments will be 10 percent of discretionary income, which is the difference between your adjusted gross income and 150 percent of the poverty guideline for your family size and state of residence (other conditions apply). Loan balance remaining after 20 years will be forgiven. Loan forgiveness is a taxable event under IRS regulations.
Income-Contingent Repayment	Direct Loans (Subsidized and Unsubsidized). PLUS loans made to students. Direct Consolidation Loans.	25 years	Payments are re-calculated each year based on adjusted gross income, family size, and total amount of borrower's Direct Loans. Loans may be forgiven after 25 years of repayment, but also considered a taxable event by the IRS.

Private Credit Loans

Private credit loans may be a viable option or complement to federal borrowing for you. Banks, finance companies, and some state-based agencies offer private credit loans to borrowers with good credit. The loans are underwritten using a process very similar to that used to evaluate other consumer loans such as mortgages, auto loans, boat loans, etc. The fundamental difference is that education lenders do not have collateral (house, car, boat) to secure the loan. Lenders can't repossess or take ownership of the education so they rely upon a borrower's general credit rather than the value of the asset to be financed.

Private credit loans may also be considered loans for both parents and students.

Most students, who will likely be in school and without a full-time job at the time of borrowing, are unlikely to pass the lender's credit test alone. Typically, they will be required to add a co-signer, likely their parent or guardian, to be approved for the loan. In the case of all loans with co-borrowers, both the student and the parents on a co-signed student loan are responsible for the repayment of interest and principal on the loan.

Why would a student ask a parent to co-sign a loan? Here are a couple good reasons:

- The parents have excellent credit, permitting the student to get a loan at a lower interest rate. In effect, the student is piggybacking on his/her parent's good credit history.

- The student has borrowed the most allowed under the federal loan program and needs a co-borrower to be eligible for a private credit loan.

- In either case, both parents and students are well advised to ensure that the private credit loans are absolutely essential and will be affordable once the repayment period begins.

Forgiveness, Cancelation, or Discharge of Federal Student Loans

As noted earlier, the obligation to repay one's student loans is difficult to escape. Federal student loans usually will not be erased or reduced even by a filing for personal bankruptcy. In rare cases, undue financial hardship may be grounds for a discharge of indebtedness, though determining whether the hardship is serious enough may require borrowers to undergo an adversary proceeding in bankruptcy court.

TIP
When student loan debt is forgiven, discharged, or canceled, it may become a taxable event for the borrower. This means that while borrowers released from their obligations gain a financial windfall, they could also face a large tax bill.

There are, however, several circumstances in which a federal student loan may be forgiven, canceled, or discharged. Some involve a student's commitment to public service. Others involve medical or financial problems.

- **Teacher Loan Forgiveness.** The Teacher Loan Forgiveness Program provides help for students who begin a career as a teacher and continue in it. To be eligible, the teacher must work full-time for five continuous academic years in elementary schools, secondary schools, or educational service agencies that serve low-income families. A combined total of up to $17,500 in Direct Subsidized and Unsubsidized loans may be eligible for forgiveness. PLUS loans are not eligible for Teacher Loan Forgiveness.

- **Public Service Loan Forgiveness (PSLF).** The PSLF Program is designed to encourage individuals to pursue careers in public service. Borrowers may qualify for forgiveness of the remaining balance of their Direct Loans after they have made 120 qualifying payments on their loans while employed full-time in certain public service jobs. Only qualified federal repayment plans can qualify, including Income-Based Repayment Plans, Pay-As-You-Earn Repayment Plans, the Income-Contingent Repayment Plan, or a standard ten-year repayment plan.

- **Total and Permanent Disability (TPD).** A borrower who has become completely disabled may qualify for total discharge of outstanding federal student loans. The borrower must provide proof of total and permanent disability to the U.S. Department of Education. The disability must last or be expected to last for a continuous sixty-month period, and certification from a physician may be required.

> **TIP**
>
> For maximum public service loan forgiveness, selecting the income-based repayment option often works best. Low public service salaries may qualify a borrower for reduced loan payments. As a result, the balance of the loan still unpaid after 120 payments will be larger, and the borrower will benefit from greater loan forgiveness.

- **Death Discharge.** If the borrower passes away, outstanding federal student loans will be discharged. Direct PLUS loan borrowers may have their loans discharged if either the parent borrower or the student on whose behalf the loan was taken passes away.

- **Discharge When a School Closes.** Federal student loans may qualify for discharge if the school closes while the student is still enrolled in pursuit of a degree. If the school closes within 120 days after the student exits, the loan may still qualify for discharge. The loan may not be discharged if the student is able to continue in an educational program at another institution.

> **TIP**
>
> Student loan discharge or forgiveness may not, by itself, harm your credit rating, but a spotty record of repayment prior to cancellation of the debt could well be noted in your credit history, with adverse consequences.

Education Loans for College Graduates

College graduates generally follow one of two paths. They either find a job or they go directly to graduate school. Of course, some may take some time to find their first job and others work for a while before going to graduate school. In any case, graduates may be in need of additional or different types of loans to help pay for graduate school or to help manage their existing debt through consolidation loans.

Loans to Finance Postgraduate Education

Graduate students, Ph.D. candidates, law students, and many others in advanced-degree programs are eligible for loans through the Federal Direct Loan and Direct PLUS programs. These loans are all unsubsidized, meaning that the government does not pay the loan interest while the student is in school, as it does for subsidized college loans. They include:

- **Direct Unsubsidized Loans.** Graduate students can receive up to $20,500 in fixed-rate direct unsubsidized loans each academic year. (Medical students are eligible for up to $40,500 per year.)

- **Direct Grad PLUS Loans.** Graduate students may also apply for a Federal Grad PLUS Loan, which are designed to cover all school costs. All applicants are approved, as long as they do not have an adverse credit history, making credit scores irrelevant. All applicants receive the same fixed interest rate and pay the same origination fees. On or after October 1, 2015, and before October 1, 2016, the Grad PLUS Loan will have a 4.272% origination fee. This is rather high when compared to other types of loans with origination fees. There is no option to restructure the terms unless the loan is repaid or otherwise consolidated into a different program. Please check www.StudentLoans.gov for updated origination fees and interest rates for the Grad PLUS program.

- **Private Loans.** Private loans may also be available for graduate students, much like private loans for undergraduates. These loans require a creditworthy borrower and some post-grads will qualify for private credit loans on the strength of their own credit profile.

Consolidation Loans

After students have taken their last exam and received their last grade, their biggest test still awaits them: finding a way to repay their student loans. Many students who have taken new loans for each semester or year of undergrad study now benefit from a consolidation loan program that allows them to, in effect, refinance each of those into a single new loan.

For graduates starting a new job and trying to live and work independently for perhaps the first time, making large monthly loan payments may be more than they can handle. Consolidation loans can ease this financial burden, stretching out loan maturities and reducing monthly payments.

The Federal Direct Consolidation Loan Program calculates the new effective interest rate by taking a weighted average of all outstanding federal loans. The result is that borrowers do not get the benefit of a lower interest rate if rates have dropped since the original loans were made. If interest rates have dropped, private consolidation affords borrowers a true opportunity to refinance at the new lower the interest rates. But it's important to read the fine print: Federal Direct Consolidation Loans may have higher interest rates but the repayment terms, such as income-based repayment, are likely to be more flexible than in private Consolidation Programs.

Private Credit Refinance or Consolidation Student Loans

Banks, credit unions, specialty finance companies, and state agencies make private credit refinance and/or consolidation loans to recent graduates who have established a positive credit history. The common attribute of these programs is their requirement that applicants undergo a credit test in order to obtain a loan. In addition to checking for defaults on other student loans and a pattern of delinquencies and other "knock-out" criteria that would cause a lender to reject an application, lenders use a credit score as a significant factor in making a loan decision. The credit score is a predictive tool that uses current information and recent behavior to give lenders a snapshot of the applicant's risk profile at the time of the credit application.

Lenders also use the credit score to determine the interest rate they will charge. Lower credit scores result in higher interest rates because lenders believe that the loan is at a greater risk of nonpayment than loans made to borrowers with higher credit scores. Although every lender perceives risk differently, most would agree that a strong credit score is generally above 750 and a low score is below 700. There are many successful private credit borrowers with scores between 700 and 750.

Chapter 12 includes a discussion of credit scoring that will help you under-stand how lenders view credit scorecards, one of which may be the FICO® score, as part of their decision making for private credit loans as well as what your student can do to establish a good credit score themselves.

SMART BORROWING BEST PRACTICES FOR PARENTS AND STUDENTS

Here is some expert advice that both parents and students should keep in mind when borrowing money for college:

- **Pay interest while in school and avoid Capitalized Interest.** Borrowers benefit not just from borrowing as little as possible but also from paying loan interest while still attending school. As discussed before, when interest is not paid during college, it is added to the loan principal, to be repaid later. The result is paying significantly more interest over the life of the loan. By paying the interest while in school, borrowers spare themselves from (a) having a debt at graduation that is larger than the debt they took at the time of borrowing and (b) having to pay interest on the capitalized interest.

- **Get a co-signer (a.k.a. co-maker), and look for programs offering a co-signer release.** If a student is rejected by a lender due to an inadequate credit record or a low FICO® score, don't despair. Today, nearly all private credit student loans are made with a creditworthy co-signer. Co-signers, also called co-makers, assume responsibility for making loan repayments when primary borrowers miss a payment. In student loan borrowing, co-signers are generally only required for private loans, where application approvals depend on screening for credit. Undergraduates with no credit history almost always need a co-signer. By attaching to the co-signer's credit, the student not only dramatically increases the odds of getting a loan but also increases the likelihood of receiving a lower interest rate.

More About Co-signers

Since federal student loans do not require the same credit checks as private loans, they do not require co-signers. The closest thing to a co-signer on a federal loan may be found in Direct PLUS loans to a single parent. Some single parents ask a former spouse to add his or her credit to the application as an endorser who will repay the debt if the primary parent borrower cannot.

Save money over time by paying interest while in school.

Agreeing to co-sign a student's loan is a major responsibility for a parent or guardian. Both students and parents should understand its seriousness and have a clear repayment plan before going forward.

Parents and students should also look for private student loans that offer the possibility of a co-signer release. If, over time, the student-borrower meets certain requirements, such as having a regular income and a history of consistent repayments, the student can ask that the co-signer be released from future obligations. Only the borrower, not the co-signer, can make this request. Also know that private student loan consolidations may offer co-signer release as well, so be ready to compare requirements to find a preferred option.

Position your children for a successful co-signer release process by getting them on track with loan repayment as soon as they graduate. It's only after the borrower makes anywhere from twelve to forty-eight consecutive on-time payments and has sufficient stand-alone credit that the co-signer release can be enforced.

For illustration purposes, let's assume a loan of $7,000 and an interest rate of a 6.8 percent. The following is an example of how making interest payments on the loan while the student is still enrolled may lead to greater interest savings. Remember, unsubsidized loans will generate interest on the debt over time, and, until the borrower begins repayment, that debt will grow.

Program	Loan Amount	Interest/ month @ 6.8% Interest	Pay interest while enrolled?	Interest costs after 48-month deferment	Loan Amount at Graduation
Direct Unsubsidized	$7,000	$39.67	No	$1,904	$8,904
Direct Unsubsidized	$7,000	$39.67	Yes	$0	$7,000

Assuming both borrowers begin a ten-year repayment schedule, the graduate with $8,904 can look forward to a monthly payment of $102.49, with total estimated interest costs of $3,392, while the graduate with $7,000 will have a monthly payment of $80.56 and total estimated interest costs of $2,666.55, a savings of $725.45. That's more than a 20 percent reduction in total interest costs! It's very important to recognize and share this concept with college students who are using loans, as they can learn the importance of debt-management skills as they impact their own financial future.

DEFAULTING ON STUDENT LOANS

If a borrower misses payments or, in the federal program, is unable to get a forbearance or deferment and cannot obtain loan discharge or forgiveness and simply ceases to pay, the result is a default. The consequences of default can be severe and lasting:

- **Impact on Credit Score.** A student loan default typically remains on a credit report for seven years. Whether the loan was federal or private, a failure to pay will greatly lower the borrower's credit rating, preventing the borrower from obtaining other loans—mortgage, car loan, etc.—as well as any other type of financial aid for education. However, a default on a Perkins Loan may remain on the credit report until the loan has been fully repaid, which may be longer than seven years.

- **Ongoing Collection Efforts.** The government is relentless in trying to collect on federal student loans. It may garnish wages, seize tax refunds, and block the borrower from obtaining or renewing professional licenses. It may also turn loans over to a collection agency, with added costs to the borrower. If the student loan is private rather than federal, some of these tactics are off-limits, but private lenders may still sell a borrower's debt to a collection agency, which will pursue the borrower in and out of court.

CREATE YOUR FAMILY'S LOAN PLAN

Putting together your family's loan plan is a simple way to keep student loan debt manageable after graduation. Taking a little bit of time early on to ask yourself a few key questions can save both time and money later.

Identify Your Needs and Use Your Resources

Know the costs and how much you have saved, and select schools that will require a minimum of borrowing.

- **Estimate the total costs of all years of school.** A college degree takes years to complete, and costs can increase 1 percent to 5 percent per year. Students may take longer than four years to graduate for a variety of reasons—a change in major or a school transfer, for example. They may also decide to pursue an advanced degree. Your estimates of borrowing needs should reflect these possibilities.

- **Compare the amount of debt needed for each school.** Even rough estimates of the costs of each school your student is considering can be helpful. Scholarships and grants are part of the equation. You should also be mindful of whether financial aid will be renewed from year to year. For example, maintaining an academic scholarship may be contingent on a 3.5 GPA at one college and a 3.0 GPA at another. Need-based financial aid is based on your family income, which could change. Including all of these factors can help clarify your thinking.

- **Use a calculator and resources, such as InviteEducation.com, to project costs, identify your needs, and help determine how you can afford a college.** To understand the impact of taking on debt, use a loan calculator to help you zero in on possible debt totals, payment amounts, and interest costs. They are not hard to use and are ideal for running estimates of future repayment plans or creating budgets for college students. While affordable monthly payments are important, also consider the total cost of repayment, with interest, over time. This will help your family understand the complete costs of educational choices.

Keep an Eye on the Big Picture

Students and parents generally hope for the successful completion of a degree program, followed by a career in a related field. Along the way, however, circumstances may change, goals may shift, and financial plans may need to be adjusted accordingly. Staying focused on actual progress and results can help you estimate appropriate debt levels, avoid unnecessary borrowing, and minimize future financial stress. Be concrete: If a student's major is shifting, understand what that means for future earnings and the assumption you made with regard to how much debt is manageable.

Pick Your Loan(s) Carefully—You May Need More Than One!

You have access to a basket of lending resources to meet your educational financing needs. The Federal Direct Loan Program permits some borrowing by students; Direct PLUS loans enable parents to borrow even more. Private lenders generally provide loans in the student's name but may require a co-signer for loan approval. The terms and repayment options of each loan will determine your family's future finances.

- Federal loans are often the most attractive options for undergraduate students but are capped based on the year of study.

- Families with high incomes may find private credit loans with interest rates below the federal loans, but they will sacrifice the access to specific loan terms, repayment plans, and forgiveness programs found in the federal program.

Federal Direct PLUS and Private Loans: Comparison	
Federal Direct PLUS loans	**Private Loans**
6.84% interest + 4.272% fee for 2015–16	Interest rates and repayment terms will vary based on lender criteria and borrower's credit profile.
Credit check: Does not consider parent applicant credit score or debt-to-income ratio. Only credit approval criterion is that applicants have no adverse credit history, allowing many to be approved.	Credit check is required. But borrowers with excellent credit may qualify for lower interest rates than they would receive in the Direct PLUS program.
FAFSA® form + promissory note required.	FAFSA® is not required. However some schools require that all of their students file a FAFSA® before any loan funding is processed on behalf of student.
Flexible repayment options: The federal student loan program can provide more deferment and forbearance options to borrowers in need of assistance in avoiding default. However, this may increase certain interest costs over time.	Repayment terms are usually less flexible than under Direct PLUS program.

Define Your Repayment Strategy

Mapping out a repayment strategy early and establishing priorities can reduce costs and ease future burdens.

- **When will repayment begin?** Repayment of student loans can generally be deferred until after graduation, but there may be an option to begin partial or full repayment immediately. Early repayment has increased in popularity as a way to reduce long-term interest costs while introducing students to healthy credit habits.

- **Who is responsible for repayment?** The person who signs for the loan is ultimately responsible. Early on parents may help, but repayment responsibilities should be directed to the student as soon as possible. Direct PLUS loans are provided exclusively to parents and remain with the parent until repaid.

Is Your College Plan Worth It?

No one questions the value of a college degree, but there are occasions when high costs require a change in strategy. Graduates of certain degree programs are much more likely to be able to repay their student loans than graduates of others. It may be useful to step back and consider the amount of debt required to obtain a particular degree or attend a specific college and the likely future income of a student in that field.

If there is a large disparity between the cost of a degree and a student's expected earning power, some reassessment is in order. No student should abandon a field of interest simply because it is not lucrative. A great deal of worthwhile work does not pay very well. But it does mean that you should consider some adjustments so that a student can follow his or her passion without incurring an unsupportable level of debt. Practical decisions about school selection, living arrangements, part-time employment, and other areas can help make a student's choices more feasible and avoid crushing long-term debt.

Other Borrowing Options

In addition to federal and private credit loans, some families may be able to access additional monies by borrowing from existing financial assets. In effect, you are making a loan to yourself—a sometimes appealing idea but often not the best alternative to finance college. Why? Because each of these assets were primarily purchased for another important purpose: insuring against death, owning a home free and clear of a mortgage, or ensuring a nest egg for retirement. If the loan cannot be repaid, you likely sacrificed these long-term goals with little time left to repair the damage. In our view, these options should not be considered as a primary means of financing education and should only be considered after fully understanding the risks and long-term consequences of the borrowing.

Borrowing from Insurance Policies

It is not possible to borrow against term life insurance policies, but owners of whole life insurance policies may borrow against the cash surrender value of their policies. If this type of borrowing is an option for you, consult with your insurance agent to understand the company's policies and procedures for borrowing against your insurance policy. Borrowing against insurance policies is usually very simple: there is no credit check, the interest rate is low, the repayment terms are fairly flexible, and the money is not considered income for tax purposes. Money saved in an insurance policy has the advantage of not counting toward financial aid eligibility. It does, however, have to be paid back, or it will be deducted from the amount your insurance beneficiaries ultimately receive.

Borrowing Against the Equity in Your Home

Home equity may be accessed through a home equity loan, in which you receive the entire loan amount at once, or via a home equity line of credit, with which you may borrow periodically up to some maximum amount approved by the bank. Just as with a borrowing against a whole life insurance policy, the process for borrowing against your home equity is usually pretty straightforward. The first step is to ensure that you have enough equity in your home to make this a viable option. You will be best served by consulting with your lender and, above all, making sure you understand the risks of borrowing against your home to pay for college. In the worst case, the bank could foreclose on your home if you're unable to make the payment.

Borrowing Against Your IRA or 401(k)

If you are considering this option, it is important to contact your plan administrator so you can clearly understand the myriad issues involved with this option. In addition to the obvious result—you will have less principal invested in your retirement so your earning will be less and you will have less available for retirement—borrowing against your retirement account is more complicated than borrowing against an insurance policy or your home equity. The type of account matters—is it an IRA or a 401(k)? There are different rules for each plan. The type of plan also matters because some may require immediate repayment of the loan if you lose the job. To further complicate the matter, if you can't repay the loan, it will then be considered taxable income, which will also have to be reported on the next FAFSA® filling. If you are under 59½, you many also be liable for paying an early withdrawal penalty of 10 percent of the loan amount. Finally, you contributed to the account on a pre-tax basis, and the repayments are made on an after-tax basis, which is a significant hidden cost.

One last point: Each of these borrowing options is your loan—not your student's obligation to repay. In each case, you are risking your insurance, home, or retirement if the loan can't be repaid. This very important point should be carefully considered before accessing these funds.

Chapter 5 Takeaways:

- Be aware that most financial aid packages from colleges include federal loans, which must be repaid.

- When savings and free financial aid money do not cover college costs, student loans may be good options to help you pay for college, as long as you don't borrow too much.

- Loans come from both the federal government and private lenders and are available to both students and parents.

- Federal loans offer easier credit, subsidies for some students, flexible repayment options, and loan forgiveness. Private loans have more demanding credit requirements and fewer repayment options but may offer better interest rates. No one solution is right for every family.

- Consolidation loans—combining several student loans into one loan with a longer maturity and/or lower rates—can make monthly payments more affordable.

- Private lenders may require a parent or other adult to co-sign a student's loan.

- Paying interest right away saves money. If interest payments on a loan are deferred while a student is in school, interest is added to the loan principal, resulting in larger loan payments down the road.

- Most student loans cannot be discharged or canceled, even by a personal bankruptcy filing. Some federal loans, however, can be forgiven when there is extreme financial hardship or when a borrower has chosen certain public service careers.

- Defaulting on a student loan can wreck your credit rating. The government may seize wages, tax refunds, and other income, and both government and private lenders may turn your debt over to collection agencies.

- FICO® scores are credit ratings based on a borrower's financial history and behavior, as recorded by leading credit agencies. A good FICO® score can make borrowing easier and cheaper; a bad score may result in higher interest rates or denial of credit altogether.

- Student loans are an opportunity for young people to begin establishing a good credit history.

- When taking on debt, students and parents should keep the big picture in mind, including a student's future career, expected income levels, the ability to repay loans and the post-graduation life style the student hopes to have.

- Using a loan calculator can simplify the process of determining which schools are affordable and how much debt you can take on.

- Borrowing from insurance policies, retirement accounts, and home equity loans may be another way to pay for college, though each of these options has potential long-term negative consequences that should be carefully considered.

Chapter 6

Tax Benefits for Higher Education—Tax Credits and Deductions

In addition to direct payments of financial aid and the subsidies provided under the federal student loan programs, the federal government offers a number of education tax benefits, including tax benefits and deductions to help families pay for college expenses.From 2010 through 2013, American taxpayers took advantage of an average of approximately $19 billion of these incentives annually. Some of the savings strategies discussed in Chapters 1 and 2, such as 529 Savings Plans and Education Savings Bonds, also depend on tax deferrals and tax exemptions that are not reflected in these tax credits and deductions.

This chapter is primarily focused on the federal government's tax programs for individuals—not on educational assistance programs designed for employers. Also, we are not offering tax advice but rather want to make you aware of the types of programs the government uses to encourage students to attend institutions of higher learning.

It's always smart to check with a tax professional before claiming the following:

- A tax deduction: a reduction to the amount of income on which you are taxed.

- A tax credit: a dollar-for-dollar reduction in the amount of taxes you owe.

Tax Benefits for Education

Tax Credits (direct offsets to your tax bill)

- The American Opportunity Credit:

  - Previously known as the Hope Credit.

  - Available for first four years of post-secondary education.

  - Tax credit up to $2,500 per student per year for qualified education expenses.

  - Eligibility dependent on taxpayer's modified adjusted gross income of $80,000 or less ($160,000 for joint filers).

- The Lifetime Learning Tax Credit: A tax credit for 20 percent of the first $10,000 of tuition, with a capped credit of $2,000 per student per year for qualified education expenses that you incur on behalf of your child, your spouse, or yourself.

Note: You cannot claim both credits for the same student in the same year. The IRS considers it double-dipping and may impose penalties if you fully cover qualified educational expenses with a 529 distribution and then also claim one of the tax credit programs in the same year. Furthermore, if the credit reduces your tax liability to less than zero, you may be eligible for a refund. (See IRS Publication 970 for more details.)

Tax Deductions (reductions in your taxable income)

- Student Loan Interest Deduction: Up to $2,500 per year may be deducted by eligible borrowers having a modified adjusted gross income of $75,000 ($150,000) or less and paying interest on qualified loans.

- Tuition and Fees Deduction: Families not qualifying for either the American Opportunity Credit or the Lifetime Learning Tax Credit may be eligible for an adjustment to income of up to $4,000 under the Tuition and Fees Tax Deduction using Form 8917.

TAX CONSEQUENCES OF SCHOLARSHIPS

Generally, scholarships are not considered taxable income to the recipient as long as the student is a candidate for a degree at an eligible educational institution and the scholarship money is used to pay qualified education expenses, including:

- Tuition and fees to attend an eligible educational institution.

- Course-related expenses for required items such as books and supplies.

It is important to check the fine print of the scholarship to ensure that its terms do not require that it be used for nonqualified expenses such as room and board, travel, research, clerical help, or equipment not required by the college or the course.

TIP
Be sure to check with your tax advisor and/or IRS.gov for the most recent eligibility requirements and definitions of qualified expenses. Parents of dependent students may be able to claim some of these tax benefits for education.

Chapter 6 Takeaways

- Education tax credits and deductions may help lower the cost of college.

- You cannot claim both The American Opportunity Tax Credit and The Lifetime Learning Tax Credits in the same year.

- Avoid possible penalties by ensuring that you do not "double-dip" by covering qualified educational expenses with tax-free 529 distribution and then claiming a tax credit for the same expenses in the same year.

- Consult a tax advisor to help determine your eligibility to utilize these programs.

PART ②

Preparing for and Applying to College

Chapter 7

The College Admissions Process—
Prepare, Prepare, Prepare

Benjamin Franklin is often credited with the adage, "By failing to prepare, you prepare to fail." There have been similar adages from wise men and woman throughout history, and they are as apt as ever for today's college-bound students. The college application process is a gauntlet of tests, applications, essays, interviews, and other challenges. Years before the ordeal begins, students and parents must begin planning for the admissions process and ultimately for a successful outcome. Choices made well in advance of application deadlines can have a huge impact on a student's college options. Preparation not only matters, it is a precondition for success.

Previous chapters have focused on issues related to preparing and how to pay for college. We now turn our attention to the actual process of applying to college. Families with pre–high school students will find specific useful information in order to begin preparing for the admissions process. Parents of high schoolers will be guided through each step of the process:

- Building a strong high school resume.

- Preparing to take the standardized tests.

- Completing the college application.

- Dealing with the colleges' decisions.

Although the process may feel very complex and overwhelming, there are a discrete number of tasks and steps that need to be taken. When the emotion is removed and the right steps are followed, it's actually not overly complicated: do well in high school, take standardized tests, select the right college fit, fill out an application, and voila, you're in. Knowing what sequential steps need to be taken and when they must be completed is more than half the battle. Empowered with this information, a plan, and a detailed calendar, students and parents can take control of the process, affect the outcome, and minimize the grueling emotional aspects of the experience ranging from building a record of achievement to completing college applications to handling both acceptance and rejection.

TIP

Social Media Alert: With increasing frequency, college admission officers are checking an applicant's social media activities including Facebook, Instagram, and Snapchat. Students are best advised to scrub their accounts at the beginning of junior year and not post any pictures or other potentially embarrassing information that college admissions professionals could find.

SELECTING COLLEGES

Identifying and selecting which type or category of college your child might apply to is the critical first step in the college application process. Fortunately, there are a lot of readily available resources to begin to narrow the college list and select those that are the best fit academically, socially, and financially. College view books and online college search engines, such as Petersons.com, provide very detailed descriptions of virtually every accredited college in the country. High school guidance counselors and college advisors can also provide detailed information about the quality of a college, its program offerings, and admissions requirements. By the time the student is in high school, you and your student should have a general idea of the type of college he or she is interested in, if the admissions requirements are realistic for your student, and whether you can afford the projected cost.

By the mid part of junior year, it is important to develop a preliminary college list with a sense of the culture of the individual colleges and figure out whether a particular college is a good fit. College fairs can be a cost-effective way to learn about many schools at once and meet their admissions staff. As the list continues to narrow, college visits are the best way to get a sense of what it might be like to attend a particular school. Take a tour and meet the students and admissions representatives to gain a first-hand understanding of admissions requirements and financial aid policies.

Taking the time to research and select a type of college will pay great dividends both in terms of time and increasing the chances that the selected colleges are a good match for your child.

EARLY PLANNING PAYS OFF

Regardless of the type of college, all college admissions offices have the same two goals:

1. Maximize Net Tuition Revenue while recruiting students to fill all available seats for the incoming freshman class initially and then select qualified transfer students to fill other available seats.

2. Assemble a broadly talented, diverse, academically accomplished, interesting group of students who will succeed academically and socially while at school and become productive alumni. They seek students who have shown strong academic performance in challenging courses, have good character, and have participated in meaningful extracurricular and/or community activities.

What does that mean to you and your child? Before a student even enters high school, parents can encourage their children to find areas of interest and aptitude. We do not advocate assembling a predetermined rigid "College Preparation and Career Path Plan" for middle school students. Obviously, their interests and desires will change and after all, they are still kids. So let them be kids, but start to take notice of their fundamental personality traits, interests, and aptitudes and adapt your plan accordingly.

Even if some traits are difficult to identify at first, as the years progress, a student's natural inclinations, interests, and abilities will become increasingly evident. Many students benefit from formalized aptitude and interests testing to help them understand their strengths and weaknesses.

Some school districts include aptitude and skills testing in middle school to try to:

- Pinpoint a child's inherent abilities and interests.

- Better understand how a child can use these to be successful.

- Consider how these abilities can eventually lead to the selection of the right college, major, and career.

Aptitude tests generally measure a student's capacity and interest in various areas as well as potential to learn. Students cannot study for these assessments, as they do not test subject-area knowledge like math or chemistry. There are aptitude tests for elementary school students—often to identify gifted or special needs students or those with special talents in math or foreign languages. Middle schools often test for mental function (processing speed, visual processing, storage and retrieval, and other psycho-motor abilities) and early career interests. It is critically important to identify as early as possible any learning issues or disabilities so you can take appropriate remedial steps to address them in conjunction with your school district and other professional experts.

Ask your child's teacher or the school's guidance counselor whether the school offers these tests, or consider third-party assessment tools.

For college application purposes, a student's overall record in high school is a primary decision factor. But actions taken earlier can help your children position themselves in the most favorable light given their abilities, interests, and learning styles. Paying attention to a child's abilities, interests, strengths, and weaknesses in middle school can prepare a student for high school and establish a solid foundation for college and career success thereafter.

Time will pass quickly, so understand that decisions made during the middle-school years may help and positively affect the college application process that will begin in just a few short years. As middle school draws to a close and high school approaches:

- Identify a student's intellectual abilities, personality characteristics and interests and possible careers that best match those interests or is of interest to the student.

- Consider the type of college the student is likely to attend by involving the student in discussions of possible college options.

- Enlist the help of a guidance counselor to help develop a four-year academic plan appropriate for the student's abilities and type of college of interest to them. Will they need honors classes or Advanced Placement® courses to be considered by the schools?

- Help students find extracurricular activities that complement their interests and are enjoyable, not undertaken simply to pad their college application.

TIP

Understanding students' innate abilities, learning style, interests, and skills early reduces frustration and helps students focus on types of studies and careers in which they will thrive. Some post-secondary schools offer more specialized career and vocational training than others. A four-year liberal arts college is not for everyone.

Building the High School Record: The Ticket to College

After three years of high school, your children will have a track record of academic performance, test scores, participation in extracurricular and community activities, and perhaps some awards and demonstrations of leadership. Their mission (with help from you and others, such as their guidance counselor) is to package and present their record and who they are in the best possible light to the colleges they are applying to.

It is important to understand the admissions requirement and level of intense competition at different colleges. The chance of acceptance varies by type and category of colleges. For example, along with the Ivy League colleges, there are approximately 150 highly selective public and private colleges that seek out the most qualified and accomplished achievers from around the world. Those standards and qualifications—whether it be class rank or average test scores—are clearly identified on their admissions sites as well as in a variety of college admissions books or online sites. Unless there are exceptional or unusual personal circumstances, these colleges are less likely to stretch their standards to admit students who do not meet them.

If your student is not in the top 10 percent of the high school class, does not have nationally competitive test scores, or has a good but not outstanding high school resume, fear not, as there are many outstanding private and public colleges across the country that accept a broad range of students with solid grades and good test scores. That is why it is important beforehand to understand how your student matches up vis-a-vis the admissions requirements to the colleges on their list. Managing admissions expectations is an important part of the college preparation process. By identifying whether a college is a "Reach," "Match," or "Safety" school, you can help your student prepare for the process and manage expectations throughout.

> **Establishing and maintaining strong academic and extracurricular performance early in high school sets up more college options.**

For students with average grades, late bloomers, or those who weren't motivated in high school to do class work or just "didn't get it" for one reason or another, there are many very good college choices that may be a perfect match and enable the student to grow and flourish in an appropriate academic and social environment.

Wherever your child falls on the spectrum of achievement, motivated students will find a college that is a good fit and leads to post college success.

HOW COLLEGES EVALUATE APPLICANTS

Colleges have a fairly standard process for evaluating candidates and offering admission to students they believe will be most successful at their respective institution. Each year, the profile of the entering class may change slightly, but the selection criteria for a particular college usually does not change. These include:

- A candidate's high school performance, including
    - Grade point average.
    - Class rank (if provided by the high school).
    - Course load and rigor.
    - Honors and awards.
    - Extracurricular activities.

- Results of standardized tests such as the ests, such as the ACT®, SAT®, some SAT Subject Tests™, and AP® exams.

- College applications and essays. Admissions committees carefully review these, with at least two admissions officers usually reading each application.

- Letters of recommendation and interviews, which offer additional viewpoints from those who know the student or the college very well.

- Special circumstances, or what is known in admissions circles as a "hook," and an applicant's "story," which may add nonacademic and nonquantitative factors that weigh in the candidate's favor and differentiate him or her from other similarly academically ranked students.

Colleges will also evaluate the consistency and overall packaging and presentation of the application:

- Are grades and class rank in alignment with standardized test scores? If not, are there circumstances that explain why? Examples may include English as a second language, a learning disability, an immigrant or first-generation college applicant, or testing anxiety supported with documentation.

- Do the personal essays and letters of recommendation reinforce the same message and positioning of the applicant?

- Is the intended major consistent with grades and test scores related to the major? It may be a mistake for a student with a low SAT® or ACT® math score to attempt to apply to a college with a declared math or engineering major.

Students whose standardized test scores may not match up to the level required for admission to a college's science, math, or engineering department don't need to give up entirely. In some cases, it would be smarter for the student to initially not declare a major when applying, take and excel in some skill-building courses, and then pursue math or engineering as a major. Often, once accepted and in school, a motivated student may demonstrate success in basic entry-level courses in the area of interest and then be able to transfer to his or her desired major. Of course, if a student consistently scores low in courses needed for high-level math, science, and engineering programs, it may be wise to re-evaluate and consider another major.

Another example of an application mistake is when a student indicates in an essay or interview a desire to major in business management, but the school has no business management major. Unfortunately, these types of "major" mistakes happen all too frequently. So, before applying, make sure your student does his or her homework and knows the programs available at that school and the requirements needed to be considered for admission.

Selective and Highly Selective Colleges

To be considered by selective and highly selective colleges, a student's academic profile should include the course work below. Ideally, most of the courses should be honors or Advanced Placement® (AP®) courses, if these are available at your child's high school. Some of the most selective colleges may require a certain number of AP® courses. Admissions officers are more impressed by strong grades in honors and AP® courses than by outstanding grades in lower-level courses.

- 5 Academic subjects per year
- 3–4 years of mathematics:
    - Algebra I
    - Algebra II
    - Geometry
    - Trigonometry
    - Calculus
- 3–4 years of laboratory sciences:
    - Biology
    - Chemistry and/or Physics
    - Earth Science
- Social studies:
    - U.S. History
    - U.S. Government
    - World History
    - Geography
- 2–3 years of a foreign language
- English and English literature

TIP

- A student should avoid declaring a competitive major if his or her grades and SAT®/ACT® scores related to that major are not very strong. A more successful outcome could result from declaring an undecided major or a major that is less competitive and then declare or switch a major once admitted.

- Not all students are up to the challenge of Advanced Placement (AP®) courses, and this is fine. Some students thrive under less pressure and go on to have very successful college and professional careers. Just be sure to seek colleges that do not demand this demonstration of academic rigor. There are plenty of them!

A Strong Finish

No matter how well or poorly a student has performed in high school, particularly in the freshman and sophomore years, there is time to recover from a poor performance or to impress even more if performance was excellent by finishing strong. A sprint to the finish line will be rewarded. Colleges are impressed by intellectual growth and development and want to see a positive upward trend. So if in the freshman year the student has a mix of Bs and Cs, but by junior and senior year has mostly As, the admissions committee may discount class rank and look favorably on the student's commitment to perform at a higher level. The reverse is also true: if the student starts strong and has mostly As and ends up with mostly Bs, the committee will question both the student's drive and academic ability. Hard work, even late in the game, will be reflected in improving grades and better recommendations, and colleges will take notice.

Throughout high school, students should try to:

- Develop new interests and enhance academic strengths.
- Select and succeed in challenging courses through the end of senior year.
- Show a trend of consistent improvement.
- Select courses that match areas of interest and academic goals.
- Participate in related clubs and activities in school or internships/jobs out of school that correspond to their particular interests and strengths.

Students should, ideally, combine work and play so that they emerge from high school as well-rounded, mature individuals with diverse interests. Admissions officers like and value well-rounded students with diversified interests and activities.

Extracurricular Activities

Preparing for college involves more than excelling in the classroom, as daunting as that task may be. It is also essential that your child pursue extracurricular and community activities that complement his or her interests. It helps if these activities are enjoyable and a commitment is made to them. It does not help when a college applicant assembles a long list of activities but demonstrates no involvement or consistent commitment. This is a quality, not necessarily a quantity, exercise. For example, when we interviewed college applicants, we saw that many students from the same high school listed the same community volunteer activities and organizations with the same number of hours dedicated to each. This is, no doubt, a formula recommended by the high school guidance counselors or college advisors, but admissions officers and alumni interviewers will be quick to discount those activities.

Active participation in extracurricular activities will not only contribute to your child's personal growth and make high school a more rewarding experience, but it will also impress admissions (and financial aid officers) considering your child's application. Many applicants to a college will present similar academic qualifications, so meaningful extracurricular community activities or demonstrated leadership ability in those activities could make the difference between acceptance and rejection.

Beginning these activities as a freshman in high school is recommended. Your child will also have a better chance of achieving a leadership position in a particular club or activity by senior year, further impressing schools. Serving as a president or chair of a club or committee is a noted sign of leadership and commitment. A lesser officer's position or leadership role of some type will also help demonstrate commitment, interest, and well-rounded social and leadership skills. A long-term commitment shows dedication and seriousness of purpose when the time comes to apply to college. In addition to extracurricular activities during the school year, summer jobs and internships can be a way to accomplish these goals.

Combining Work and Play

Successful students:

- Choose quality over quantity of extracurricular activities.
- Seek out leadership roles at any level to help set them apart.
- Show dedication and consistency of involvement in an activity.
- Select activities that they genuinely enjoy. Choices can include community service, school clubs, sports, and the arts.

Standardized Tests

Along with GPAs, standardized tests help colleges measure a student's academic readiness for college. These tests give colleges a common scale with which to evaluate students nationwide. A standout performance can open the door to many schools and to the possibility of merit-based scholarships. Bad or low scores will be a serious disadvantage in the more competitive admissions process of selective colleges. Unless the student and recommenders can explain poor test results or there are special circumstances, poor scores will most likely close the door to selective colleges.

TIP

A growing number of very good colleges are not requiring standardized tests or are making them optional. If your student does not score well on standardized tests, identify and consider these schools early in the process.

The following is a summary of the standardized tests most colleges use and some commonly asked questions about each. Your child will likely have to take one or more of them so understand what they are, what they test, and how they may affect your child's college application. Is one test better suited to your child's aptitudes, interests, strengths, or learning style than another? That may well be the case, so spending some time now understanding how to help your student design a favorable testing strategy is time very well spent. Your student's guidance counselor and others may help you devise an appropriate preparation and testing strategy for your child.

- Preliminary SAT®/National Merit Scholarship Qualifying Test (PSAT/NMSQT®)
- Scholastic Aptitude Test (SAT®)
- American College Testing (ACT®)
- SAT Subject Tests™
- Advanced Placement Exams (AP®)

TIP

Parents should:

- Know which tests are required by the colleges that will be on the college list.
- Understand the differences between the tests.
- Know which test your child is most likely to score the highest on.
- Help students develop a strategy for preparing for the test.
- Consider encouraging their student to apply to colleges that do not require standardized tests or a less competitive college if he or she does not score well.

PSAT 10 and PSAT/NMSQT®

The College Board administers the Preliminary Scholastic Aptitude Test/National Merit Scholarship Qualifying Test (PSAT/NMSQT®), to prepare students for the Scholastic Aptitude Test (SAT®). Although the College Board offers a PSAT 8/9 for students in those grades, we will focus on the two exams that many students take to prepare for the SAT®:

- The PSAT 10
- The PSAT/NMSQT®

The PSAT 10 is a 2-hour, 45-minute exam offered in the spring of the sophomore year. It is the same test as the PSAT/NMSQT National Merit Scholarship Qualifying Test (NMSQT). So what's the difference? Eleventh-grade students taking the PSAT/NMSQT®, usually administered in the last two weeks of October of the junior year, are automatically entered into competition for National Merit Scholarships. Since 1955, the National Merit Scholarship Program has honored high-scoring students with commendations and scholarships. Currently, students scoring in the top 3 percent of test-takers in a state are eligible for additional recognition. Two-thirds of these scholars receive Letters of Commendation. The remaining third qualify as National Merit Scholarship Semifinalists.

Semifinalists then submit additional information and a pool of approximately 15,000 are chosen to be Finalists. Among the Finalists, approximately 7,400 receive one of three Merit Scholarships, including the $2,500 National Merit Scholarship awarded annually. Finalists and Semifinalists may also be eligible for consideration for scholarships offered by corporations and others who use the PSAT/NMSQT® as their screening exam.

In fall 2015, the PSAT/NMSQT® changed to prepare students for the newly revised SAT®. Both the PSAT/NMSQT® and the SAT® have been redesigned with a focus on:

- Words in Context: Gone are the days of memorizing arcane vocabulary words via flash cards. Now there is an emphasis on commonly used words and phrases.

- Command of Evidence: Students are tested using tables, charts, and graphs to support reading passages.

- Math sections: Questions cover algebra, geometry, probability, and statistics, but they focus on real-world problem solving and data analysis, with problems often relating to situations in social studies or history as well as science.

For more information about the new test design, go to:
https://collegereadiness.collegeboard.org/psat-nmsqt-psat-10

TIP

Students can find free practice test questions online for the PSAT/NMSQT® and the other exams mentioned in this chapter.

When is the PSAT/NMSQT® given?

High schools choose the date based on options provided by the College Board. The PSAT/NMSQT® is generally administered on a

Wednesday in mid- to late October. The schools may offer the PSAT 10 in a range of dates offered by the College Board, usually between late February and early March. Homeschoolers need to call their local high school principal to make arrangements to take the exam.

Who takes the PSAT/NMSQT®?

Students may take the test in their sophomore year, but most wait until junior year. Those who take it earlier must retake it as juniors to be considered for a National Merit Scholarship.

Why is it important?

The PSAT/NMSQT® is excellent practice for the SAT® and an opportunity to compete for a National Merit Scholarship. Moreover, the score is a good indicator of the student's admissions possibilities at various colleges and can help manage student expectations. If, for example, the student scores a combined total of 860 out of 1520, unless there are special circumstances or extraordinary skills and accomplishments, it will be a challenge to gain admission to a highly selective college. Most students who retake the SAT® are able to increase their score, but they need to be realistic about the gains that are possible, even if they study and/or are tutored for the exam.

Students can also receive information from colleges and scholarship providers by checking "yes" on "Student Search Service." Colleges and scholarship providers market to students based on PSAT/NMSQT® score ranges. They do not receive your student's actual test score, grades, phone number, or social security number.

The College Board and Khan Academy have also joined forces to provide specialized SAT®-study recommendations based on your child's test results.

How many questions are there?

Reading . . . . 47 with a 60-minute time limit

Writing and Language . . . . 44 with a 35-minute time limit

Math . . . . 48 with a 70-minute time limit

Total . . . . 139 with a 165-minute time limit

How is the PSAT/NMSQT® scored?

The PSAT scoring system is somewhat complicated with students receiving five sets of scores:

Total Score . . . . Ranging from 320–1520

Section Scores . . . . Ranging from 160–760

Test Scores. . . . . Ranging from 8–38

Cross-test Scores . . . . Ranging from 8–38

Subscores. . . . . Ranging from 1–15

How do students sign-up?

High schools register students for the PSAT/NMSQT®.

When are the scores sent?

Scores are usually sent to high schools approximately six weeks after the testing date. Test-takers may also access their scores and receive customized feedback based on their score by establishing an account at My College QuickStart™ at http://quickstart.collegeboard.org.

What accommodations will the College Board offer students with special needs?

The College Board cautions that it may take as long as seven weeks to process accommodations and recommends that students work with their high school's Services for Students with Disabilities ("SSD") to file online requests for accommodations. There are a variety of accommodations for students with documented disabilities, including extra time, computer use for essays, large print, Braille, dictated to scribe, large-block answer sheets, taking the exam over multiple days, small-group setting, private rooms, and others depending on the student's disability.

TIP

Be aware of special early deadlines and necessary documentation to request accommodations.

TIP
If your child will be taking more than four years to complete high school, contact the National Merit Scholarship Corporation (http://www.nationalmerit.org) to determine when your child should take the PSAT/NMSQT® to compete for a National Merit Scholarship.

AP Potential®

It's possible that results on the PSAT/NMSQT® could signify which AP® courses your child should take. The College Board is currently utilizing a new product called AP Potential® that provides participating high schools with predictions on how students will score on the twenty-three AP® exams, based on their PSAT/NMSQT® results. The tool is designed to help high schools identify which AP® courses to offer and which students are most likely to score a 3 or higher.

SAT®: It's Not Your SAT® Anymore

The Scholastic Aptitude Test (SAT®) was redesigned, and the new format was first used in March 2016:

- The writing section is now optional (check to see if your college choices require it).

- There is no longer a penalty for guessing.

- Arcane vocabulary memorization has been dropped.

- Philosophically, the test has moved toward evidence-based reading and writing, with an emphasis on actual subject knowledge in math, and contextual understanding of words and phrases.

The SAT® is usually taken in the spring of the junior year and often a second time in the fall of the senior year. The "new" SAT® takes between 3 hours (no essay) and 3 hours and 50 minutes (with essay):

TEST SECTION	Number of Questions	Time Limit
Reading	52	65 minutes
Writing and Language	44	35 minutes
Math (No Calculator and Calculator Sections)	58	80 minutes
Essay (Optional)	1 Essay	50 minutes

How is the SAT® scored?

The "new" SAT® scoring system ranges from 200 to 800 with the essay results reported separately:

- Evidence-based Reading and Writing: 200–800

- Math: 200–800

- Essay: 2–8 on each of three essay dimensions

What should my student know about the new essay?

Each essay is read and scored by 2 readers, each of whom awards 1–4 points in each of the three dimensions: Reading, Analysis, and Writing. The scorers have a rubric to follow:

- 4 Advanced

- 3 Proficient

- 2 Partial

- 1 Inadequate

The student's final score is calculated by adding the readers' scores.

For more information see:
https://collegereadiness.collegeboard.org/sat/scores/essay

When is the SAT® offered?

The College Board administers the SAT® seven times a year, from October through June. Fifty percent of students take the SAT® twice, and most improve their scores. It is important to understand that students cannot take the SAT® and SAT Subject Tests™ on the same day, so plan and schedule accordingly.

How do students sign up?

Students must set up an account with the College Board and are highly encouraged to register online. The registration process requires students to include a photo, which will then appear on their Admissions Ticket. Once students register, they will not be able to change the name, gender, date of birth, or photo they provided at registration. Students older than 13 are required to bring a photo ID to the test site.

What is the cost?*

The SAT® currently costs $43 without the essay or $54.50 with the essay. The College Board offers fee waivers. There are additional fees for registering late ($28), registering by phone ($15), or changing the test date or test center ($28). The Registration Fee entitles students to send their scores to up to four colleges. Additional reports may be sent at a cost of $11.25/report. Students may also receive their scores by phone ($15/call) or on "rush order" for $31.

Costs of these exams are subject to change annually. Check http://Collegeboard.com for current fees.

When are scores sent?

Test results are usually available at http://Collegeboard.org approximately three weeks after the test date.

What accommodations will the College Board offer students with special needs?

As with the PSAT/NMSQT®, the College Board cautions that it may take as long as seven weeks to process accommodations and recommends that students work with their high school's Services for Students with Disabilities ("SSD") to file online requests for accommodations. There are a variety of accommodations for students with documented disabilities, including extra time, computer use for essays, large print, Braille, dictated to scribe, large-block answer sheets, taking the exam over multiple days, small-group setting, private rooms, and others, depending on the student's disabilities.

*At the time of publication the costs were confirmed. Please check with the test maker for updates.

American College Testing Exam (ACT®)

The American College Testing exam (ACT®) was established as a competitor to the SAT® in 1959. The ACT® historically placed more emphasis on what a student has learned, as opposed to the general aptitude and reasoning ability once tested by the SAT®. In 2011, the ACT® surpassed the SAT® in total number of test-takers and is now accepted by all four-year colleges and universities.

The ACT® consists of multiple-choice tests in English, math, reading, and science, with an optional writing test required by some colleges. A composite score is calculated by averaging the scores from each of the tests and rounding to the nearest whole number. Test scores are based on the number of correct answers, with no penalty for wrong answers. Scores can range from zero to a high of 36.

The ACT® is also embarking on a number of new initiatives to help students, parents, and educators assess student's relatively preparedness for college and careers. Beginning in 2015, the test added some minor new features, including a number of new scores:

- A Science, Technology, Engineering, and Mathematics (STEM) score, based on a student's answers in the math and science sections

- An English Language Arts (ELA) score, which is an average of the English, Reading, and Writing scores

- A Progress Toward Career Readiness score to help evaluate a student's preparedness for a particular career path. This indicator will also be a predictor of a student's performance on another new ACT® assessment called the ACT® National Career Readiness Certificate.

- A Text Complexity Progress Indicator to assess a student's capacity to understand more complex tests they will encounter in college and in their careers.

In 2016, the ACT® is expected to add new reporting categories to align with Common Core State standards.

Should students take the test more than once?

According to the ACT® website, of test-takers who graduated in 2014 and took the ACT® more than once:

- 57 percent were able to increase their Composite Score.

- 22 percent saw a decrease in their score.

- 21 percent had no change.

- Students who initially scored between 13 and 29 increased their score on average by 1 point.

Generally the lower the score, the greater the probability of increasing the score.

When is the ACT® offered?

The ACT® is administered six times per academic year, from September to June. In the past, students usually took it in the spring of their junior year and, if necessary, again in the fall of their senior year. More now take it during the fall of their junior year to allow for more flexibility in retaking the test or to leave time for taking the SAT® or SAT Subject Tests™.

How do students sign up?

Students register online with ACT® and establish an online account. Students can print their admissions tickets from the account. Students younger than 13 or those who are unable to pay with a credit card may register by mail. Students will be asked to provide a photo of themselves, which will be printed on the Admissions Ticket and on the score report sent to the colleges designated to receive the scores. Check the ACT® website to ensure that the photo will be acceptable. The ACT® is very specific about the pose, style, and size of the image.

A photo ID is required to be shown at the Testing Center on the day of the exam.

What is the cost?*

The current test fee is $39.50. Many students also take the optional writing section for an additional $17 for a total fee of $56.50 for the ACT® with writing. These fees entitle the student to send the test results to up to four colleges in addition to their high school and themselves. To send scores to additional schools, there is a fee of $12 per college. There are additional fees for registering late ($25), registering by phone ($15), and changing the test date ($24) or test center ($24). If a late registration deadline is missed, students may request stand-by testing for an additional fee of $49, which will be refunded if the testing center does not have space on the day of the exam.

Fee waivers for the basic test (not extra services such as late registration, standby service, additional score reports, etc.) are available under special circumstances and should be requested through the high school, not directly from the ACT®.

Costs of these exams are subject to change annually. Check http://ACT.org for current fees.

How long is the test?

The test is designed as follows:

- English. . . . . 75 questions; 45 minutes
- Math . . . . 60 questions; 60 minutes
- Reading. . . . . 40 questions; 35 minutes
- Science . . . . 40 questions; 35 minutes
- Total . . . . 215 questions; 2 hours 55 minutes
- The Optional Writing Test is 40 minutes.

When are scores available?

Scores for the multiple-choice portion of the test are generally posted to the student's ACT® online account approximately two weeks after a test date and are released to the colleges within three to eight weeks. If a student takes the Writing Test, the writing score

*At the time of publication the costs were confirmed. Please check with the test maker for updates.

is often available about two weeks after the multiple-choice results are posted. A student's "Official Score" will be released after all of the scores are in—usually five to eight weeks after the test.

The ACT® advises that scores are generally released on Wednesday and Friday in the weeks they are processed.

What accommodations will the ACT® offer students with special needs?

The ACT® accommodates students with documented special needs, including:

- National Standard Time with Accommodations—wheelchair-accessible rooms, large-type test booklets, and marking responses in the test booklets. Hearing-impaired students can receive up-front seating to lip-read spoken instructions, printed copies of spoken instructions, or the services of a sign language interpreter for spoken instructions.

- National Extended Time—providing 50 percent more time.

- Special testing (at the student's high school)—providing, for example, more than time and a half, testing over several days, or the option of responding orally.

Which test to take, ACT® or SAT®?

Not too many years ago, this was a relevant question for students because the ACT® and SAT® tested for different skills and knowledge, and not all colleges were accepting ACT® scores. Moreover, historically there was a regional bias as students on the East Coast generally tended to take the SAT®, while students from the Midwest and West took the ACT®. That difference is closing quickly as most colleges now accept both tests.

With the advent of the new SAT®, the choice between tests is not as clear. Previously, students were able to choose between the SAT® and ACT® based on their individual strengths and learning style. Some performed better on the SAT®, which measured reasoning and verbal abilities with strong emphasis on memorizing vocabulary. Others excelled on the ACT®, which has always been designed as more of an achievement test measuring what a student has learned in specific subjects, such as math. The ACT® tested material not found on the SAT®, such as trigonometry.

Today, most schools accept both ACT® and SAT® scores. Over the next several years, data from test-takers of the redesigned SAT® will be compared to ACT® test-taker data, and differences between the tests will become more apparent and perhaps offer some guidance about which test may be more appropriate for students with different learning styles and needs.

For now, the best advice is to consult your student's guidance counselor and have your student take a few practice tests to help decide if one test is better suited than the other.

TIP

Pick the test on which your child will excel, or have your child take them both and report only the highest score. Colleges will accept either.

SAT Subject Tests™

These assessment exams administered by the College Board focus on specific topics to provide students with the ability to demonstrate college proficiency in a particular subject. Colleges use them to assess a student's mastery of an academic subject area and readiness for college-level courses. Colleges often require at least one SAT Subject Test™. Many require at least two, and some of the most selective colleges require three. It is important for students to:

- Know if, or how many, SAT Subject Tests™ are required by a particular college.

- Select subjects carefully, based on which is likely to produce the highest scores.

- Plan a schedule of when each exam will be taken.

Tests are 1-hour, multiple-choice exams. Students may take up to three SAT Subject Tests™ per session, but not on the day they are taking the SAT®.

When are the tests given?

The College Board offers SAT Subject Tests™ six times per year, from October to June. Not all tests are available on every testing date. "Early Decision" or "Early Action" applicants need to take the tests by October or November of their senior year.

TIP

Plan carefully. Not every SAT Subject Test™ is given on every test day. Students are also not permitted to take SAT Subject Tests™ on the day they take the SAT®.

What subjects are tested?

There are 20 SAT Subject Tests™ divided into five categories: English, History, Math, Science, and Languages.

Academic Tests	Language Tests
Literature	French
U.S. History	French with Listening
World History	German
Math Level 1	German with Listening
Math Level 2	Spanish
Biology/EM	Spanish with Listening
Chemistry	Modern Hebrew
Physics	Italian
	Latin
	Chinese with Listening
	Japanese with Listening
	Korean with Listening

TIP

Take the test shortly after any related course work is completed, including as early as sophomore or junior year. Students taking language exams often do better after two years of language study.

How are SAT Subject Tests™ scored?

The College Board uses a scale of 200 to 800. For the 2015 graduating seniors, the College Board reported these average scores:

- Literature 618
- U.S. History 645
- World History 618
- Math Level 1 619
- Math Level 2 690
- Biology–Ecological . . 625
- Biology–Molecular . . 652
- Chemistry 666
- Physics 667

What does it cost?*

Currently, the Basic Test Fee, essentially a registration fee, is $26. In addition, students are required to pay per-test fees:

- $18 for each Subject Test that is not a language with listening
- $26 for each Language with Listening Test

The Registration Fee includes sending the scores to up to four colleges. The College Board currently charges an additional fee of $11.25 per college after the fourth school.

Under special circumstances, the College Board will waive the fees. Approximately 500,000 students each year receive fee waivers.

Costs of these exams are subject to change annually. Check http://Collegeboard.com for current fees.

How do students sign up?

As with the SAT®, students must register with the College Board.

*At the time of publication the costs were confirmed. Please check with the test maker for updates.

When are scores sent?

Scores are available online approximately three weeks after the testing date. Students may obtain their score via phone for an additional fee. Scores are sent to the student's high school approximately five weeks after the test date. Colleges listed on the test registration form will also receive the scores.

What accommodations does the College Board offer students with special needs?

As with the PSAT/NMSQT® and SAT®, students with documented disabilities are eligible for accommodations that include Braille or large print, preferential seating, extended test time, and extra time between sections. Be aware of special deadlines to request accommodations.

Advanced Placement® Exams

Some high school courses are designated as **Advanced Placement®** or **AP®** Courses. These permit high school students to be eligible for college credits if they score well enough on Advanced Placement® exams related to the course work—usually 3 or higher on a 5-point scale. Receiving college course credits before attending can help reduce the number of courses needed to receive a degree, saving students time and money and permitting them to graduate earlier or take more electives.

According to the College Board, in 2015, 2.5 million students in over 19,000 high schools took more than 4.5 million AP® exams.

AP® exams assess college-level knowledge, skills, and abilities. Tests are approximately 3 hours long and consist of multiple-choice and free-response sections. Though AP® courses and exams are usually optional, colleges view taking them as an indication that students have challenged themselves. Test results can also lead to scholarship opportunities and provide insights into a student's academic strengths and career potential.

When are AP® exams given?

Most high schools administer the AP® exams in May. Most students take an exam only after completing course work related to the topic.

What are the subject areas of the exams?

Students can take exams in thirty-four subject areas:

Art History

Biology

Calculus AB

Calculus BC

Chemistry

Chinese Language and Culture

Computer Science A

English Language and Composition

English Literature and Composition

Environmental Science

European History

French Language and Culture

German Language and Culture

Government and Politics: Comparative

Human Geography

Italian Language and Culture

Japanese Language and Culture

Latin

Macroeconomics

Microeconomics

Music Theory

Physics 2: Algebra-Based

Physics C: Electricity and Magnetism

Physics C: Mechanics

Psychology

Spanish Language and Culture

Spanish Literature and Culture

Statistics

Studio Art: 2-D Design

Studio Art: 3-D Design

Studio Art: Drawing

United States History

United States Government and Politics

World History

What does an exam cost?*

The fee for each AP® exam is $92. Low-income students may qualify for a $30 fee reduction. There is a $55 per exam late-order fee. On the day of the exam, students select one college to receive the score. If a college is not indicated at that time, or if the student wants more than one school to receive the score, additional score reports may be ordered online for a fee. There may be an additional fee for rush requests.

Costs of these exams are subject to change annually. Check http://Collegeboard.com for current fees.

*At the time of publication the costs were confirmed. Please check with the test maker for updates.

How do students sign up?

Most high schools have an AP coordinator, often one of its guidance counselors. Check with your school to find out who coordinates registration for AP® courses and which AP® courses are offered.

How do students get credit for taking an AP® class?

Each college has its own policy on accepting AP® credits and not all do. To receive credit, a student usually completes an AP® course and takes the AP® exam related to it. The student must get a score of 3 or higher and must also request that the College Board send the official score to the college.

CLEP®: Get College Credit in Advance

> Students can receive free college credit for what they already know by scoring well on AP® and CLEP® exams.

Students may be able to receive college credits before they even take their first class in college. The College Board administers the College-Level Examination Program (CLEP®) exams, which give students an opportunity to earn credit for specific areas of knowledge.

Like AP® credits, CLEP® credits can help students meet college course requirements and reduce the number of semesters needed to graduate, saving on tuition and housing costs. For students not interested in graduating early, they allow more leeway to take electives. Nearly 3,000 colleges and universities participate.

TIP

Contact the college as soon as possible to find out the score it requires to grant credit, the number of credit hours granted, and the courses that can be bypassed with a satisfactory score.

What is the CLEP®?

The CLEP® is an opportunity to earn from 3 to 9 college credit hours by earning a high enough score on any one of thirty-three exams offered in five subject areas. Subjects include:

- History & Social Sciences

- Composition & Literature
- Science & Mathematics
- Business
- World Languages

How is the CLEP® scored?

Tests are 90 minutes long and range from 80 to 140 questions. Scores range from 20 to 80. A score of 50 is regarded as the lowest score test organizers believe would qualify a student for college credit. However, each college has its own minimum qualifying grade and credit allocation.

Multiple choice tests are graded by computer with the results reported instantly. For written exams, results are generally available within four weeks.

When are the CLEP® tests offered?

CLEP® examinations take place throughout the year at over 1,800 test centers in the United States and abroad.

Why is it important?

Passing an exam saves the cost and time involved in taking a course and speeds progress toward a degree at more than 2,900 schools. By helping students satisfy course requirements, it can also enable students to take an elective instead.

How do students sign up?

Students should:

1. Check with the College Board to ascertain whether a particular college accepts CLEP® credits.
2. Register with the College Board. Students may use existing accounts.
3. Pick a Testing Center.

What is the cost?*

$80 per examination. Some test centers also charge an administrative fee.

*At the time of publication the costs were confirmed. Please check with the test maker for updates.

Chapter 7 Takeaways

- As early as possible, identify your child's strongest aptitudes, weaknesses, interests, and college preferences, so you can work on a high school and college plan that best positions your child to accomplish the work required to increase the chances of a successful admissions decision and outcome.

- College fairs can be a cost-effective way to learn about many schools at once and meet the admissions staff of the colleges.

- College visits are the best way to get a sense of what it might be like to attend a particular school.

- High school guidance counselors can be helpful in selecting colleges, finding scholarships, and formulating an application strategy. Unfortunately, they are often stretched too thin. Recommend that your student stay in regular contact with his or her counselor to avoid being forgotten, and, if necessary, retain a paid college advisor.

- Preparing for college involves more than excelling at challenging course work. Complementary extracurricular and community activities are also essential.

- Even if a student is off to a shaky start in high school, don't give up. Colleges will be impressed by improvement and intellectual growth.

- Standardized tests matter. Understand the differences between the tests (SAT®, ACT®, SAT Subject Tests™), prepare for them, and have a strategy for choosing those that will result in the highest scores.

- Advanced Placement® courses and exams may be helpful when applying to selective colleges and, if students score high enough, will also enable them to receive college credits before even attending.

- The College-Level Examination Program (CLEP®) enables students to earn college credit in advance. Like AP® credits, these can help students meet college course requirements, graduate in fewer semesters, take more electives, and save on tuition.

Chapter 8

The College Application—Pulling It All Together

Many years of hard work culminate in the collection of information and the press of a button to file the college application. Knowing what to expect and how the process operates will be a big leg up and very advantageous for you and your student.

The job of college admissions officers is to create an interesting, dynamic class of students who complement each other and enhance the reputation of the college. The student's job is to write the application and position his or her candidacy in such a way that the admissions officer concludes that he or she would fit in well and contribute to the thriving intellectual and social culture of the school.

The months will pass quickly, so try to dedicate some time by the fall of the junior year to understanding what's required on a typical college application. Starting to plan in junior year gives students plenty of time to begin thinking about how to successfully package themselves and consult with guidance counselors and others about what can be done to improve weak parts of their application. Time still exists for a corrective course of action, but it has to be done now.

How you stand apart determines how well you will fit in.

The summer between junior and senior year is time that can be very valuable. In addition to getting some well-deserved vacation after a busy (and usually stressful) junior year and maybe getting a job or internship, many successful rising seniors also do the following:

- Study for final sittings for the SAT® or ACT® in the early fall.

- Line up teachers and coaches to write letters of recommendation.

- Work on their college essay.

- Finalize their college list and determine if they will apply Early Action or Early Decision.

High school seniors have many balls in the air as application deadlines approach—grades, extracurricular activities, standardized tests, college visits, college selection, interviews, letters of recommendation, scholarship applications, and more. It's a lot to juggle, but preparation and knowing what to expect pays dividends. A detailed schedule and checklist that is discussed and updated regularly is critical to helping avoid missteps and the stress that inevitably accompanies the final compressed sprint to the finish line.

To-Dos for High School Seniors

- Lock down the final college list:
  - Select five to eight colleges: one or two that are a "reach"; two to four that are a "match," and two to three that are a "safety school."
- Decide whether to apply to one of these schools Early Decision and/or Early Action to any other schools.
- Meet with your guidance counselor and/or other advisors.
- Know the application requirements and deadlines for each school.
- Finalize senior-year test plans:
  - Retake the SAT® and/or ACT®.
  - Retake SAT Subject Tests™ and/or AP® exams, if necessary.
- Know how and where to file applications, i.e., which schools use:
  - The Common Application.
  - The Universal Application.
  - Another application form or their own.
- Sew up loose ends:
  - Finish the college essays.
  - Collect letters of recommendation.
  - Do as many college interviews as possible: practice pays!
  - Make final campus visits.

What You Need to Know About the Application Itself

Times have changed when it comes to applying to college. Not too long ago, each college had its own unique (paper) application with some common questions about grades and test scores and the much-dreaded essay questions and personal statements. As the Internet and online college search engines made it much easier for students to identify potential colleges, the colleges also sought to streamline their application processes using technology. Today, many colleges will accept the Common Application or the Universal Application, enabling students to fill out one application and, with the press of a button, apply to multiple schools.

The ease of applying to multiple schools has resulted in increased admissions competition for students as colleges are receiving record numbers of qualified applicants. Unfortunately, many top students with similar academic profiles are applying to larger numbers of the same selective colleges where in the past they might have applied to just three or four. For example, in April 2016, Stanford University reported its admission acceptance rate for the new Class of 2020 to be 4.69 percent. Harvard's acceptance rate was 5.2 percent, down from 5.33 percent the previous year. Today's technology makes it fairly common for the top students from each high school around the country to apply to the same ten or fifteen schools. Competition is intense and the job of an admissions officer is increasingly more difficult as they select a class, try to differentiate between applicants, and determine if in fact the student will end up attending their college if admitted. That is why a well-thought-out positioning strategy is critical in order to maximize the chances of success.

Colleges have different methodologies for evaluating applications, weighing quantitative measures, and determining how a student's high school course load compares to the academic demands of the institution. At some colleges, the admissions committee painstakingly reviews each application while at others a more automated method is used for the initial screening. No matter what the format or how the application is evaluated, colleges generally require the same scores, personal information, and supporting documents.

Common Requirements of College Applications

- Quantitative Measures
    - Grades: a high school transcript through the junior year and a mid-year report for senior year
    - Test scores: ACT®, SAT®, SAT Subject Tests™, and/or AP® results (a selective few do not)
    - Class rank (required by some colleges)
- Accomplishments: descriptions of achievements, awards, demonstrated leadership, extracurricular activities, community involvement
- Athletic participation
- Personal statement—an essay, short answers, and/or supplemental writing
- Personal information
- Letters of recommendation
- High school information
- Family details (e.g., mother's/father's name, is the student the first in the family to attend college?)
- Disciplinary history: Has the student been suspended? Does the student have a criminal record?
- Other details
    - Semester to start school
    - Will the student live on campus?
    - Will the student apply for financial aid?
    - Which major or field of study is the student interested in?
    - How did the student hear about the school?
    - What other colleges are the student applying to?
- Interview—some schools require or encourage an interview on campus, with an alumnus, or by Skype.
- Application fee

The Common Application: What Is It?

In 1975, fifteen private colleges banded together to adopt a single application form that a student could complete to apply to several schools. Now, more than 600 public and private colleges use "The Common App." Each member school determines the nonrefundable filing fee it will charge, usually between $40 and $100. Students cannot access the Common Application website until August 1st just prior to their senior year.

How to Access the Common Application

Students create accounts at www.commonapp.org. The student's e-mail address is the user name and the primary means of communicating with the Common App.

The Student Dashboard icons will guide students through the application process for each college. Recent versions of the Common Application have included six sections, each with numerous subsections:

- **Profile:** eight parts seeking personal and demographic information
- **Family:** five parts seeking information about parents and siblings
- **Education:** nine parts seeking basic information: class rank, GPA, current-year courses, honors, career interests
- **Testing:** multiple sections, depending on which tests are taken
- **Activities:** allowing applicants to list up to ten activities
- **Writing:** up to four parts, including a 650-word personal essay and, if necessary, space to explain any disciplinary or legal infractions

The Common Application is not offered in printed form or as a downloadable document. Students applying to colleges that accept the Common Application should open an account at www.commonapp.org and complete the form online.

The Common App is available on August 1st of each year for use in the next academic year commencing in September. At the end of July each year, all Common Application accounts are deleted so you will need to recreate an account if you started one prior to August 1st for the next academic year.

The Universal College Application

More than forty schools now accept the Universal College Application. You can find a current list at www.universalcollegeapp.com. The Universal App collects many of the same details as the Common Application, though in a different format. It requires answers to basic questions about:

- Personal data: contact information, citizenship, ethnicity, family members
- Family information
- Academic information
- Standardized test scores
- Additional information, including academic and other awards
- Extracurricular activities, volunteer activities, and work experience

Students are asked to provide a personal statement of not more than 650 words. There is also room to provide links to multimedia information and to discuss any unique talents or activities a student wishes to highlight.

Some colleges that accept the Universal App may also require other supplemental information, i.e., mid-year reports, letters of recommendation, or essays. These requirements are listed in the Universal Application's Check List, which also provides deadline information.

Other Application Formats

Colleges not using the Common App or Universal App offer online or printed versions via their websites or admissions offices. These schools still require the same information: quantitative measures (grades and test scores); one or more essays, including a personal statement; and letters of recommendation.

The Coalition for Access, Affordability, and Success

In September 2015, approximately 80 colleges announced the formation of The Coalition for Access, Affordability, and to help provide useful information and facilitate the college admission process. The Coalition's new application platform is available to students as early as freshman year to use as a place to accumulate information to eventually be used in their college applications. As of the time of this book's printing, the Coalition expected to have its own application for admission to member schools available during the summer of 2016.

THE COLLEGE ESSAY OR PERSONAL STATEMENT

The summer after your student's junior year is the time to focus on the college essay, particularly for Early Decision or Early Action applications. Because the essay is such a critical part of the application, students should start early, select a personally relevant topic, and seek feedback on both the topic and content from trusted advisors or parents to help them put their best foot forward.

> The college essay is a unique chance to express who you are— in 650 words or less.

TIP

- Students should not write what they think the admissions committee wants to hear. They should write from the heart about a subject that they are passionate about or that is uniquely meaningful.

- Remember that admissions committee staff members read hundreds of essays and applications during a two-month period, so students should take the time and effort necessary to craft a compelling, well-written essay that adds context to who they are.

- Unless there are exceptionally special circumstances or an amazing story, students should avoid writing about religion (unless they are applying to a faith-based institution) and/or how important their parents are to them, unless there are exceptional, rare, and compelling reasons to do so.

The college essay is a very personal statement that can move an application to the "Admit" from the "Decline" or "Wait List" pile—and vice-versa. Students who are otherwise qualified could be declined admission because their essay did not enhance their application or was subpar.

Successful essays include personal touches. It is the one guaranteed opportunity students have to use their own voice to impress admissions officers. Students should:

- Reflect rather than recount. Tell a story to make a point.
- Showcase personal qualities, activities, or experiences that are memorable, special, and different.
- Avoid listing or boasting about accomplishments and awards. Applications contain other sections for this.
- Create a killer "hook" or attention-getter to engage the reader from the start.
- Begin early and write several drafts.
- Put drafts away for several days before rereading the essay.
- Make sure the final draft retains the student's voice.

If there are "special or unusual circumstances," such as a difficult home environment, family circumstance, or personal crisis the student had to overcome or deal with, the essay will be the best opportunity to communicate how this affected the student. Too often students omit critical personal and family information because they may be embarrassed to reveal it, but it may provide the admissions officer with ammunition to place you in "the special circumstance pool" where chances of admissions are higher.

Given the importance of the college essay, many students seek additional help from a trusted person: guidance counselor, parent, or professional with experience helping students write college essays. Admissions officers recall exceptional essays, so be careful not to replicate another essay from a book or have a college coach write one.

To save time, students can create basic components, such as a personal statement, for use in more than one application. It is always a mistake, however, to try to force existing material into an essay question that calls for a slightly different response. Read essay questions carefully, and make sure that any material your student recycles or repurposes is on point and fits perfectly. If this is not done, admissions staff will infer that the student is not committed to that particular school.

Frequently Asked Questions About College Essays

How do colleges use essays to evaluate applicants?

Each college has its own philosophy about how the essay factors into admissions decisions. Colleges generally use essays for four purposes:

1. To assess a student's ability to meet the school's academic standards and the student's writing abilities.
2. To assess whether the student would be a good fit for the school.
3. To help them understand who the student is, what passion they might have, or what drives them beyond grades and test scores.
4. To understand special or unusual circumstances that have affected the student's life and possible academic record.

What do admissions committees look for in an essay?

Admissions committees read thousands of essays each year. They want to see essays that use grammar and sentence structure properly, have accurate spelling, and prove that a student writes proficiently. Committees also see the essay as an opportunity to learn about a student's background, personality, and interests. They usually require that the essay not exceed 650 words. Admissions officers will be most impressed by essays that engage them from the start and have a central thesis, illustrating a noteworthy experience or passion in the student's life.

Is it okay to use humor in the essay?

Sure. When used correctly, humor can be effective, particularly if it is genuinely part of the student's personality. Self-deprecating humor is often very appealing. Forced or off-color humor can be a significant negative. Avoid it.

What types of essays do colleges ask for?

In general, college application essay questions can be categorized as the following:

- Personal—focused on the student's unique characteristics, experiences, or special or unusual circumstances.
- College-centric—creatively describing why the school is ideal for the student.
- Creative—prose that tells a story or paints a picture.

LETTERS OF RECOMMENDATION

Letters of recommendation are an important part of the college application because they afford opportunities for people who have observed the student in various situations (in the classroom, on an athletic field, in volunteer activities) to point out distinguishing attributes that make the student special. These letters also provide professional context as they are often written by one professional (a teacher or coach) to another (the admissions officers) who together see hundreds and even thousands of students over their careers. Students should pick those who will take the time to write their letter of recommendation carefully. Ideally, the recommender will have unique personal experience with the student and will highlight attributes of the candidate not found elsewhere in the application.

Throughout their school years, students should try to establish great relationships with a few teachers. Apart from the educational benefits, this can be helpful when the time comes to ask for letters of recommendation. The better a teacher knows a student, the easier it is for the teacher to write a letter filled with stories, anecdotes, and examples of a student's accomplishments and character.

It may not be enough just to have a longstanding relationship with a teacher, however. As college applications approach, students should try to do extra work, participate actively in class, and make an effort to distinguish themselves so teachers are excited about supporting their college quest.

Letters of recommendation are an opportunity for admissions officers to hear from someone with professional credibility who knows the student well.

Students seeking to apply Early Action or Early Decision (discussed later in this chapter) need to identify letter writers by the end of their junior year or immediately upon returning to school for their senior year. Others can wait for the start of senior year. In either case, remember that many students are competing for recommendations from teachers. The early birds catch the most worms.

Students should select letter of recommendation writers carefully and with the advice of a guidance counselor to ensure that the strongest possible letters will be written. Most colleges want at least two and often three letters of recommendation. These should be from:

- The high school guidance counselor
- One or two core subject teachers
- An extracurricular advisor, coach, or internship/job supervisor

---

TIP

- Most students waive their rights to reading the letter of recommendation. College officials prefer confidentiality. Not waiving the right to see the recommendation is often viewed as a negative.

- When requesting a recommendation, the student should ask that the writers emphasize certain qualities or achievements. A teacher might be asked to emphasize specific intellectual abilities, a research project, and classroom performance while a guidance counselor might be asked to emphasize overall leadership and contribution to the school community.

How to Maximize the Impact of Letters of Recommendation

To gain the greatest benefit from letters of recommendation, students should try to do the following:

- Understand how the high school processes letters of recommendation.
  - Will the high school collect letters and submit one package, or should each teacher mail them independently?
  - Is there an electronic system for handling recommendations?
- Discuss the choice of letter writers with advisors and guidance counselors.
- Approach letter writers in person (not by e-mail) as early as possible—at least six weeks before the letter is due.
- Soon after a letter of recommendation writer agrees to write the letter, follow up with an electronic package that includes the following:
  - A resume containing pertinent information about academic performance, extracurricular activities, and honors/awards, particularly if the activities took place outside of school
  - Special or unusual circumstances that the writer may not be aware of to include in the letter
  - The names of the colleges and their deadlines
  - A written description of why the student is applying to the colleges, so the letter writer can tell relevant stories or cite examples of work that support the application. Include statements about college and career aspirations.
  - Phone number(s) and e-mail address, so the letter writer can get in touch with the student if there are any questions
  - All required forms that the letter writer must complete
  - A personal thank-you note, preferably handwritten, recognizing the time and effort of the letter writer
- Three weeks before the deadline, politely remind the recommender of the deadline.
- One week before the deadline, ask if the recommendation has been sent.
- Upon receiving a college acceptance letter, be sure to let the letter writer know that the application was successful, and thank him/her again for their support.

THE APPLICATION IS READY: WHAT'S NEXT?

Once the information has been collected, tests completed, and the essays written, it's time to file the application. But when? Based on their level of interest in attending a particular college, students can choose one of the following paths:

- Early Decision (ED): Students are contractually obligated to attend if accepted. Do not file more than one Early Decision application. At most colleges, the only way to get out of an ED acceptance is if the student applied for financial aid and the aid package is not sufficient.

- Early Action (EA): Students are not contractually obligated to attend if accepted. Some students file multiple EA applications.

- Regular Decision: Students are not contractually obligated to attend if accepted.

Each college has a schedule of deadlines to accept applications in each category. Be sure you know when applications are due. Some colleges, particularly state schools, have rolling admissions policies.

TIP

Throughout the process, have the student stay in touch with the college or the college's admissions representative assigned to his or her high school. Showing genuine interest in attending the school can help when the Admissions Committee reviews the application. It also helps high school counselors to determine priorities when admissions representatives call to discuss candidates.

Approximately 450 colleges have "Early Decision" or "Early Action" plans. Some have both or other early acceptance plans, including one known as Single-choice Early Action, in which the student is not bound to attend the college if admitted but agrees not to file another ED or EA application at another institution. Be sure to check the colleges' websites to understand their EA and ED policies.

As the names imply, ED and EA candidates will receive answers early—often before December 1. Some colleges offer ED II plans, with deadlines in January. But the real benefit is that many ED and EA colleges allocate a percentage of seats in their freshman class to early applications with the knowledge that nearly every candidate who is admitted will matriculate.

This helps colleges manage their yield—the percentage of applicants who accept the acceptance. At some colleges, competitive candidates have better odds of admission during the EA or ED periods.

Pros and Cons of Applying Early

Applying early may work well for those who are confident that one school is right for them and that they stand a good chance of admission. For others, it may not be the best strategy. Below are some of the considerations:

Pro	Con
• Often (but not always) gives qualified students a better chance of getting in	• May force a student to commit to a school without fully exploring other options
• Avoids the time and stress of waiting until spring for a decision	• Leaves little time to file other applications if student is not admitted early
• Saves the trouble and expense of applying to multiple schools	• Does not leave time for demonstration of good performance in the first semester of senior year or additional standardized test scores to be included in an application
• Gives students who are admitted early more time to focus on other things during their senior year and to prepare for college	
• Enables rejected students to still apply to other schools, though under time constraints	• Requires standardized tests, recommendation letters, and other materials to be completed early
• Allows students who aren't admitted early but are qualified to be placed in a reconsideration pool during the regular admission process	

TIP

If applying Early Decision or Early Action, the final application steps, including test taking and lining up letters of recommendation, need to be accelerated in order to meet the early deadlines and not compromise the quality of the application.

THE INTERVIEW

After colleges receive the application, some may offer an informational interview or require a more formal interview either with a staff member or an alumni interviewer. Admissions committees use interviews to get a third-party evaluation of a candidate's drive, intellectual curiosity, and personality, based on direct observation. Sometimes, the interviews are conducted on campus with Admissions Officers; sometimes, volunteer alumni living near the candidates do the interviews. Interviews may or may not make or break a candidate, but they are a great opportunity for students to express interest in a college, collect information, and make a favorable impression. Colleges weigh alumni interview reports differently, so it is important to be prepared and impress the interviewer with personal as well as intellectual abilities. Harvard, for example, has a detailed 10-page alumni interview form that is divided into four categories:

College interviews are much like job interviews: an exchange of information to see if there is a "fit."

1. Personal Qualities

2. Extracurricular, Athletic, Community, Employment, and Family Commitment

3. Academic Qualities

4. Overall Appeal

Alumni are asked to rate each interviewee numerically on a subset within each category and then write a narrative on each category that supports the rating, along with a final recommendation.

Not all colleges require interviews, however, so students should:

- Know which schools require them and which offer them for informational purposes only.

- Find out when they are scheduled to take place.

- Determine who will be conducting the interview. If it will be a member of the alumni, try to learn more about him or her so that you will be better equipped and able to engage the interviewer. Google, LinkedIn, and other online networks are a good source for information such as when the interviewer graduated, his or her career(s), civic involvement, and so on.

Most high school students have little experience interviewing. Interviews can be a stress point and cause anxiety; however, through preparation, including mock interviews, the anxiety can be significantly lessened.

Likely Interview Topics and Questions

There are a number of topics students should be prepared to address and questions they should be able to answer in an interview. Some involve specific accomplishments detailed in their resume. Others are about a student's life, values, and ethics. Here are some of the most common:

- Tell me about yourself or how would your friends describe you? (Every student should have a short, general self-description in mind if asked this common interview icebreaker.)
- Why is this particular school of interest or a good match for you?
- What talents and experiences do you bring to the college?
- What did you get out of high school?
- What are your best and worst traits?
- How have you improved or learned from a negative experience?
- What are the strongest influences in your life?
- What are your academic passions and favorite classes?
- What are your favorite activities outside of the classroom and why?
- What books have you read outside class requirements? Tell me about them?
- Is there anything else you would like me to communicate to the Committee about you?

The best interview is a conversation, not a Q&A session. The student should engage the interviewer in a give-and-take conversation, using the information he or she learned about the interviewer both during and prior to the interview. Ask about the interviewer's major, experience at the college, their career, and if their major was relevant to their current career.

The interview is a two-way street. Applicants should ask questions to find out more about a college or clarify answers to questions not fully addressed on the website or in brochures. Questions might include:

- Are there any changes planned in majors I'm interested in? When do I have to declare a major?
- Are courses taught by professors or by teaching assistants?
- What qualities are considered when matching roommates?
- If appropriate, what is the school's financial aid policy?

Interview Dos and Don'ts

Do	Don't
• Arrive about 10 minutes early.	• Whine or make excuses.
• Dress nicely (no jeans or T-shirts).	• Expect your parents to participate in the interview. You are the one applying to the school, not your parents.
• Be polite and cordial. Everyone you interview with could have an impact on your overall evaluation.	• Bring your parents if the interview is with an alumnus.
• Research the school and interviewer before the interview.	• Make a speech.
• Engage the interviewer and ask questions about their experience and careers; seek advice.	• Chew gum.
• Try to schedule your lower-priority schools first so you can practice and gain experience and confidence for the interviews that really count.	• Have a cell phone in hand. Before the interview starts, turn off the ringer and put the phone away.
• Practice answers out loud. This is effective and may help you appreciate how a particular answer will sound. Mock interviews are very helpful.	
• Show interest and enthusiasm.	
• Bring up anything about your application that needs some elaboration or clarification, e.g., a bad grade or disciplinary action or special personal or at home circumstances.	
• Send a thank you note.	

TIP

Most interviews are scheduled for half an hour. Be aware of the time, and make sure to communicate the most important points you wish to make. Have a plan and practice your anticipated answers so that they are concise and to the point.

Many polished public speakers practice a speech or answers to questions out loud so they can hear what it will sound like. They often rearrange ideas or words to ensure that the most important points are properly emphasized. This is a good practice for students and one way to help avoid leaving an interview wishing something had been said another way.

DECISION TIME—AND WHAT TO DO

Soon after the sigh of relief at having submitted a completed application, the anxiety of waiting for THE DECISION takes over. The long road to college admission can end happily, unhappily, or, in some cases, ambiguously. Ideally, students will be accepted by at least one of the schools they have applied to. If not, all is not lost. Even in the worst case, there are further steps high school seniors can take.

At some point, an e-mail is likely to arrive in your student's inbox followed by some snail mail announcing:

- Good news: an acceptance.
- No news: a deferral or wait-list status.
- Bad news: a rejection.

Good News

E-mail has taken the fun and/or anxiety out of checking the mailbox every day to see if today is the big day. Is there a large envelope full of admissions material or a letter-sized envelope containing the dreaded rejection letter? Thankfully, it's the acceptance envelope. But is it really party-time? Most likely, but just like everything else in this process, it really depends on your student's goals and unique situation.

- For Early Decision candidates, it *is* party time. Now obligated to accept the college's offer of admission unless there is a glitch with financial aid, the long process of being admitted to college has been successfully concluded. Hooray!!!!

- For Early Action and Regular Decision candidates: Congratulations! The shoe is now on the other foot. Rather than the student having to compete for a spot on a college's campus, the college is now com-peting for the student. Now your student gets to determine which college will be the best fit. To make the final decision among one or more options, your student can:
    - Revisit schools as part of an "Admitted Student Day" or at another time to get a better feel for the campus, the school's culture, and the types of people who attend.

- ◆ Compare financial aid packages. Even high–net worth or high-income families may receive merit-based institutional aid that could be an important consideration.

In any case, the clock is ticking toward May 1, the day deposits are due for matriculating students.

Not So Good News

Your student did receive some news—deferred or wait-listed—not the "yes" he or she was hoping for.

There is a difference between being deferred and wait-listed:

- For deferred applicants who applied Early Action or Early Decision, a deferral means that the application has been placed into the Regular Decision pool of candidates. Read the deferral letter carefully as it may yield clues as to what is the probability of admission in the Regular Decision pool. At least one school we know instructs Early Decision–deferred candidates that their chance of admission in the Regular Decision pool is not high, in effect encouraging the student to apply elsewhere.

- For deferred applicants who applied Regular Decision, the college is likely to request more information (another test score or perhaps the following semesters grades) before making a final decision on their application.

- Colleges use wait lists to say no to students without having to outright reject them. They're saying that the student is not their first choice but could be admissible if other candidates decide not to attend. The student may be perfectly well qualified and "good enough" for acceptance, but there was simply another candidate who fit the college's profile better.

Wait-Listed: What to Do?

The Wait List is not a great place to be. Colleges do not even begin to consider wait-listed applicants until after the May 1 deposit deadline for admitted students. Most colleges either rank students who are wait-listed or have a priority group. What should a wait-listed student do?

The first and most important step your student needs to take is to decide whether he or she wants to wait for a decision. If so, your student should do the following:

- Contact the college and ask about the wait-list policy. Ask specific questions to gather information to determine if there is a real chance of gaining admission. Here are some good questions to ask:
  - What percentages of students in the last three years were accepted after being wait-listed?
  - Is there a wait-list ranking? Where am I ranked on the current list?
  - Is there something specific that concerned the Admissions Committee that I could correct with additional and/or updated information?
  - If I were eventually accepted, would first-year housing still be available?

- Send in the wait-list acceptance form, including a letter reaffirming a desire to attend, and update the admissions office staff as to any post-application achievements or honors that have been attained.

- Establish personal contact with an influential or at least well-informed person involved in the admissions process. This could be a regional representative, alumnus interviewer, or someone working in the office.

- Encourage his or her high school guidance counselor to follow up with a phone call to the admissions staff.

- Begin a soft self-marketing strategy to show a genuine passion to attend. Without being a pest, periodically inform the college about new achievements—academic or extracurricular—and emphasize why the student and the school are a great match and what the student would contribute. The energy, spirit, and intelligence your student demonstrates during this process may make a difference.

While taking the steps previously noted, wait-listed students are best advised to be very realistic. Many times a very low percentage of wait-listed students actually gain admission. In fact, in many elite schools, the acceptance rate exceeds the number of available seats, and there is no opportunity for wait-listed students. It is possible, but it takes patience, effort, and good fortune.

In most circumstances, unless a student is close to the top of a wait list, and the college has a track record of matriculating students from the wait list, the best option is to choose another school that has accepted him/her and send in the deposit needed to reserve a space. If it turns out that admission to the wait-listed school materializes—and offers to attend sometimes arrive within days of freshman orientation—you would, of course, lose the deposit that you sent to the other school to secure your student's spot.

TIP

This is the student's battle. Students, not parents, make the best case for gaining admission from the wait list.

Time is of the essence. Move quickly!

Frequently Asked Questions About Wait Lists

Why do colleges have a waiting list?

Colleges do not always correctly estimate the "yield" from their offers of admission, i.e., how many applicants will matriculate. Wait-listing some applicants gives colleges a margin of error. If too many accepted applicants enroll elsewhere, leaving the college with fewer incoming students than desired, the college can fill the open slots from the wait list.

When do colleges admit from the wait list?

Colleges begin admitting students from the wait list after the May 1 decision deadline has passed and they know if there are available spots.

What is the best strategy for managing the wait-list process?

Students on multiple wait lists should prioritize them and determine which to pursue. They should pay the deposit for a college that offered admission and continue to pursue the wait list, knowing that the deposit may be lost. They can also consider whether it makes sense to begin college at one school and then try to transfer. Check the desired college's transfer policy.

Students' Wait List Dos and Don'ts	
Do	**Don't**
<ul><li>Immediately contact the admissions office and find out the following:</li><ul><li>How many wait-listed students were accepted last year?</li><li>How does the admissions staff choose which students are tops on the list? Is there a ranking?</li><li>Where do I stand on the list?</li><li>Does the admissions office think I have a chance of being accepted?</li></ul><li>Write a letter to express your strong interest in attending. In addition:</li><ul><li>Provide new information: better test scores and grades if available, a significant award, new demonstration of leadership.</li><li>Explain why the college is your first choice.</li></ul><li>Ask for an opportunity to meet an admissions officer to make a final presentation on why the school and you are a great match and why you belong there.</li></ul>	<ul><li>Be rude or argumentative or call in parents or alumni to make the case.</li><li>Try a "clever" or "creative" trick.</li><li>Become a pest to the college's admissions office.</li></ul>

Rejection: What Can Be Done?

Nearly all colleges reject more students than they admit. Some colleges admit fewer than 25 percent of all applicants. The most highly selective colleges offer admissions to approximately 5 percent of applicants. At the most selective schools, many of the rejected applicants would perform well if allowed to attend, but it just wasn't in the cards for them to be part of this freshman class. The admissions process can be a numbers game with some arbitrariness about who wins and who loses. Unfortunately, there may be a number of students with the same exact record being discussed by the admission staff, but they are charged with admitting just one. Sometimes it's simply a matter of luck and several other factors, including the following:

- Timing of when a student's application is reviewed—sometimes the Committee at a particular meeting may have already accepted 2 or 3 students with similar resumes and/or from same high school or geographic region.

- Pool of candidates already admitted by category—although equally qualified, the Committee seeks other types of students to balance the entering class.

- Geographic region—the Committee may be looking for students from particular states or regions of the country and the world.

Students may deal with the rejection better if they understand that reasons like these or seemingly arbitrary factors sometimes prevail. Every year, perfectly well-qualified students, including valedictorians and students with perfect test scores, are not admitted to the college of their dreams. It's not personal.

Some students will be rejected by some colleges and accepted at others—presumably colleges they wanted to attend at the time they applied.

> As painful as a rejection is, at least there is an answer, and it should not be taken personally.

Whether admitted to another college or not, parents and students often ask two questions:

1. **Are there any concrete actions that can be taken?** As disappointed as parents and students may be, the best thing that both can do is try to move forward constructively.

   - Remember that there is more than one college that suits a student's needs, abilities, and interests.

   - A great college experience does not hinge on attending one particular school.

   - If the college is the absolute, must-have dream for a student, he or she should become familiar with the college's transfer policy. Perhaps the student can start somewhere else and end up at the college of their dreams.

- Consider a community college as a place to begin. Students can then reapply or transfer to other schools. In some states, four-year colleges routinely accept transfer students from community colleges. Students who plan to transfer should look into transfer policies, in particular how transfer credits are applied and what GPA is required.

2. **Can the rejection be appealed?** Few colleges overturn their initial decisions, but students may feel better if they send a letter to the admissions office appealing the decision.

TIP

If the student is rejected at all the schools he/she applied to or is not happy with the one(s) offering admission, check with the National Association for College Admission Counseling (NACAC). In early May each year, NACAC posts the names of schools with openings in their upcoming classes: www.ncacnet.org.

AFTER THE DECISION: PLENTY TO DO

Knowing what to do upon arrival can greatly ease a student's transition to life on campus.

Once a student has been admitted to college, a series of communications will begin to arrive on everything from tuition and housing to freshman orientation. Summer is a good time to address all of these issues. Make note of any key dates, and create TO DO lists for the financial, logistical, and academic challenges ahead. These may include weighing course selections, going to medical appointments, shopping for clothing and dorm room supplies, and other preparations.

Summer Schedule: Selected Action Items

- **Review your savings and finances** and begin to budget and plan for the expenses that you will incur in the next 90 days and in the year ahead.

- **Make travel arrangements.** Once you know when your student is expected to be on campus and where the residence is, your family should make plane, train, and/or hotel reservations ASAP. Hundreds of families may be traveling to the same destination at the same time, and reservations may become scarce. Make plans to ship supplies to your student's dormitory address if that seems easier than carrying them. If you'll need a small truck or minivan, make a reservation now.

- **Send in your deposit and make your first payment.** Most schools require a deposit in May to secure a spot in the incoming class. The first payment of 50 percent of the freshman year tuition will most likely be due in August.

- **Explore the college's handbook and course catalog.** These two publications will guide you throughout college. The college handbook usually contains college rules, procedures, policies, and information about official student organizations. It may explain minimum degree requirements and eligibility for honors. The course catalog will have a list of courses available in the coming years. Summer is a good time to focus calmly on potential course selections, core requirements, classes necessary for particular majors, and electives.

- **Establish banking relationships.** Obtain a student loan, student checking account, debit card, and/or credit card as necessary.

- **Attend orientation and contact the faculty advisor.** Some schools offer advance registration and pre-orientation programs to enable students to get to know the campus and classmates before upper-class students arrive. They will send information and schedules for these in materials that arrive during the summer. If a faculty advisor has been assigned, your student could send an introductory e-mail, asking appropriate questions. If a faculty advisor has not yet been assigned, you can prepare appropriate questions to ask in the fall, e.g., what is the best way to use core courses to help decide on a major? What are the options for taking required and elective courses? When does a major have to be officially declared?

- **Consider time-tested strategies.** Faculty advisors will know the ins and outs of the college's academic and administrative systems, but some time-tested strategies are worth remembering as you plan for freshman year and beyond.

    ◆ Fulfill core courses as soon as possible to free up spots for electives later on.

    ◆ Make balanced course selections. Don't take too many similar or demanding classes (e.g., heavy reading or writing, extensive labs).

    ◆ Try to take a mix of small and large classes to get a feel for how they differ, and manage time by spreading classes out over the week to allow time for studying, work (if necessary), and a few extracurricular activities.

    ◆ Consider taking a writing course, even if it's not required. It will help with other course work and with any future career.

    ◆ Attend freshman orientation events to get acquainted with the new surroundings, understand policies and procedures, and have a structured opportunity to meet other entering students and make friends. The more students learn going into the first weeks of classes, the easier it will be to settle into a routine that works for them and succeed.

- **Register early.** For certain classes, there are sometimes more students than spots available, so the earlier students register, the more likely they will be to get the choices they want. If a course is already fully enrolled, there will be time to adjust and select worthwhile alternatives. Although difficult for some freshman, appealing directly to a professor can sometimes open the door to a closed class.

Chapter 8 Takeaways

- Whether they use the Common Application, Universal Application, or some other format, most colleges will require the same basic information about a student's record, accomplishments, and background.

- The college essay is a unique opportunity for applicants to tell a college who they are. It should be written from the heart, grab the reader from the outset, and have a thesis. Spelling, grammar, and writing style matter.

- Interviews are an opportunity for students to present their personal qualities and intellectual abilities, explain anything in their record that requires explanation, convey unusual or special personal circumstances, and find out more about a school.

- Applying Early Decision or Early Action may enhance a student's chances of getting in, but it can also mean fewer options and a tighter application schedule.

- Students should choose Letter of Recommendation writers carefully, provide them with all the information they need well in advance, and strongly consider waiving their right to see the letter.

- A final and detailed "application checklist" can help students (and parents) stay organized and meet all requirements as deadlines approach.

- Wait-listed students realistically have very little, if any, chance of getting into selective and highly selective schools and should probably make a deposit to secure a place in another school that offered admission.

- Students who are determined to try to get in from a wait list should make contact with the school's admissions office and embark upon a self-marketing strategy that is enthusiastic but not counterproductive.

- Rejection should not be taken personally. Students should remember that a positive college experience does not hinge on attending any one school.

- For students not accepted at any school, check the National Association for College Admission Counseling (NACAC) website in early May for the names of schools that still have openings.

- Use the summer before freshman year to set the stage for a successful entry. Get bank accounts and financial affairs in line, take time to think about course selection, arrive on campus and register for classes early, ask questions of faculty advisors, and attend pre-orientation and orientation events. The more students know, the more easily they will adapt to college life.

Chapter 9

Financial Aid—The Second College Application Process

Chapter 3 provided a general overview of key concepts and the language of the financial aid process. This chapter digs deeper into what is, in effect, the second part of a college application for many families. One important difference: you (the parent) are most likely responsible for collecting the financial information and filing the financial aid package.

In this chapter, we'll discuss:

- Deadlines

- An Overview of the Forms Required in the Process:

  - FAFSA®

  - CSS/Financial Aid PROFILE®

- The Importance of Your Financial Aid Base Year

- Strategies for Maximizing Financial Aid

- How to Appeal (a.k.a. Negotiate) for More Financial Aid

DON'T MESS WITH DEADLINES

Before taking another step, realize deadlines are deadlines. If you miss a financial aid deadline—even by a day—you may be disqualified from being considered for aid.

In general, here are the most relevant dates and deadlines for financial aid:

Key Dates in Financial Aid Process	
Oct. 1	FAFSA® & CSS/Financial Aid PROFILE® are available.
Nov. 1	Earliest deadline for CSS/Financial Aid PROFILE®.
Feb. 1	Earliest regular decisions deadline for financial aid applications. Some colleges request taxes by this date.
March 1	A small percentage of colleges *require* tax information by this date.
March 15–April 10	Most financial aid is awarded.

Every college has different financial aid deadlines, requirements, and policies for awarding aid, which may vary from year to year. It's important to check each college's financial aid website to see exactly what they require and when.

Although a large percentage of aid is awarded in the March 15–April 10 window, there are exceptions. Colleges may send merit awards with an Early Decision or Early Action acceptance or shortly after accepting a regular decision student who is truly outstanding and a special fit for the incoming class. Some will also send need-based awards as soon as they receive the FAFSA® from admitted students. Also, some colleges make awards after the March 15 to April 10 period and right up to the May 1 reply deadline and sometimes beyond. The financial aid award process is fluid and may work in your favor if the circumstances are right. You should feel free to contact the school's financial aid office to ask when award letters are sent out.

FILE THE FORMS: THE FIRST STEP ON THE ROAD TO RECEIVING NEED-BASED FINANCIAL AID

You won't be surprised to learn that there are forms required to qualify for aid programs. For financial aid, you may need to file more than one form based on the source of the aid:

- **FAFSA®:** An acronym you will get to know all too well. It stands for the Free Application for Federal Student Aid. The FAFSA® is required to receive federal financial aid of any kind.

- **CSS/Financial Aid PROFILE®:** In addition to requiring a FAFSA®, over 400 private colleges (and a very few public schools) use the CSS/PROFILE® to determine eligibility for need-based aid from the college (a.k.a. Institutional Aid).

See Chapter 10 for a more detailed discussion about the FAFSA® and the CSS/PROFILE® and how to file these important forms.

The FAFSA® is the most important filing you will make in the process of applying for financial aid. Why? Because the Federal Student Aid Program (FSA), in conjunction with the college, uses the information to calculate your Expected Family Contribution (EFC)—the amount of money a family would be expected to contribute toward a child's education for the next academic year.

For example, if a school has a Cost of Attendance of $40,000 per year, and your EFC is $25,000, the college determines the student has $15,000 in financial need. However, this does not guarantee the student will receive $15,000 in funding to cover the difference. It may be that the student receives only $10,000 in funding, leaving the student with unmet financial need of $5,000. Policies and procedures regarding a student's EFC and financial need can vary at each institution, but, generally speaking, the lower the EFC, the more likely a student can qualify for financial aid.

In recent years, the government has modernized and streamlined the FAFSA®-filing process from paper to electronic filing. While a definite improvement, the FAFSA® still confuses families, sometimes resulting in mistaken entries that could have a negative effect on their financial aid eligibility. Nevertheless, thousands of families do successfully complete the FAFSA®'s lengthy but very important process to obtain their EFC.

How is your EFC derived? The FAFSA® collects information such as your income and assets, the number of children you have in college at the same time, and, most importantly, your children's income and assets, if there are any.

For purposes of determining your EFC, the federal government considers assets, including all nonretirement savings and investments including real estate, but not your primary home. A parent's and a student's 529 savings account are both treated as assets and are assumed to be contributed or assessed at 5.64 percent. Note that other non-529 Plan assets (passbook, CD, or mutual funds) in a student's name are assessed at 20 percent. A grandparent or relative's 529 Plan that benefits your child is not counted in the EFC formula until a distribution is made. Once identified, a grandparent/relative-owned 529 account is technically considered a gift to the student and treated as untaxed income for financial aid purposes. This treatment can impact a student's aid eligibility in subsequent years because 50 percent of the distribution amount would be considered as income to the student and therefore assessed at the usual rate of 50 percent of student income the following year. So if possible, grandparent/relative-owned 529 distributions should be made in the student's junior and senior year so as not to be counted as income to the student of financial aid purposes.

Ultimately, as indicated in the following chart, the type and ownership status of assets can affect financial aid eligibility. Assets will weigh against financial aid eligibility, as is to be expected.

Assumed Parent and Student Contributions According to the EFC		
	Parent's Contribution	Student's Contribution
529 Accounts	5.64%	5.64%
Other Assets	5.64%	20%
Income/AGI < $100,000	15%	50%
Income/AGI from $100,000 to $170,000	22%	50%
Income/AGI > $170,000	25%	50%

Can I get a preliminary indication of what my EFC might be before filing the FAFSA®?

Yes. It's a very good idea to get an indication of your EFC as early in high school as possible—you can start as early as you like by accessing free online tools and calculators. Knowing how much colleges will expect your family to pay is very important early in the college selection process. With this information and adequate time to act, families may see the benefit of advantageously and smartly moving assets to reduce their expected family contribution.

There are many calculators that provide high-level indications of your EFC using a few factors such as current income and number of students in college simultaneously. If you have more detailed financial information available, try the Department of Education's FAFSA4caster at http://Fafsa.Ed.gov. Using any of the EFC estimators provides only preliminary indications of your estimated EFC. These may, or may not, be good indicators of the actual EFC calculated from your information on the FAFSA® you eventually file.

Also, these calculations only affect need-based aid. Your student could receive unexpected merit aid. At this point, continue to be open-minded about the affordability of a particular school. You may not want to rule out any of your selected schools until after the financial aid award letters arrive and you know how much need- and merit-based aid is offered by each college.

TIP

Don't rule out a college if your preliminary EFC seems too high. The full aid picture could change considerably by the time it is time to file: your financial situation may have changed or your student may qualify for merit aid.

Finally, there is relief for families with lower incomes:

- Parents with Adjusted Gross Incomes of less than $50,000 and family members filing 1040EZ or 1040A do not have to report their assets on the FAFSA®.

- The EFC for parents with income under $24,000 is $0.

In order to continue receiving need-based financial aid after the freshman year, students must file a new FAFSA® after October 1 and before the college's deadline in each subsequent year the student is enrolled. Moreover, the school may have a different FAFSA® filing deadline for institutional/campus-based funding each year. It behooves students to file the FAFSA® on time every year or risk reductions in funding.

Some colleges also have their own institutional forms in addition to requiring the FAFSA® and/or CSS/PROFILE®. Check the college's website to determine precisely which forms are required and when they are due.

THE BASE YEAR IS VERY IMPORTANT

Before you dive into the forms, take note of a critical benchmark known as your Base Year. Establishing a base year is common when trying to compare one year to another. For financial aid purposes, the Base Year refers to the year of the tax return that you need to use to first provide information required by the FAFSA®. For example, a freshman entering college in September 2018 would include information from the family's 2016 tax return—that student's Base Year—on the FAFSA®. Freshmen entering in 2017 will use information from the family's 2015 tax return.

Why is the Base Year so important? The federal financial aid formula is income driven and therefore your income will be the largest single factor in determining whether you qualify for financial aid and the amount of aid you qualify for. As we have discussed, financial aid calculations treat assets owned by parents and students differently. In most cases, parental assets are assumed to contribute to college costs at a much lower rate than student assets. Therefore, ensuring that assets are categorized as parent or student assets in the Base Year can help to maximize aid eligibility. Finally, the Base Year simply moves forward as the student moves through college. Need-based financial aid can also change year to year, reflecting changes in your family's evolving financial circumstances.

Wise planners recognize that simple steps can be taken to improve your ultimate financial aid award. Be sure to make changes that will increase the likelihood of receiving financial aid before the Base Year. This means that you may need to switch assets to be used to pay for college from the child's name to the parent's name before the Base Year. In the example above, for college freshmen enrolling in 2017, these assets would need to have been moved prior to January 1, 2015, so all of the account activity is reported on the parent's 2015 tax return. For those starting college in September 2018, assets would have to have been moved prior to January 1, 2016. This is very important and will be discussed in more detail in the upcoming "Strategies to Maximize Financial Aid" section.

One word of caution: When it comes to moving assets or taking on debt to maximize financial aid, be careful to ensure such advice is coming from a trusted source and is right for your financial picture. Be wary of financial aid consultants or financial advisors who suggest you take on more debt, reduce your income, or hide assets in order to qualify for more aid.

STRATEGIES TO MAXIMIZE FINANCIAL AID

Maximizing financial aid can be accomplished by:

- Lowering your EFC.

- Carefully selecting colleges that have reputations for providing significant aid.

- Applying to schools that would consider your student an academic star or potential campus leader or someone who would add geographic diversity to the entering class.

Death and taxes, they say, are the only two givens. Our society also understands that paying a fair share of taxes by taking advantage of all legal means of minimizing taxes is appropriate. The same is true in the world of financial aid. Before your Base Year, you should take steps to ensure that your income and assets and those of your children are aligned to produce as low an Expected Family Contribution as possible. It's perfectly legal, and you should consider which strategies work best for your situation.

TIP

If your child has any non-529 assets (a bank savings account, mutual funds, etc.) in his/her name, consider transferring them to a 529 account where they will be assessed at 5.64 percent vs. 20 percent for financial aid purposes.

Seven Ways to Lower Your EFC and Receive More Financial Aid

The lower your family's EFC, the more aid you will receive. Here are several steps that can reduce your EFC and increase your financial aid:

1. Remove assets held in your child's name to your or another family member's name before January 1 of their high school sophomore year (i.e., in the year prior to their Base Year).

2. Rely on relatives to help pay because their assets are not included on the FAFSA® so they are not included in the student's EFC calculation.

3. If relatives have opened 529 savings accounts to benefit your child, realize that once the funding is provided to the student it becomes a traceable income event for the student, decreasing financial aid eligibility relevant to that tax return's financial aid Base Year. In such cases, it's best to wait until the student's last two years of college to liquidate the 529 account to avoid having this funding count as student income when determining financial aid eligibility.

4. Keep savings or assets in your business during the college years. Business assets have a much smaller impact on your EFC than personal assets. If you own investment property, consider structuring/retitling the property as a business.

5. It is to your advantage to have more than one child in college at the same time. Both the FAFSA® and CSS/Financial Aid PROFILE® take this into account and split Expected Family Contributions accordingly.

6. Place savings in retirement accounts, such as an IRA, 401(k), 403(b), or pension plan. These are rarely considered in the EFC calculation. You must do this before January 1 of sophomore year in high school (i.e., in the year prior to their Base Year).

7. When reporting the value of your primary residence or other real estate on the CSS/Financial Aid PROFILE® form, use the measure that produces the lower value. This is not the time to inflate the value of your home. Consider the lower of the Housing Index Calculator (HIC), the assessed value, or another documented value indicator. Also confirm if any debt on the property would weigh against total value.

Another way to maximize your financial aid is to target schools based upon the ratio of your EFC to their Cost of Attendance (COA) . If your EFC is substantially less than the college's COA, you may be more likely to be eligible for need-based aid. The result will be that your actual out-of-pocket costs for college will be closer to your EFC than the college's COA. As discussed earlier, be aware of the type of aid you are being offered: loans, even government-subsidized loans offered in financial aid packages, need to be repaid. Also be aware of the maximum Expected Family Contribution limits for federal programs, like Pell, or various state-backed, need-based grant programs.

TIP

If you are unable to qualify for either need-based or merit-based financial aid, you can still seek out "value" colleges. These are high-quality public and private institutions that have a lower Cost of Attendance relative to their peers, making them more affordable, perhaps even without financial assistance.

Need-Blind Admission

A school's admission policy may be "need blind," which means that students seeking financial aid are not at a disadvantage in the admission process. Such schools typically have access to large endowments that enable admitted students to be fully funded if unable to pay out of pocket. This presents an excellent opportunity for some exceptional students at institutions capable of supporting such a generous budget.

Colleges offering 100 percent financial aid to students from low-income families often require detailed, verifiable information, including all family income and asset data, in order to confirm eligibility. Policies are designed to be solid in principle but flexible in action, where year-to-year funding is dynamically distributed. Funding can vary based on the total number of students applying to the school and asking for aid. Some offer a sliding percentage of costs based upon the income level of families. For example, some private and public colleges provide 100 percent of need for families with income under $65,000 and ask families to pay only 10 percent if their gross income is less than $120,000 to $180,000.

> ### TIP
>
> Do not narrow college choices simply because you don't *think* you can afford it. In fact, some high-priced colleges may end up costing you less than a lower priced or in-state public college because of how the federal-aid formula works and the financial aid policies of various high-priced colleges. Bottom line is that a combination of need-based and merit-based aid is widely available, and high-priced colleges should be ruled in, not out, due to tuition costs.

If maximizing financial aid is important, it's smart to apply to a number of colleges and make the final decision after comparing the financial aid packages. You may be pleasantly surprised if one school provides unexpected merit aid.

NEGOTIATING THE BEST POSSIBLE FINANCIAL AID PACKAGE

A college's offer of financial aid is not always grounds for celebration. Sometimes it falls short of expectations. Unless your child is the rare genius or one of a select group of athletes or performers, you may not receive a 100 percent scholarship. The percentage you do receive may be less than you need. Some families find that after receiving their financial aid package, the cost of attending the college still exceeds their EFC and aid package. In this situation, you may decide to try to get a second bite of the financial aid apple.

The first offer of financial aid does not have to be the last. While financial aid administrators do not "negotiate" aid packages, they do listen to reasonable, fact-based appeals.

> ### TIP
>
> When asking for more aid, avoid the word "negotiate," and do not approach financial aid officers as if you are negotiating for more money.

Financial Aid Decisions Can Be Appealed—for the Right Reasons

Each college's Office of Financial Aid has the ability to review the appeals from students regarding family financial circumstances that may have drastically changed their ability to afford college. Most often this involves a loss of employment, but other circumstances, such as death, disability, or natural disasters, could be cause for an appeal as well. Often, specific documentation will need to be submitted and approved before any new financial aid can be awarded. Most commonly requested forms include tax returns, pay stubs, records of assets, and documentation that proves a reduction in household income.

The process begins simply enough by contacting the school's Financial Aid Office and/or submitting a brief but concise letter identifying the student, the situation, and request for assistance.

By their nature, financial aid administrators want to be helpful and offer as much as possible, but there is only so much they can do. They are professionals who can usually tell when a family is trying to game the system and when more assistance is truly needed. You should recognize that you have little, if any, leverage in the discussion, so be reasonable in your approach.

TIP

The words "Special Circumstances" are important when appealing for financial aid. Use these words and provide documentation with them.

Your goal should be to understand the aid process, file all forms accurately and on time, and make changes if family circumstances change. Above all, you need to present a well-supported rationale for requesting an increased financial aid package.

TIP

Family accountants are not always experts on financial aid. There are fee-based advisors specializing in this arcane area who may be more helpful. However, be wary of fee-based advisors who are selling financial products or recommend you take on significant debt simply to qualify for financial aid.

Seven Steps to Appeal for More Financial Aid

1. Ask for more aid, but be polite and courteous. Don't be confrontational. Frame communications as a request for reconsideration. Don't use the word "negotiate."

2. Know the process the school uses to reconsider aid. Your odds for a successful appeal are higher at colleges with larger endowments: mostly private colleges and flagship public universities.

3. Check the accuracy of the FAFSA® and CSS/Financial Aid PROFILE® forms that were submitted. Perhaps you overstated assets, lost significant assets since the filing, or simply made a mistake in the rush to file.

4. Ask the financial aid administrator if your tax deductions were counted as income. Some colleges do not accept all tax deductions and, instead, view some as untaxed income. If you know what deductions the college converted to income, it may be possible that your true financial need is greater than they think.

5. Write a letter that includes documentation of "Special Circumstances" and/or changes in your family's situation since the FAFSA® or CSS/Financial Aid PROFILE® was submitted. There are many special circumstances. Here are a few:
    - ◆ Divorce
    - ◆ Death of a wage earner
    - ◆ Unexpected, unreimbursed medical bills or costs associated with caring for special-needs children
    - ◆ Tuitions for private elementary or secondary schools
    - ◆ One-time retirement in the Base Year
    - ◆ Necessary home repairs: roof, heating, windows

6. Have a follow-up meeting or call to make the appeal directly to the financial aid administrator.

7. For new potential freshmen, politely present a more generous financial aid package from another school, if your child received one. Try to get the schools to compete by showing that another peer school came to a different conclusion.

Chapter 9 Takeaways

- Aid is usually based on need or merit. Need, for purposes of federal financial aid, is determined through the FAFSA®. The amount of need-based aid you receive is based on your EFC. "Merit" may take the form of academic excellence, but notable talent in sports, the arts, and other areas may also be sufficient.

- Check with the college to see if it requires the CSS/Financial Aid PROFILE® or another form provided by the college to be considered for Institutional Aid. Private colleges may ask more questions than the federal government, but they may also be more generous.

- Know the FAFSA® and CSS/Financial Aid PROFILE® deadlines for each college.

- Resubmit applications for need-based financial aid annually for a student to continue receiving aid after freshman year.

- If you do not receive a financial aid offer adequate for your needs, you may be able to appeal successfully for more aid.

- If you do not receive sufficient aid, consider "value" colleges. These are high-quality public and private institutions that have a lower Cost of Attendance relative to their peers, making them more affordable, perhaps even without financial assistance.

Chapter 10

Filing Financial Aid Forms—It's Worth the Effort

In previous chapters, we discussed the financial aid process and outlined strategies for minimizing the Expected Family Contribution (EFC) and maximizing your financial aid eligibility. In this chapter, we dive into the weeds of the two primary forms used by colleges in the financial aid process:

- Free Application for Federal Student Aid (FAFSA®)

- CSS/Financial Aid PROFILE®

NO FAFSA®: NO FEDERAL AID FOR YOU

If nothing else, the government did a great job of naming its form: The Free Application for Federal Student Aid (FAFSA®). As the name implies, there is no charge to file the FAFSA®, and it is required to be considered for federal financial aid.

Essential facts about the FAFSA®:

- DO NOT MISS THE DEADLINE! High school seniors must file a FAFSA® form after October 1 of their senior year and before the college's deadline. Each college may have a different deadline so be very careful to file before the first deadline.

- Several agencies depend on FAFSA® information, including state higher education groups and institutions of higher education awarding additional need-based funding. They may have internal funding deadlines requiring strict adherence to qualify.

- The FAFSA® filing is an annual ritual. A new FAFSA® form must be filed annually if your student is to receive any aid for the next academic year. It's identical to the process used by twelfth-grade students applying for aid for the first time: the form will be available beginning October 1 and must be filed before any deadlines. The best advice is to file the FAFSA® each year in October.

- The required information tracks very closely to your tax return. You can use a link to download tax return information you filed with the IRS onto the FAFSA® form to be filed with the U.S. Department of Education (DOE). If your taxes are not completed prior to the college's FAFSA® deadline, you may use estimates. Simply update your FAFSA® once you have completed your taxes.

- The information required to be filed or the process used to file the FAFSA® may change each year.

In order to successfully file the FAFSA®, you need to understand:

- How to set up your account to file the form.

- What information is required to be filed.

Don't be overwhelmed. It's just an information-gathering process. Albeit somewhat time consuming, this isn't difficult, and there are resources at FAFSA.ed.gov to guide you—you just need to get it done. Also, some college financial aid offices will be glad to answer questions and provide assistance, so be sure to check with them as well.

A Step-By-Step Guide to Filing the FAFSA® Form

Obtain a Federal Student Aid (FSA) ID in three easy steps:

1. Go to: https://fsaid.ed.gov.

2. Register by providing personal information.

3. Get your FSA ID and use it to e-sign important documents.

Compile your personal, tax, and financial information. Estimates are okay, but you should update the information once your taxes are finalized.

Go to https://fafsa.ed.gov:

- The Federal Student Aid program (FSA) works in conjunction with your college's financial aid office to facilitate the application and funding process for much aid. After initially filing the FAFSA®, an official Student Aid Report (SAR) is generated, with a copy made available to the student. Families should review the SAR and make corrections as necessary.

- FSA officially forwards the FAFSA® data to all colleges listed on your SAR. This is referred to as the ISIR (Institutional Student Information Record), and colleges receive thousands of requests for financial aid from all students who are considering attending.

EFC will affect financial aid eligibility, but total award eligibility may vary depending on funding availability at each school.

Colleges use the ISIR to determine the amount of institutional aid you will receive but may request verification documentation to confirm reported tax and FAFSA® information.

ABOUT THE FEDERAL FSA ID

The federal FSA ID is a user name and password registered with the U.S. Department of Education to provide access to the student's personal information as well as to permit users to e-sign federal financial aid documents in a legally binding format. If you are a parent of a dependent student, you and your child must separately establish FSA IDs.

It's easy to establish your secured federal FSA ID:

1. Go to FAFSA.ed.gov and look for one of the several places to click to create the FSA ID.

2. You will be prompted to provide a user name, establish a password, and enter personal information, including:

   - Social Security Number
   - Date of birth
   - Address
   - Contact information
   - Answers to five challenge questions used for security purposes

After agreeing to the Terms and Conditions and verifying your e-mail address, your account will be ready for use. Use your FSA ID to e-sign important documents.

Do you already have a Federal Student PIN? It won't work anymore. To enhance security and improve users' experience, the federal FSA ID replaced the Federal Student PIN as the tool for e-signing in May 2015. If you currently have a Federal Student PIN, you can link your PIN to the new FSA ID. If it expired, you will need to register with a new FSA ID.

TIP

You will be prompted to change your FSA ID password every 18 months if you don't change it before. Changing it as you begin each new academic year process will keep it fresher in your mind.

FILING THE FAFSA®

The FAFSA® form and the process for filing a FAFSA® is subject to change, so it pays to check the FAFSA® website to ensure you have the most current form and process. As previously noted, the Department of Education changed the log-in system for the FAFSA® in May of 2015—basically at the time families were in the process of finalizing their aid packages and financing arrangements for the 2015–16 academic year. It pays to stay up to date every year, so you can proactively manage the process.

TIP
It is not unusual for the federal government to make changes to the FAFSA® form each year. You can find more information about the current FAFSA® form requirements at https://fafsa.ed.gov.

What You Need to File Your FAFSA®

The FAFSA® form, now due after October 1 of your student's senior year, is fairly long and tedious, but it's necessary if you want to be considered for federal or institutional financial aid.

Here's how to start the process of filing the FAFSA®. Remember that this is the student's FAFSA®, so it is written from his or her perspective. (i.e., use the student's Social Security Number). As a parent, you are providing information to support the student's application for financial aid.

1. Obtain federal FSA IDs.

2. Collect the following personal information:

    - Student's driver's license number, if they have one.

    - Student's Social Security Number—and parents', if student is a dependent student.

    - Alien Registration Number if you are not a U.S. citizen.

3. Gather the following documents:

   ◆ Most recent tax records for the student and parents of dependent students. The FAFSA® link provides an IRS record retrieval link—the IRS Data Retrieval Tool (IRS DRT).

   ◆ Documentation of any untaxed income (Social Security, military benefits, child support, welfare) for the student and parents of dependent students.

   ◆ Current bank and investment statements, as well as any real estate holdings, but not information about your home.

   ◆ Business records.

4. Go to FAFSA.ed.gov after October 1 of the high school senior year and start your FAFSA® form. When you have entered all of the information and are ready to file, here is what you need to do next:

   ◆ Use your FSA ID to sign the FAFSA®.

   ◆ Check the confirmation page—select the option to automatically transmit the data to the FAFSA® for a sibling, if applicable.

TIP

When filing the FAFSA®, you may also see a prompt to automatically apply for aid in your state—don't miss this opportunity. Be sure to click it.

CSS/FINANCIAL AID PROFILE®

In addition to the FAFSA®, some 400 colleges require you to make this supplemental filing if you want to be considered for their institution's financial aid. The College Board administers the CSS/Financial Aid PROFILE® application process. On October 1 each year, the College Board releases the CSS/PROFILE® form to be used for consideration for aid to be awarded in the following spring.

Unlike the FAFSA®, the CSS/PROFILE® involves a filing fee, which is subject to change. Recently, the fees were $25 for the first school and $16 for each additional school. The College Board does offer fee waivers for families with lower income and/or few assets. Visit CollegeBoard.com to find out whether the schools you are considering require this filing as well as the current fee structure.

The CSS/PROFILE® asks for additional information beyond what is required on the government's FAFSA® form and makes separate financial aid calculations for purposes of qualifying for a college's institutional financial aid programs. You can find more information about the CSS/Financial Aid PROFILE® at http://student.collegeboard.org.

If you have a high school senior—particularly one who plans to apply for Early Decision—be sure to know when the college requires the CSS/PROFILE® to be filed. It can be as early as the beginning of October at some colleges. These are deadlines you do not want to miss.

The requirements for completing the CSS/PROFILE® vary from institution to institution. It often has different deadlines than the FAFSA® and asks more questions because it relies on different financial assumptions to determine need. For example, it requests data on some assets not counted by FAFSA®, including:

- Your home's equity

- A small business

- Retirement accounts

- Insurance policies

Though they may require more detailed information, schools using the CSS/Financial Aid PROFILE® may also provide more generous assistance than the federal government as they may also have more flexibility when determining a student's need.

TIP

Some schools require the CSS/PROFILE® in the fall of the senior year for Early Decision or Early Action applicants. Know the deadlines early in your search process, and file your CSS/PROFILE® two weeks before the deadline.

A Step-By-Step Guide to Completing the CSS/Financial Aid PROFILE®

1. Set-up an account at the College Board (https://www.collegeboard.org).

2. Collect information from your tax returns.

3. File the CSS/PROFILE® online at the College Board website.

4. Receive your CSS ID number.

5. Complete the verification process:

   ◆ Many colleges require a copy of federal tax returns and W-2s from students (if applicable) and parents. Financial aid will not be finalized until you've submitted tax returns.

   ◆ Complete your tax returns as early as possible after your base income year. Some colleges request tax returns as early as February 1.

   ◆ Some private colleges use a central processing agency—the Institutional Documentation Service (IDOC)—to collect and process your verification documents. You will receive e-mail notification from IDOC in early February with instructions on how and where to send tax returns and W2s.

A Note on Two-Household/Divorced Families: When there is more than one parent, the custodial parent must complete and file the CSS/PROFILE®. After it is submitted, the non-custodial parent must complete and file the Non-Custodial Profile ("NCP"). Some colleges do not accept the online NCP. Consult with each of your colleges to confirm.

Once you have filed all the necessary paperwork and received financial or institutional aid, your work is not done. The FAFSA® (and, if required by the college, CSS/PROFILE®) must be filed annually during your child's college years for your child to continue receiving aid. Need-based aid does not automatically renew at the start of a new academic year. Also, in cases of multiple children, each will need to complete a separate FAFSA® or CSS/PROFILE®.

FAFSA® and CSS/PROFILE® Compared

FAFSA®	CSS/PROFILE®
Uses standardized, universal application form and same methodology for all schools.	Asks questions specific to the private school the student is applying to.
No fee to submit application.	Fee for each school.
Relies primarily on income, assets, family size, and the number of children in college at the same time.	Relies on income, assets, family size, and the number of children in college, but also includes other assets, such as your home, small business, retirement accounts, and life insurance policies. Also assumes a minimum contribution by the student.
EFC does not vary based on school attended or special circumstances.	Eligibility and amounts vary. Financial aid counselors have flexibility and can give weight to special circumstances when determining a student's need.
Available after October 1 of senior year. Deadlines vary by school or state. Students may receive aid on first-come, first-served basis.	Deadlines vary. Students receive aid on first-come, first-served basis.

Chapter 10 Takeaways

- The financial aid process at all colleges is driven by the required federal form (the FAFSA®).

- To be eligible for their institutional aid, some (mostly private) colleges also require the CSS/Financial Aid PROFILE® is to be filed in addition to the FAFSA®.

- Deadlines are hard and true. Research, verify, and recheck them on each college's website. DO NOT MISS THE DEADLINES.

- The federal financial aid formula is income driven, and, therefore, your gross family income will be the largest single factor in determining whether you qualify for financial aid and the amount of free aid you qualify for.

- If your EFC is relatively high or low, schools may use need-based and merit-based aid awards to make their school attractive. Don't count yourself out of the financial aid process too early.

PART ③

Pulling It All Together

Chapter 11

Financial Literacy—For High School and College Students

Since the financial crisis of 2008, financial literacy has become an increasingly important concept. The National Financial Educators Council defines financial literacy as "possessing the skills and knowledge on financial matters to confidently take effective action that best fulfills an individual's personal, family, and global community goals." Although critically important for all to master or at a minimum to understand the basics of good financial management, it remains a challenge for people of all ages who are confused by basic financial terms, products, and transactions. Study after study has documented that most high school and college students are ill equipped with even the most basic knowledge of interest rates, credit cards, bank fees, and student loans to effectively manage their finances. Parents can help their children immeasurably by helping them become financially literate.

Although the topic of financial literacy is worthy of its own book, we will focus on a few foundational concepts that will help you focus your young adult on financial literacy that is meaningful to them and can have a long-term beneficial impact on their lives. Here, we will discuss:

- Budgeting

- Credit Scoring

- College Loan Refinancing

BUDGETING

Making some money is usually not the issue. Earning enough money to afford current and projected lifestyles becomes the challenge.

High school juniors and seniors and college students often struggle with how they will manage the money they have to pay the bills they incur. For many it is difficult to project what their earnings will be after college and to plan accordingly. In college, they struggle with an important chicken-and-egg issue: Will their college major lead to their job or will their desired job dictate their major? However that goes, students need to think about what interests them and where they envision themselves, even generally, in the work force. Will their first paycheck come from the military, the private sector, or from the not-for-profit or public sector? Will their eventual job provide ample income to support their college loans and the lifestyle they desire after graduation?

Having some focus on the selected college major with an eye toward post-college employment and income picture is relevant because it provides a general indication of the projected capacity to repay college loans and have sufficient income to cover other basic expenses, such as rent and car payments. All too often, students take out college loans and don't under-stand how much they will repay in aggregate or the exact amount of the monthly payments. This is all knowable well in advance of the required first payment. Recent graduates can avoid having the total amount of student loan debt and resulting monthly payments from seriously impacting their budget and quality of life—as long as they are realistic about how much they may earn and about their expenses, including student loans.

The college financing discussion, choice of major, and expected employment and income serve as a good starting point to focus on the bigger picture of budgeting and the consequences and trade-offs of economic choices. The Faustian Pact (Chapter 5) needs to be avoided, and students should only borrow what they can reasonably expect to repay based on their projected earnings. Using loan-repayment calculators linked to starting salaries will provide valuable insight into a student's capacity to repay based on their projected careers. Students and parents need to be smart about how much student loan debt is used to finance an education and the value of a par-ticular major they select and college they may attend.

We prioritize the importance of understanding the link between starting salary and college loans before budgeting, because too often students doom themselves early in college by signing on for more loans than their eventual desired jobs can support. Avoiding this trap is a strong first lesson in being financially literate.

Budgeting is the foundation of any financial plan. One key concept is knowing the difference between needs and wants. For example, today's students would consider a cell phone as important a necessity as food, clothing, and shelter. It has evolved into a need. But are all of those paid apps also a need? Financial literacy should make students aware of nuanced financial choices and teach them how to best allocate their scarce earnings.

The fundamental principles of budgeting are the same no matter the life stage: high school, college, graduate school, or after. Here are some basic essential elements to create a workable budget that you can share with your children:

- Set the time parameters. Will the budget be for the semester, an academic year, or a calendar year?

- Identify the sources of income.

  - Wages from work after taxes

  - Financial aid

  - Gifts or other family contributions

  - Withdrawals from savings

- Categorize expense categories.

  - Fixed expenses

    - Rent or room and board

    - Tuition and fees

    - Loan payments

    - Insurance payments

  - Variable Expenses

    - Transportation

- Utilities, cell service, etc.
- Personal care items
- Clothing
- Groceries and snacks
- Entertainment
- Student activities
- Interest on credit card debt

- Design a savings plan.
  - For contingencies—the rainy-day fund
  - Longer term for:
    - Future large purchase, such as a car or house
    - Retirement

- Balance and review the budget monthly. Do comparative analysis of actual versus forecasted expenses and income to develop an intuition for how spending and income patterns are changing—or need to be changed.

Related to budgeting for college students is the issue of keeping current on requirements to maintain or reapply for financial aid and loans—critical income items for college and postgraduate students. Recipients of need-based funding must reapply for aid each year, which means filing the FAFSA® and, perhaps, the CSS/Financial Aid PROFILE® if it is required by the college. Some merit-based aid awards and scholarships require a minimum grade point average or impose other requirements, so the student should be mindful of meeting those and not jeopardize the free money.

CREDIT SCORING

As technology began to replace human banking interactions, the concept of underwriting credit (i.e., evaluating the borrower to determine the risk that they will not be able to repay a loan) migrated from a subjective, relationship-based activity to an objective, data-driven analysis. Companies such as Equifax, TransUnion , and Experian collect data on how we pay our bills, how long we've had a credit history, and other information. As will be detailed a little later in this chapter, a company originally called Fair, Isaac, and Company (now known as FICO®) developed credit scorecards to help lenders systematically gauge a borrower's capacity and propensity to repay obligations. Equifax, TransUnion, Experian, and others use these credit models to produce a credit score for each of us. As a result of the type of information one company or another may track or emphasize, our FICO® credit score from each company will likely be different.

Understanding how credit scoring works generally, and specifically for student loans, will help students know early on how important it is to pay their bills on time and develop a good credit score.

For many students, applying for a private credit student loan or a credit card is the first time they are evaluated for credit purposes. Most require a co-signer because students have not yet built a strong repayment history.

Student loans are an opportunity to gain financial literacy and build strong credit while still in school.

In addition to making school affordable, student loans can, by themselves, serve an educational purpose in financial literacy. Borrowing while in college is an opportunity to learn the value of credit and acquire healthy debt-repayment habits. Life after college will present new challenges, and financial lessons learned ahead of time can help a student transition smoothly into independent and fiscally responsible adulthood.

Build Positive Credit Habits in College

Most students enter college without much credit history. Until they graduate, they can build positive credit habits that will last a lifetime. Building good credit requires a record of borrowing and making consistent, on-time payments. The college years offer the time, space, and resources to help students graduate with a strong credit history.

There are three main requirements for establishing good credit. Students need:

1. Access to credit.

2. A source of income.

3. A strategy for making consistent debt payments.

Here's how students can do it:

1. Establish credit: College students typically have access to a variety of credit opportunities, including federal and private student loans as well as credit cards in their name or jointly held by the parent and student.

2. Earn income: Students may qualify for work-study or find other on- or off-campus employment, satisfying requirement number 2.

3. Make timely payments: The most common stumbling block is the third item, which requires students to design and execute a consistent plan for all required payments, including loans, utilities, credit cards, etc. Becoming knowledgeable about this topic should be a priority for both students and parents, who may need to help to get them started.

What Is a FICO® Score?

The term "FICO®" began as an acronym for Fair, Isaac, and Company, a firm that developed predictive analytics based on an individual's payment history to determine their ability to pay debts and bills on time. Fair, Isaac, and Company has since changed its name to FICO® because of its widespread recognition.

FICO® rates borrowers using scores that help lenders predict future debt-management and bill-payment behavior. FICO® analytics have grown to provide forecasts of which accounts are most likely to be profitable and which are most likely to end up in bankruptcy. Lenders ultimately use FICO® scores to approve or deny loan applications. Some employers may also request that candidates agree to pull a credit report as part of the job application process. While employers do not receive your credit score, they can view the report to check for any major delinquencies that could flag a potential employment risk.

FICO® is not actually a credit-reporting agency. Its role is to create a score for an individual based on data collected by the three major credit reporting agencies: Equifax, Experian, and TransUnion. These agencies keep detailed records, including name, address, Social Security number, date of birth, and employment information, as provided by individuals when applying for credit.

> In today's job market, having a good credit profile can be as important as a high GPA, as many employers do credit checks.

Records contain "trade lines" or "trade references," representing a borrower's financial activity. Trade lines include reports on such debt as student loans, credit card borrowing, auto loans, and home mortgages. Data collected include the date an account was opened, the original loan amount, current account balances, and payment history. Credit inquiries appear on the report whenever an individual requests credit from a lender. Reports also rely on public record and collections information from the court system and from collection agencies to determine whether a borrower has experienced any bankruptcies, foreclosures, suits, wage garnishments, liens, or judgments.

What Goes Into a FICO® Score?

FICO® scores can range from 300 to 850, with higher numbers signifying that a borrower is less of a risk for a lender. A good credit score is based on a number of data points that reflect a borrower's consistency and diversity of accounts. Each is weighted differently:

- Payment history (35%). Are payments made on time or does the file include "derogatories," such as late payments, bankruptcies, liens, or judgments?

- Debt Burden (30%). Incorporates a number of measures, including amounts owed compared to the amount of available credit and number of accounts with balances.

- Length of credit history (15%) (Time in File). Includes the age of the oldest account and the average age of all accounts.

- New credit in the last 12–18 months (10%).

- Mix of credit (10%). Include credit cards, retail accounts, installment loans, finance company accounts, mortgage loans.

Some factors that do NOT affect your FICO® score may surprise you:

- Age, sex, marital status, race, color, religion

- Salary

- Debt ratio: total outstanding debt divided by total assets

- Income

- Length or place of residence

- Length of employment or a credit pull by an employer

Why Do FICO® Scores Matter?

FICO® scores are critically important because they determine whether you will be able to acquire credit and, ultimately, what interest rate you will have to pay. A high (good) FICO® score provides access to credit of all kinds: private student loans, credit cards, auto loans, mortgages, and other credit products. Lenders have credit policies that put consumers into categories of risk based on the FICO® score. Consumers with higher FICO® scores are eligible for the lowest interest rates and most favorable repayment terms because they are judged to be less risky than low-FICO®-score borrowers. Conversely, a lower (bad) FICO® score indicates increased risk in lending, so the interest rates will be correspondingly higher to offset the greater risk of nonpayment. A low score may result in a lender declining to make the loan at all.

A credit report with a high FICO® score is useful for a variety of needs apart from borrowing. Information on a credit report can be a factor when applying for an apartment rental, a job, or certain types of insurance, such as an automobile or homeowner's policy.

TIP

Have your student periodically check his or her credit report. Every twelve months, all consumers are entitled to receive a free credit report from each of the three major credit bureaus at www.AnnualCreditReport.com. Be wary of sites advertising free credit reporting. Some will provide free reports for a limited time and then continue to provide the reports for a fee.

NOTE: FICO® scores are not used in the federal student loan program, but private credit student loan lenders use them.

How to Raise a FICO® Score

The first realization is that it will take some time to raise a FICO® score or to repair a low score after some credit stumbles. The credit score premise is to measure and predict your ability and willingness to pay over a long period of time. Establishing good credit habits early will provide students with opportunities to gain credit for cars and homes in the future. With this in mind, here are a few steps and tips:

4. **Ensure that the report is free of errors.** Monitoring credit reports quickly identifies any errors that may appear and negatively affect the credit score. The reports identify the lender (loans, credit cards) or vendor (utilities, phone companies, etc.) and if there is a delinquency on the account. Check to ensure that you have an account with all of those listed on your credit report. Occasionally, a lender or vendor incorrectly posts a delinquency to the wrong account; make sure you owe what the report says you owe. This is also a handy way to ensure that you are not the victim of identity theft.

   Once comfortable that the information on your credit report is accurate, you may take measures to actively manage and increase your FICO® score. Setting up payment reminders or arranging for direct payments from your accounts are two ways of ensuring that payments are made on time.

5. **Make consistent, on-time payments.** The simplest way to increase your FICO® score is to pay bills and borrowings on time. While in college, this is most quickly achieved by responsibly utilizing a credit card and paying the amount due on time. Paying 100 percent of the balance each month is preferable to avoid the high interest rates associated with virtually all credit cards. Students can also use responsible amounts of student loans to build a healthy debt-management habit by making payments before graduation. Some loans require only interest payments while in school. Student loans in a deferred status, i.e., making no payments until after graduation, will not negatively affect a student's FICO® score because they are not contractually obligated to make payments on the loans. Some students choose to pay at least interest while in school to avoid capitalizing the interest and increasing the total amount they will have to eventually repay. See Chapter 5—Student Loans.

6. **Set up automatic payments.** To make loan repayment easier, set up a checking account to make monthly student loan payments automatically using Automated Clearing House (ACH) or other banking tools. With automated payments, students will always make payments on time.

7. **Have several different active trade lines, all in good standing.** For example, a person with a credit card, auto loan, and student loan that

are all current and in good standing will likely have a higher credit score than a person with just a credit card, all other things being equal. Demonstrating the ability to manage multiple accounts can prove the borrower's effectiveness in debt repayment.

More Ways to Improve FICO® Scores

- Get current on missed payments ASAP! And, continue making timely payments on all outstanding bills.

- Do not cancel credit cards. Canceling cards decreases "capacity" and could lower your score.

- The credit ratio matters: keep credit card balances as low as possible. Manage the ratio of your outstanding balance to your available credit by spreading expenses over different cards. Keeping your outstanding balance/available credit ratio low on each card will improve your score.

- Pay down debt.

- Stop or slow down opening new accounts. Opening new accounts will lower your average account age. Higher account age will improve your credit score.

- Establish a consistent track record of timely payments.

- Move "revolving debt," (e.g., credit card debt or other open-ended debt) into "installment debt"—a one-time loan with a fixed schedule for repayment.

What Causes a Decrease in a FICO® Score?

Credit scores can decrease as a result of a few financial missteps that adversely affect a borrower's credit history. These can include:

- Missed payments.
- Over-borrowing from available lines of credit.
- A high number of applications and inquiries for new credit.
- Canceling a credit card.
- Too many revolving loans and not enough installment loans.
- Student loan delinquencies or default.

While student loan delinquencies can damage a student's credit record, they can sometimes be rectified through good communication with student loan services and a few extra payments. Default is a much bigger problem. Student loan debt remains part of a borrower's credit until the debt is resolved and repaid. As noted above, absent certain types of discharge or forgiveness, even bankruptcy in most cases will not be enough to cancel student loan debt. With sufficient awareness and proactive steps, students and parents can avoid these problems

Jump-start Your Student's Access to Credit: Authorize Them on Your Credit Card.

A simple strategy to help rapidly improve your child's credit profile is to utilize the option to "authorize" their access to your credit card. Providing authorization allows your child direct access to credit through your pre-existing account. You can authorize a limited amount of credit for your student, preventing them from running up unnecessary debt, but providing just enough to handle necessary expenses and pursue a speedy repayment process. When you authorize your child's access to credit, you are essentially adding years of parent credit history to your student's newly minted credit report. This creates an immediate increase to your child's credit. But be careful. If you have a poor credit history, this method can backfire as years of negative credit could also be added to your student's report. Just note that your child is not liable for repayment of the debts incurred by you on the credit report.

Think big picture: You want your child to have strong credit and understand the nuances of managing it over time. Simply adding your child as an authorized user can help bridge the gap toward independence when they can begin qualifying for credit on their own after graduation. Contact your financial institution for details about credit authorization and ways to extend smart credit to your child.

Credit Pulls

When a lender contacts one of the credit bureaus for an authorized review of credit, it is known in the industry as a Credit Pull. It is important to know the difference between the two kinds of credit pulls: soft versus hard.

Soft Credit Pull

A soft pull of credit is most commonly associated with background checks for employment but is also industry standard for those "pre-approved" financial product offers you may receive in the mail. Soft pulls occur when individuals check their own credit or companies seeking to market financial products review credit profiles. Sometimes, soft credit pulls are authorized for verification of identity, apartment rentals, or car rentals. When preparing to apply for a loan, some borrowers gain a soft pull of their credit to observe any anomalies on the account and begin the process of correcting them before requesting an official hard pull of credit. This is a wise strategy as it prevents unpleasant surprises that may arise from an unexpected loan denial due to incorrect or outdated information on a credit report. The amount of data provided on a soft credit pull is more limited when compared to an actual hard credit pull, but it remains sufficient as an overview and very helpful for monitoring purposes. So it is important to understand the difference and ask beforehand if it is a soft credit pull or not.

Hard Credit Pull

A hard pull of credit occurs whenever applying for new credit. Mortgages, car loans, and credit card applications all trigger a hard pull by the issuing financial institution to determine if the borrower can be approved and the risk associated with lending to this individual. A hard pull of credit provides detailed information on a credit report, including total lines of credit, payment history, record of delinquencies or defaults, and a credit score. Based on this information, the lender will determine an interest rate reflective of the risk in lending. Consequently, lower interest rate loans are provided to borrowers who have demonstrated positive repayment habits, while higher interest rates are provided to borrowers with greater risk in repayment or default. Each time a hard-pull credit inquiry is authorized, the credit score can reduce slightly. The logic is that a person requesting additional credit translates into an increased risk. In practice, requesting new credit normally only reduces an already strong credit score by a few points. If several requests occur over a 45-day period, for instance, when "rate shopping" for mortgage, auto, or private student loans, the credit score may reduce nominally. However, excessive numbers of credit inquiries over a long period of time can serve to deteriorate a credit score, so carefully plan requests for credit to keep scores optimal. This is especially important when orchestrating college plans, as private student loan borrowers can position themselves to qualify for low interest rates to supplement their college expenses or gain a low rate consolidation after graduation.

TIP

Do a soft pull of credit with your children so they may check their own credit and begin to learn how to use credit to their advantage. This lesson can be refreshed annually, as each person is entitled to at least one free soft-pull credit report every year.

How to Fix an Error on a Credit Report

The three major credit bureaus now accept disputes online. In general, contact each of the three credit bureaus and the credit provider that provided the disputed information with an explanation of what you are disputing and why, and include any documentation you have to support your claim. Based on your state of residence, you may be eligible to receive a free credit bureau report to verify that your dispute has been corrected.

COLLEGE LOAN REFINANCING AND CONSOLIDATION

Recent college graduates have opportunities to consolidate their student loans into one loan. In many cases, consolidation loans substantially benefit borrowers by streamlining payments to one lender, reducing the interest rate and extending the term of the loan to make repayment amounts lower. The potential downside of consolidation loans: the longer a loan is extended, the more total interest that will be paid on the loan.

As with other loans, college consolidation loans are offered by the federal government and by private lenders.

Federal Direct Consolidation Loans

In a federal consolidation, all of a student's federal student loans are combined into a single loan with an interest rate based on a weighted average of all the loans' interest rates rounded up to the nearest one-eighth of one percent. This rate then remains fixed for the life of the consolidated loan. There are no fees associated with federal loan consolidation.

Consolidation loans help streamline repayment after graduation, making loans more manageable.

TIP

Federal student loan consolidations are available through the Federal Direct Loan Program and there are no additional fees to process your application. If prompted by a third-party loan processor to pay an out-of-pocket fee for a federal student loan consolidation, take a closer look. You can simply apply for your federal consolidation loan at www.studentloans.gov and avoid paying unnecessary fees. Be sure to continue making payments on the loans to be consolidated during the application process.

While this type of loan consolidation does not reduce the overall interest rate, it does make it possible for the term of a loan to be extended, which can make repayment easier. This benefit also means that the borrower will be paying more in total interest because of extended payment periods. Benefits of federal loan consolidations include:

- Guaranteed approvals in nearly all cases, with fixed interest rates

- Income-based repayment plans that can reduce minimum monthly payments to meet a percentage of income while extending the loan term to 20+ years

Issues to consider when evaluating a federal loan consolidation:

- Once loans are consolidated, they cannot be undone or consolidated again, unless a new Direct Loan was taken after the initial consolidation. A new consolidation loan is possible to include the new loan.

- If the loans to be consolidated have special features, such as borrower benefits (i.e., an interest rate deduction or loan forgiveness), those features will likely be lost in a consolidation.

- Private credit loans cannot be included in a federal loan consolidation.

- The borrower will pay more in total interest if the loan period is extended.

Private Consolidation Loans

Relatively new to the student loan market, private consolidation loans differ from Federal Direct Loan consolidations in some significant ways:

- Private credit loans are credit tested, which means that some borrowers will be rejected because their credit profile is inadequate. A co-signer may be needed for a borrower to gain approval.

- Borrowers with good credit may receive a lower interest rate on the new consolidation loan resulting in actual savings, unlike the federal consolidation program, which does not reduce the interest rate.

- Private credit consolidation loans permit the refinancing of both federal and private loans.

- Fixed and variable rate loans are generally available.

Important issues to consider when evaluating a private credit consolidation loan:

- While borrowers may gain access to lower interest rates by consolidating their federal loans in a private loan consolidation, they forfeit some attractive features in the federal loan program, including income-based repayment and loan forgiveness options available with Federal Direct Loan consolidations.

- Not all borrowers will qualify for a private credit consolidation loan because of the credit test.

- Consider a co-signer release option. Private consolidation loans rely on credit for approvals and may need a co-signer, with duties again often falling to the parents. Private student loan consolidations may offer a co-signer release. Co-signers may be released from their repayment obligation when the primary borrower makes a designated number of on-time monthly payments (chosen by the lender but often 24, 36, or 48 months). Once released, the co-signer is no longer liable for the debt. This increases a co-signer's capacity to take on new credit and is especially helpful for families with multiple children. Not all private student loan consolidations have a co-signer release, so always check before finalizing an application and confirm the exact eligibility requirements.

Private Loan Consolidations Offer True Refinance

A true refinancing of a loan means that debt is reissued by the lender with a new and, ideally, lower interest rate. In student lending, a Federal Direct Loan consolidation is not a true refinancing, because it uses a weighted average of the loans' existing interest rates to set the new interest rate.

True refinancing is available only through private consolidations, when borrowers benefit from lower rates and savings on interest. Not all borrowers will be eligible for a private consolidation loan as a result of the requirement that applicants undergo a credit check. Also, private credit student loan borrowers forego more favorable repayment options associated with the federal loan programs.

A Good Idea: Pay Interest on Student Loans While the Student Is in School

Student loans generally permit borrowers to defer all payments (interest and principal) until after graduation. For federally subsidized loans, the federal government in effect pays the interest for the student, so the amount the student borrows does not increase. For private credit loans and unsubsidized federal loans, interest is accruing and will ultimately be paid by the student. While in school, students may pay the interest as it accrues or they may capitalize the interest, which means simply permitting the interest amount to be added to the outstanding principal amount.

Here's a simplified comparison. Student A (Alison) takes out a $10,000 loan at 5 percent in her freshman year and enters a 48-month payment deferment until she graduates. Student B (Brian) takes the same $10,000 loan at 5 percent but agrees to make interest-only payments while he is in school over the next 48 months.

Initial Student Loan	Interest Rate	Time in School	In-school Monthly Payment	Debt at Graduation	Required payment on 10-year schedule	Total debt + interest to repay
Alison: $10,000	5%	48 months	$0	$12,000	$127.28	$15,273.43
Brian: $10,000	5%	48 months	$41.67	$10,000	$106.07	$12,728

A little bit of diligence goes a long way, as Brian was able to save about $2,545 in total interest costs through interest loan payments beginning his freshman year.

In addition, the student builds the positive habit of debt management on a month-to-month basis, making sure he has financial means, as well as tools like a checking account, to accomplish this goal. This is a simplified illustration, but it demonstrates a true path to establishing good debt-management habits.

Chapter 11 Takeaways

What you can do to help your student who is in high school or at the start of college become financially literate and responsible:

- **Use the college selection and financing process to talk to your high school student about cost and budgeting.** Use the college selection and financing discussion, choice of major, and expected employment and income as a good starting point to focus your high school student on the bigger picture of budgeting—and the consequences and trade-offs of economic choices.

- **Ensure that students understand how credit is obtained, the importance of maintaining an excellent credit record, and how FICO® scores can change.** This discussion is an important step in helping your student take responsibility for their financial future. How students plan to manage their money, use financial products, and budget in college will lay the foundation for their financial future.

- **Postgraduate student loan consolidation may help students reduce their monthly payments, but be sure to understand the benefits and trade-offs between the different consolidation options.** Consolidating under the federal program will not reduce the interest rate on the loans but will stretch out lower payments over a longer period of time, resulting in a greater total amount of interest and principal paid. Private loan consolidation or refinancing programs may lower the interest rate for some borrowers, particularly those with strong credit scores, but could result in less favorable repayment options.

- **Check FICO® scores annually at** www.AnnualCreditReport.com.

- There is no single best solution for all students because each has unique financial circumstances and goals.

Chapter 12

Create a Family College Plan—You'll Be Glad You Did!

Let's finish up where we started—with the very first words of the book:

Fortunately, there are only two questions that students and families have to answer when it comes to college:

- *Can the student get into the school they want?*

- *How can families pay for it?*

HERE'S WHAT YOU NEED TO DO

That's the theme of this chapter. So here's what you need to do: Find the relevant grade category below for each of your children, and follow the financial and academic guidance to build a comprehensive college plan for your family.

- Pre-Schoolers Through Fifth Grade (page 226)

- Sixth Through Eighth Grade (page 230)

- The High School Years (page 234)

    - Ninth Grade: Freshman Year (page 237)

    - Tenth Grade: Sophomore Year (page 242)

    - Eleventh Grade: Junior Year (page 247)

    - Twelfth Grade: Senior Year (page 253)

For each of those grade cohorts, you will find guidance to address these two important topics:

- **College Affordability:** Steps to take now to minimize debt and maximize college options, including how to save for and finance college, access financial aid, and utilize scholarships.
- **College Admissions Preparation:** What you and your student need to know about the admissions process and steps to take during the high school years to prepare for and subsequently manage the senior-year college application process.

In addition, each grade discussion includes the following:

- A "Student Financial Literacy" section that generally introduces activities and topics that are appropriate for the age cohort
- Three important focal points to help you and your child prepare for eventual success in the college selection and admissions process

As the years go by, the emphasis evolves from mostly financial planning for younger families to academic preparedness as your student gets closer to actually selecting colleges and submitting admissions applications.

Before we dive in, make sure to obtain a Social Security Number for your child. It's an important detail that should not fall through the cracks, as you will need this number for a variety of reasons, including establishing a 529 savings plan.

Pre-Schoolers Through Fifth Grade

Yes, college seems far away, but it will be here before you know it. Your primary goal is to set up a disciplined savings program, monitor the cost of college, and enjoy seeing your child grow. Remember, when it comes to saving money, your most powerful ally is time: the more you have, the more your savings can compound and grow.

Here's what to do:

Understand the Financial Elements of Affording College

Project College Costs

- How much does college cost now?
- How much will it cost when your child enrolls in college?

Project Savings

- Open a college savings account for each child.

  - How much have you saved to date?

  - How much can you begin to save each month—starting this month?

  - Many families feel overwhelmed with too many current bills or saving for their own retirement to start saving for college now. Even modest amounts saved now will help a lot later: If you save $25 per week (the cost of a few coffees and snacks), in eighteen years you will have saved approximately $37,500 (assuming a 5 percent interest rate). The key is to take advantage of the power of compounding and begin saving ASAP.

  - Put some of the birthday or holiday gifts your child receives in the college savings account.

  - Encourage relatives to use a gifting program to add to the college accounts.

- Project how much you will have saved when each of your children enters college.

  - College is expensive. It may be unrealistic for you (or almost anyone) to save for the entire cost of college. Whatever you can save now will minimize college loans and make college that much more attainable for your children later.

  - Are you saving for each child individually or do you have one "college savings" account for your entire family? When the time comes, how will you determine how much each child will receive? To avoid future shortfalls for your youngest child and the commingling of funds, we recommend that parents set up a college savings account for each child.

Student Financial Literacy

Children watch, listen, and learn from everything adults do—and that includes how we think and feel about money. At a very young age, children observe us exchanging money in the form of currency, card swipes, or digitally. While we shop in stores (brick and mortar or online), they quickly grasp that money is used to buy goods and services. As they tag along to the ATM or on errands, they absorb concepts related to financial literacy. One of the earliest and seemingly unrelated lessons that can lay the foundation for future financial habits revolves around children making everyday choices—picking clothes or food at the market. Simply being aware of choices sets the stage for later life when they will ascribe value to money and understand the trade-offs of spending or delaying purchases based on their ability to afford their wants or needs.

Here are some ideas to help you introduce financial literacy to your child:

Pre-K Children:

- Start with simple activities such as sorting and counting bills and change. Let them hand over cash for store purchases. After grasping the value of currency, they will be prepared to understand the link to swipes and digital payments and, eventually, bank products such as debit and credit cards.

- Play games using fake money with them. One of our favorite board games was Prest-O Change-O, but there are many others.

- Make the connections for them: You work to earn money to buy things you need or want. Talk about your job and other people's jobs, too.

- Talk about the difference between what people need and want and how you allocate your money to each.

- *Sesame Street*'s educators suggest having three jars to help very young children understand about basic money allocations. One jar each for Savings, Spending, and Sharing.

Kindergarten Through Fifth Graders:

- Play more sophisticated games involving money—Monopoly® for children is among the best-known games.

- Start introducing the concept of earning money via an allowance for doing chores. Some believe $0.50–$1 for each year of age is a good guide for younger children.

- Talk about the link between your job, earning money, and what you do with the earnings (save, spend, donate). Have them designate their earnings for spending, saving, and giving. Consider the *Sesame Street* three-jar methodology, one each for Saving, Spending, and Sharing.

- Make them aware of the importance of NOT sharing information online.
- Open a savings account for your child—and take them along when you open it.

What You Need to Know to Build a Strong Foundation and Prepare for the Future College Admissions Process

College is a long way off, so this is not the time to stress or become too concerned about preparing academically for the college application. Kids need to be kids. Enjoy this time, and help them develop their own interests and natural abilities. For now, here are some ways that you can help your school-age child:

- Read to them regularly.
- Monitor their relative progress compared to classmates and friends to see if there are signs that they are gifted or in need of extra help. Discuss your observations with trained professionals. Getting help now for learning issues may directly affect middle school and high school performance and college choices later.
- Engage in activities of interest to them and allow them to develop their skills and talents. What they do is not nearly as important as finding things they enjoy and have fun doing. This will result in healthy levels of self-esteem.

Three important things you can do for your pre-K through fifth-grader:

1. Open a college saving account and contribute regularly. Encourage grandparents and others to contribute.

2. As your child grows, help him or her establish good study habits.

3. Help your children find and develop their academic strengths, interests, and innate talents; identify any learning and/or behavioral needs, and take remedial action.

Sixth Through Eighth Grade

College may not be imminent, but it's getting closer. The middle school/junior high school years bring fundamental developmental changes as your child transitions into the teenage years and high school. Saving for college continues to be very important. It's also a very exciting time as your child's interests, skills, and aptitudes are fully emerging and you begin to get a glimpse of what they might pursue in high school and college.

Your little child isn't so little any more. Your observations of his or her personality traits, academic capabilities, and interests are important predictors of what the high school years might bring. Is your daughter drawn toward the arts or athletics? What are your son's favorite subjects and interests? It's time for them to begin preparing for success in high school and beyond by building their academic and extracurricular foundation.

Here's what to do:

Understand the Financial Elements of Affording College

It's not too early to take a few minutes each year to begin doing some "what if" analyses on the cost of college. Tracking college costs now and the rates of increase in their costs will help you understand what you'll likely be able to afford and how much you may be dependent on financial aid and scholarships in a few years.

Project College Costs

- How much does college cost now?

- What is the cost of a specific college? Your alma mater, for example.

- How much will it cost when your student will matriculate? See what it will cost for different types of colleges:

  - Community colleges

  - Private four-year colleges

  - Public in-state or out-of-state colleges

Do some preliminary analysis now to determine if you might qualify for financial aid using an Expected Family Contribution calculator.

Project Savings

If you have a college savings account, continue contributing. If not, open one immediately.

- How much have you saved to date?

- How much can you begin to save each month—starting this month?

- How do your projected savings stack up to the projected costs of college?

- If you save $25 per week (the cost of a few coffees and a snack or two), in six years you will have saved over $9,100 (assuming a 5% interest rate). Save as much as is appropriate for your circumstances with the knowledge that every bit helps reduce the amount your student may need to borrow. By saving even small amounts, you're doing something wonderful for your child.

- Look for opportunities for your child to contribute to increase the college savings account—birthday and holiday gifts or a portion of their allowance or earnings from odd jobs, such as babysitting, dog walking, and so on.

- Encourage relatives to use a gifting program to add to your children's college accounts.

Project how much you will have saved when each of your children enters college.

- It may be unrealistic to think you can save for the entire cost of college. That's ok. Whatever you save now will make college that much more attainable. When the time comes to pay, financial aid, scholarships, and/or loans will likely fill the gap. Your sacrifice today could substantially reduce the amount that you or your child may need to borrow in the future.

- Evaluate your college savings plan. Are you saving for each child individually or do you have one "college savings" account for your entire family? How will you determine how much each child will receive? Think about setting up a college savings account for each child.

Student Financial Literacy

The middle school years are a bridge between the relatively immature spending habits of elementary school children and the evolving consumers in the middle school, who may now be purchasing online or with their friends at the mall.

- Reinforce the importance of protecting identity and credit information. Sites such as the federal government's OnGuardOnline (www. onguardonline.gov) provide great tips to keep your online transactions as safe as possible.

- Find financial literacy games that children of this age would enjoy. For instance, VISA and the National Football League created Financial Football.

- Have your student create a simple budget or list a few near- and long-term purchases he or she would like to make. Are these needs or wants? How much has been saved for each?

- Open a student saving account and perhaps provide a debit card.

What You and Your Student Need to Know and Do to Prepare for High School and the Coming College Application Process

Middle schoolers have begun to establish themselves academically and with extracurricular activities to prepare for success in high school. Continue to help them prepare for high school by doing the following:

- Reinforcing good study habits: Eighth grade can be considered pre–high school, so refining good study habits now will serve students well in high school. Organization is important:

  - Have a designated time and place to study and do homework.

  - Help your child set up an assignment-tracking system or master the e-system used in school.

  - Discuss the importance of breaking larger assignments into smaller, discrete tasks and estimate how long they will take to complete.

- Determining which activities (art, clubs, music, sports, student government, theater) your child is likely to pursue in high schools—these will evolve into important elements of the future college application.

- Encouraging your child to become engaged in community and/or faith-based activities.

- Using, if necessary, aptitude and skills-development assessments to identify your child's gifts and challenges.

- Talking with your child about their dreams, aspirations, and college and career interests.They will evolve as your child's experiences pile up. How does higher education fit into these goals and dreams?

- Encouraging students who want to get an early jump on practicing for the SAT® to take the College Board's PSAT 8/9. Likewise, the ACT® Aspire is available as early as the third grade to provide a readiness on-track indicator for students in grades 3 through 10.

Three important things you can do for your sixth- through eighth-grader:

1. Open a college savings account or continue contributing regularly if you already have one set up.

2. Reinforce good study habits and provide opportunities to explore interests, aptitudes, and skills. Engage your child in conversations about careers and jobs, the value of college, and the connection between dreams and desires and the hard work it takes to be successful.

3. Determine if your child has identified a particular college that he or she would like to attend. Become familiar with the college's admission requirements. Share the requirements, such as average grades and standardized test scores, with your child, so he or she will be motivated to work toward meeting those standards.

The High School Years

Where did the time go? Some of the days were long, but the years certainly seemed short—a great reminder that the next four years will be gone in the blink of an eye.

You may fondly remember when when getting promoted from one grade to the next was a big deal for your student. One day you will also fondly remember the day your child made it to high school. It seemed so far away not long ago, but now your child is in high school, which means the next major transition will be to college in four years. Breathe. It will be ok.

Smart planning and preparation now can strongly influence the answers to the two fundamental questions that face every family with children on the road to college:

- Which college will your son or daughter attend?

- How will you finance that college education?

IMPORTANT: In September 2015, there were two significant changes to the process for applying for financial aid:

1. Beginning October 1, 2016, the FAFSA® form will be available on October 1 of a student's senior year in high school. Previously, the form was made available on January 1 of the senior year.

2. The "Base Year" definition for financial aid, beginning with the 2017–18 school year, will be a year earlier than was previously required.

The Base Year is the year of the tax return used by the government and colleges to calculate financial aid. For graduates prior to 2017, the Base Year was the "Prior Year" tax return. So 2016 high school graduates used the 2015 tax return information on their FAFSA® and CSS/Financial Aid PROFILE®.

Starting with the class of 2017, the FAFSA® and CSS/Financial Aid PROFILE® will require the "Prior Prior" year tax return information. For those graduating from high school in 2017, the Base Year income data will come from the 2015, not 2016, tax return.

Why is this important? Beginning with the class of 2017, families that may benefit from retitling assets in their student's name (in order to qualify for more financial aid) need to complete these transfers in the sophomore, not junior, year of high school. See Chapter 9 for a complete discussion or the FAFSA® and CSS/PROFILE®.

The dynamics are changing rapidly, and it's helpful for you to begin thinking about how you're going to support your student through the high school years given these two core realizations:

1. **The responsible party is changing.** Your child is going to begin taking an increasingly active role in finding a college, and your role will lessen. By senior year, guidance counselors and colleges will expect your child—not you—to be the primary point of contact. That's the way it should be. After all, it is:

   - The student's application

   - The student's request for financial aid

   - The student's high school record that is being packaged and evaluated by colleges

   And at the end of the rainbow, your son or daughter will be the one to attend the college that is selected.

   This means that you have to acknowledge that there's a tipping point ahead: the responsible party in this process will be your student. This may not happen in the freshman year, but it certainly should by junior year. Your role will evolve to one of active, perhaps very active, support.

2. **The focus of activity is also changing.** From the time your child was born and right through middle school, the predominant focus related to thinking about college revolved around answering the "how will we afford it?" question. Establishing a program to save for college and understanding the cost of college was all you realistically could do. That's now changing quickly. In high school, teachers, counselors, and you are concentrating on preparing your student to address the other question: "which college will your child attend?"

The good news is that when the entire college application process is boiled down, very simply, here's all students need to get into college:

- A high school (or equivalent) track record with:
  - Good grades
  - Demonstrated interest and, preferably, leadership in school, community, and/or faith-based activities:
    - Clubs
    - Sports
    - Theater
    - Art
    - Music
    - Student government
- Standardized tests as required by the colleges
- Strong letters of recommendation
- Essays
- An application that tells a unique story and leads the college to the conclusion that the student will fit into the community and culture of the college he or she wishes to attend.

That's all. Stripped of the emotion, the process for applying to college is not overly burdensome. The key for you is knowing that a substantial portion of the value and guidance you will add and offer is understanding the process: what will and needs to happen in each year of high school to best position your student for success in the college process.

You and your student should utilize all of the resources available to help you through the process. High school guidance and college counselors are extremely important. Not only are they experts in the college admissions process and have relationships with representatives of the colleges, but they will also have insight into your student that you may not. They see, and hear about, your student every day at school. Eventually, counselors will be the ones to write a recommendation and help your student identify others who will also write letters of recommendation. Students should be very strongly encouraged to establish a great working relationship with their counselors and recognize that these counselors will have a substantial impact on the outcome of the college application process.

You may determine that additional assistance is necessary to complement the work of the high school counselors. The average ratio of students to high school guidance counselors nationwide is more than 100 to 1. With this heavy load, counselors need lots of lead-time and have limited capacity to meet privately with students for extended periods of one-on-one work. Some families supplement the services provided by the high school with paid services, including:

- Tutors for the standardized tests.

- College "Coaches" who work with high school seniors, and sometimes juniors, to assess interests and identify "safety," "match," or "reach schools" as well as prep for exams and/or help with college essays.

- Services to help with the college or scholarship essays.

Ninth Grade: Freshman Year

For students, the transition from middle or junior high school to high school is stressful—often with a new building with older kids and unknown expectations. As you help them transition and settle into high school, you can also begin to very subtly prepare your maturing child for the college process.

This year, the activities are focused on:

- *Getting your new high school student off to a strong start by doing well academically and actively participating in interesting extracurricular activities.*

- *Spending some time thinking about how you will pay for college.*

Here's what to do:

Understand the Financial Elements of Affording College

Project College Costs

Paying for college is on the horizon, and it's time to begin a more in-depth "what if" analysis. It's also a time for realism. You know what you have saved and can now reasonably begin to project what will be available in four short years for college. It's not too late to increase savings. It will all help. The goal now is to understand in general terms how much you may need to rely on financial aid, scholarships, and loans to pay for college. Zero in on costs for specific schools that seem to be of interest to your student. Take some time to determine how much college will cost, based on tuition, room and board, and other fees for different types of colleges:

- Community colleges

- Private four-year colleges

- Public in-state or out-of-state colleges

Project Savings

- Continue contributing to a college savings account if you have one. If not, open one immediately.

  - It may be unrealistic to think you can save for the entire cost of college now. There are very few years left to permit compounding (the Rule of 70) to carry the day. That's ok. Whatever you save now will make college that much more attainable four years from now. Your sacrifice today could substantially reduce the amount that you or your child may need to borrow in the future.

  - Determine how your current and projected savings stack up to the projected costs of college.

- Look for opportunities for your student to contribute to increase the college savings account.

- Continue contributing birthday and holiday gifts and some portion of your child's allowance or earnings from jobs.

- Encourage relatives to use a gifting program to add to the college account.

- Evaluate your college savings plan. Are you saving for each child individually or do you have one "college savings" account for your entire family? If you have one account, do you plan to allocate a portion to each student prior to college or draw from one account when each enters college? You may want to set up a college savings account or segregate these funds for use by your soon-to-be college student.

Project Financial Aid Need

- Become familiar with key elements of the financial aid process—it's not too early!

- Do some analysis now to determine if you might qualify for financial aid using an Expected Family Contribution calculator. This is a great indicator of how much you will be expected to pay.

- Determine how your current and projected savings line up with this estimate of what your expected contribution might be.

Student Financial Literacy

Begin developing your student's knowledge of the cost of college and generally how you're planning to pay for it.

- Is your student aware of how much different colleges will cost? Does he or she understand the financial choices that will be made?

  - What is the cost implication of attending a public or private college? Public in-state tuition, room and board, and fees are often significantly less than those costs for out-of-state students attending a public school in another state.

  - What are the travel and other costs associated with attending schools far from home?

  - What is the cost of living at home versus living on campus for one or more years?

  - Is there adequate campus housing for all four years?

  - What is the cost and feasibility of living in off-campus housing/apartments?

- Is your student aware of how much, even generally, you have saved for a college education? If so, does he or she know that the cost of a particular college will be a major factor in the final decision for your family?

- Is your student aware of all of the sources of funds to pay for college?

  - Savings and gifts
  - Wages from working
  - Financial aid
  - Scholarships and grants
  - Loans

- Is your student beginning to look for potential scholarships and contests? Paying for college will likely require different sources of funds. Your student may be able to enter contests now that will provide grants or scholarships to be applied to the cost of college.

- Is your student aware of the importance of protecting his or her identity and credit information—and yours, too? Sites such as the federal government's OnGuardOnline (www.onguardonline.gov) provide great tips to keep online transactions as safe as possible.

College Applications Are Just a Few Years Away

Be mindful of the fact that in three short years, students will "package" themselves in a college application. Strong performance now will increase college options later. Here's a path to success for you and your freshman to be ready for the senior year college application process:

- Identify your student's natural interests, aptitudes, and skills to help steer him or her to areas of interest to pursue in high school and eventually college.

  - Some middle schools and many high schools conduct various assessments.
  - Discuss these tests with your student and engage in discussions about the results and academic strengths and weaknesses. Guidance counselors will use the information to help with course selection to help your student achieve high school and college success.
  - Begin to discuss prospective careers based on these areas of interest.

- Engage your student in conversations about college. Does he or she know:

- College admissions requirements generally?

- The differences between highly selective and less selective colleges?

- The opportunities and challenges of public schools and private colleges?

- Choose, with the help of a guidance counselor, classes and courses of study that are appropriate for the type of college (highly selective, selective, etc.) that is attractive to the student. Excellent grades in Honors and AP® courses may be required for admission to the most highly selective colleges, but for other schools a less rigorous path may be appropriate. The most competitive colleges require:

  - Honors and/or Advanced Placement® courses

  - Five academic subjects per semester

  - Three to four years of mathematics

  - Three to four years of laboratory sciences

  - Three to four years of social studies and/or history

  - Two to three years of foreign language

  - Three to four years of English or English literature

- Determine if your student should consider taking the PSAT/NMSQT® early to experience standardized testing, evaluate how he or she performs, and identify areas of focus to improve their future scores.

- Encourage your student to join high school, community, and or faith-based activities in art, music, theater, sports, student government, or any other club of interest. Will there be leadership opportunities as high school progresses? A consistent record of participation and leadership will evolve into important elements of the future college application.

- Reinforce good study habits.

- Talk to your student about dreams and aspirations. They will evolve as experiences pile up. How does college fit into these goals and dreams?

- Find out if your student has identified a particular college to attend. Become familiar with the college's admission requirements. Share the requirements, such as average grades and standardized test scores, with your child so he or she can to work toward meeting those standards.

Three important things you can do for your freshman to begin preparing for the college process:

1. Open a college savings account or continue contributing regularly. Begin engaging your student in discussions about the cost of college and about paying for college. Do you expect your child to have some skin in the game by contributing to their college savings account?

2. Encourage conversations about careers and jobs, the value of college, and the connection between dreams and desires and the hard work it takes to be successful. Is your student taking the courses and doing well enough to be competitive candidates at the schools of interest?

3. Support activities in the classroom and extracurricular pursuits.

Tenth Grade: Sophomore Year

Sophomore year brings a stronger focus as students begin to hear more buzz about college from the juniors and seniors. Decisions they make about course selection, preparation, and activities are important. Good grades in difficult courses are better than outstanding grades in easy courses since college admissions committees seek students who challenge themselves.

High school will be 50 percent completed very soon and the track record your child is establishing is the foundation for the college application.

This year, the activities are focused on:

- *Establishing a strong record of academic and extracurricular performance as a foundation for the college application.*

- *Beginning to refine your plan to pay for college.*

- *Starting preliminary, informal exploration of the type of college or specific colleges that may suit your child and their costs.*

Here's what to do:

Understand the Financial Elements of Affording College

Project College Costs

Begin to sharpen your financial plan. Has your student expressed interest in particular colleges? Is there a preliminary list or an indication of the type of school of interest? Do some "what if" analysis based on the cost of:

- Specific colleges of interest to your student

- Different types of colleges (including your alma mater):

  - Community colleges

  - Private four-year colleges

  - Public in-state or out-of-state colleges

- Your Expected Family Contribution (EFC) if your child were applying to college this year. This is your Base Year that will be used to calculate financial aid when your student is applying to college. You should take action in retitling your and your student's assets this year to maximize eligibility for financial aid from colleges that accept them. (See Chapter 9.)

Project Savings

Continue contributing to a college savings account if you have one. If not, open one immediately.

- It may be unrealistic to think you can save for the entire cost of college now. There are very few years left to permit compounding to carry the day. That's ok. Whatever you save now will make college that much more attainable. When the time comes to pay, financial aid, scholarships, and/or loans will likely fill the gap. Your sacrifice today could substantially reduce the amount that you or your child may need to borrow in the future.

- Determine how your current and projected savings stack up to the projected costs of college.

- Look for opportunities for your student to contribute to increase the college savings account, such as birthday and holiday gifts and/or some portion of allowance or earnings from jobs.

- Encourage relatives to use a gifting program to add to the college account.

- Evaluate your college savings plan. Are you saving for each child individually or do you have one "college savings" account for your entire family? It's time to begin determining how much each child will receive to defray the college expenses. You may want to set up a college savings account or segregate these funds for use by your soon-to-be college student.

Student Financial Literacy

Refine your student's knowledge of the cost of college and how you're planning to pay for it.

- Is your child aware of what different colleges will cost?

- Is there recognition of the financial choices that will be made?

  - What is the cost implication of attending a public or private college? Public in-state tuition, room and board, and fees are often significantly less than those costs for out-of-state students attending a public school in another state.

  - What are the travel and other costs associated with attending schools far from home?

  - What is the cost of living at home versus living on campus for one or more years?

  - Is there adequate campus housing for all four years?

  - What is the cost and feasibility of living in off-campus housing/apartments?

- Is your child aware of how much, even generally, you have saved for a college education? If so, does your child know that the cost of a particular college will be a major factor in the final decision for your family?

- Is your child aware of all of the sources of funds to pay for college?

  - Savings and gifts

  - Wages from working

  - Financial aid

  - Scholarships and grants

  - Loans

- Has your student begun looking for scholarships and contests for tenth graders? Paying for college will likely require different sources of funds. Your student may be able to enter contests now that will provide grants or scholarships to be applied to the cost of college.

- Is your student aware of the importance of protecting identity and credit information? Sites such as the federal government's OnGuardOnline (www.onguardonline.gov) provide great tips to keep your online transactions as safe as possible.

What You and Your Sophomore Need to Know and Do This Year to Manage the Senior-Year College Application Process

Avoiding the sophomore slump takes some focus as students may relax now that the novelty of high school is over. This is the bridge year from being an underclassman to upperclassman. The college admissions process will begin in earnest next year, so there is increasing intensity at school and socially around the whole topic of college.

- Ensure that a strong foundation is in place from which the college application will be built:

  - Good grades in challenging classes.

  - Extracurricular activities—look for leadership opportunities.

- Take aptitude and skill-assessment exams to provide a framework of interest and aptitudes. These exams will often help a student begin to develop specified career interests, which then concretely inform the student about job and salary prospects.

- Interact with the high school guidance counselors. They play a critical role in guiding students through the coming college process.

- Begin researching colleges—learn about the different types of schools (public vs. private, colleges vs. universities, four-year vs. two-year). Which seems best suited to your student?

- Begin identifying specific colleges:

  - Which colleges have majors or courses of study in areas of interest for your student?

  - What are the pros and cons of each particular school?

- Share the admissions requirements of specific colleges or a category of colleges so your child can see the average GPAs and test scores of admitted students, and provide motivation to maintain or improve grades.

  - Is this college best known for preparing students for graduate school or for getting a job? Does this align with your student's expectations?

    - What is the job placement rate?

    - What are the average starting salaries for graduates? Are there statistics for the college telling the average starting salary by major?

  - Is the school a safety, match, or reach based on your student's evolving academic profile?

  - Which college might provide the best value for your student: a good education for the desired job at the lowest cost and the least amount of student loans?

- Begin to get a feel for college campuses and their culture. Maybe casually check out a college fair, attend an event at a local college, or simply drive through campuses when you're in the area. In two years, finding the right "fit" will be an integral part of the college selection process.

Three important things you can do for your sophomore to begin preparing for the college process:

1. Open a college savings account or continue contributing regularly. Begin engaging your student in discussions about the cost of college and about paying for college. Do you expect your child to have some skin in the game by contributing to the college savings account or by taking a student loan?

2. Encourage conversations about careers and jobs, the value of college, and the connection between their dreams and desires and the hard work it takes to be successful. Is your student taking the courses and doing well enough to be a competitive candidate at the schools of interest?

3. Begin the process of finding colleges by doing online research, perhaps informally visiting a campus or attending a college fair.

Eleventh Grade: Junior Year

This year will be action packed as the process for finding a college heats up. The new upperclassmen are becoming leaders of the school and zeroing in on how to find a great college fit based on their academic qualifications, extracurricular interests, and personality. Standardized exams are coming, along with college fairs and visits and a more intense focus from the guidance counselors.

In ten short months, your junior will be a rising senior with a near-final college list, test scores in hand, letters of recommendation to be solicited, and applications to be completed.

This year, the activities are focused on:

- *Shaping your plan to pay for college*
- *Preparing for and taking the standardized exams*
- *Assembling a preliminary college list*
- *Understanding the college application and financial aid processes*

Here's what to do:

Understand the financial elements of affording college

Project College Costs and Financial Aid

For high school students graduating in 2016 and 2017, colleges will use your tax return from this year (tax return for 2015 for both 2016 and 2017 high school graduates) as your Base Year for the purpose of calculating financial aid. You should take action to retitle your and your student's assets, this year to maximize their eligibility for financial aid from colleges that accept your student. (See Chapter 9.) In addition, it would be wise to do the following:

- Determine your Expected Family Contribution (EFC) if your child were applying to college this year.

- Spend some time understanding the required forms for financial aid:

  - FAFSA®

  - CSS/Financial Aid PROFILE®, if your child will apply to colleges that require it.

- Ensure that the college list your student is assembling matches the school list you are using to determine how affordable a particular college might be. Be very concrete and honest.

  - How much of a gap is there between the costs of the colleges your student is interested in and your savings—an indication of how dependent your family might be on financial aid, scholarships, or loans to pay for college.

  - How much financial aid have colleges on the list traditionally provided to families in your income bracket?

  - What scholarships might be available from the college or third parties? Become familiar with the deadlines and requirements now, while there's no pressure and you have time to plan and decide which are likely to be pursued.

  - How much loan money (federal and/or private) would be required for your student to attend this school?

    - What is the projected monthly payment after graduation compared to the student's projected income?

▪ After graduation, will the projected debt be affordable for you and your student?

Project Savings

- Continue contributing to a college savings account if you have one. If not, open one immediately.

  ◆ It may be unrealistic to think you can save for the entire cost of college now. There are very few years left to permit compounding to carry the day. That's ok. Whatever you save now will make college that much more attainable. When the time comes to pay, financial aid, scholarships, and/or loans will likely fill the gap. Your sacrifice today could substantially reduce the amount that you and your student may need to borrow in the future.

- Determine how your current and projected savings stack up to the projected costs of college.

- Look for opportunities for your student to contribute to increase the college savings account, such as birthday and holiday gifts and/or a portion of the allowance or earning from a part-time job.

- Encourage relatives to use a gifting program to add to the college account.

- Evaluate your college saving plan. Are you saving for each child individually or do you have one "college savings" account for your entire family? It's time to begin determining how much each child will receive to defray the college expenses. You may want to set up a college savings account or segregate these funds for use by your soon-to-be college student.

Student Financial Literacy

It's time to sharpen your student's understanding of financing their college choice, as well as introduce him or her to some basic bank products.

- Discuss how your family expects to pay for college.

  ◆ How far will savings go?

  ◆ Will you be dependent on financial aid ?

  ◆ Are there scholarship opportunities to be explored?

- Determine if federal loans and/or private loans need to be in the mix.

  - If so, how will the loan repayment schedule affect your student after graduating from college? Make the connection that debt needs to be repaid with the earnings from a job.

  - Use loan calculators to know what the projected monthly payments might be.

  - See what the starting salaries are for jobs of interest. Avoid taking debt in excess of what can be reasonably repaid.

- Talk about the importance of establishing excellent personal finance habits by saving and establishing a good track record of responsible paying.

  - Does your child understand some of the basic financial products? Does he or she have any banking relationships, such as a savings account at a local bank or credit union?

  - Does your student use a debit card that's attached to his or her checking account?

  - What about credit cards? Your student is likely ineligible for a personal credit card, but some credit card companies offer cards to 16-year-olds under a parental account.

  - Have you looked into reloadable prepaid cards? These cards are basically debit cards with an initial amount deposited and offer the ability to make additional deposits.

- Reinforce the importance of protecting identity and credit information. Sites such as the federal government's OnGuardOnline (www.onguardonline.gov) provide great tips to keep your online transactions as safe as possible.

What You and Your Junior Need to Know and Do This Year to Manage Next Year's College Application Process

Use available resources to cast a fairly wide net to assemble the preliminary college list:

- **Online research or the college's website:** take a look online at all of the information, photos, video, and more.

- **Books and printed material:** look over materials produced by the colleges and others.

- **College Fairs:** attend one or more local events. Check with guidance counselors and the local paper for events scheduled near you.

- **College visits:** develop a budget and schedule for visiting college campuses.

- **Guidance Counselors:** attend a "College Night" event, if available at your student's high school, where guidance counselors describe the process used to keep students on track in the college process.

- **Other advisors:** Will you supplement the work of the high school guidance counselor with a paid advisor, sometimes called a College Coach or College Admissions Specialist?

  - Interview one or more to get a feel for the best fit for you, the counselor, and your student. After all, you will pay the counselor to work with your student, so how this person relates to both you and your child is very important.

  - Determine what role the advisor will play?

    - Will the advisor work with your child to evaluate and identify colleges?

    - Will this advisor help with the college essay or preparing for the SAT® or ACT® ?

    - How does the advisor charge for services? Is it by the hour or is there a pre-set amount?

- **Standardized Exams:** Important standardized exams are taken beginning junior year. Students are not required to take all of these exams. Check to see which standardized exams are acceptable to the colleges to which your child will apply and which are best suited to your student's learning profile.

  - **PSAT/NMSQT®:** Usually administered either the second or fourth Wednesday in October. Required to be considered for a National Merit Scholarship.

  - **SAT®:** Most juniors take the SAT® in the spring, and many take it a second time in the fall of senior year.

- **ACT®:** Like the SAT®, most juniors take the ACT® in the spring, and many take it a second time in the fall of senior year.

- **SAT Subject Tests™:** Most students begin taking the SAT Subject Tests™ in their junior year, but the best advice is to take them as soon as possible after the course in the subject of the test is completed. Students applying early decision may need to have all of the required SAT Subject Tests™ completed before the application is due, so check with the college for its requirements.

- **Advanced Placement® Exams:** Juniors taking AP® classes will take these exams at the conclusion of the course.

- Become familiar with the college application process and determine which application colleges on your student's list require:

  - The Common Application—available on August 1 of senior year.

  - The Universal Application.

  - The college's own application.

  - The new Coalition for College Access application—to be used by more than eighty colleges reportedly in the summer of 2016.

- Understand the common elements to all applications and how your student will need to package their academic credentials, activities, leadership skills, and awards to make the best presentation.

- Encourage your student during the summer after the junior year to do the following:

  - Draft the college essay and personal statement.

  - Know who will be asked to write letters of recommendation in the fall.

  - Study for the last round of SAT® or ACT® exams.

  - Determine if your student will seek an Early Decision or Early Action admissions decision.

- Help your student compile a list of college admission representatives from the top few colleges on the list. Students should begin to appropriately network with these individuals. Showing genuine interest is very important and may help candidates on the bubble make it into the class.

Three important things you can do for your junior to begin to prepare for the college process:

1. Talk to your student realistically about how you plan to pay for college. Engage him or her in discussions about the cost of college and how you're likely to pay for college. Do you expect your student to have some skin in the game by contributing to the college savings account, taking a loan, or working while in college?

2. Manage expectations. Three quarters of the high school career will soon be over. The foundation for the college application has been laid. Where your student ranks in the high school class is now indicative of how competitive he or she may be in the college process.

3. Initiate conversations about careers and jobs, the value of college, and the connection between dreams and desires and the hard work it takes to be successful. Is your student taking the courses and doing well enough to be competitive with candidates at the schools of interest? No matter where your student stands in his or her high school class or where he or she goes to college, their future is bright. Support and encourage your student to dream, pursue goals, and achieve.

Twelfth Grade: Senior Year

The theme for this year: the time has come. It all comes together in the next few months—applications are filed, acceptances arrive, and the deposit check will be mailed.

This year, the activities are focused on:
- *Taking (or retaking) the standardized exams*
- *Finalizing the college list*
- *Applying to college*
- *Dealing with the financial aid process*
- *Selecting the college based on acceptances*
- *Determining how you will pay for the selected college*

Here's what you need to do to keep a step ahead of the game:

Figure Out How You'll Pay

Project College Costs

The deposit to hold a place in a college class will be due on May 1. It's time to zero in on how you will actually pay for each college on your senior's list.

- Be sure that the college list you are using is in sync with your child's and the guidance counselor's list.

- Know the following, whether your student is applying Early Decision, Early Action, or Regular Decision:

  - The total cost of attendance

  - Your Expected Family Contribution (EFC)

  - How much financial aid families in your income bracket have previously received from each school

  - How far your savings will carry you

  - How likely it is that your student will receive third-party grants or scholarships

  - How much of your annual income you might be able to contribute each of the next four years

  - Any other gift aid from relatives or others that might be contributed in each of the next four years

  - If a gap remains, the likelihood that you and/or your student would take out a loan to fill the gap—and the type of loan

  - Federal Direct Student Loan

  - Private Credit Loan

  - Loan from the college or university

  - How manageable the projected debt will be for you and/or your student

- Obtain and file the financial aid forms. Be sure to know the deadlines.

- ◆ **FAFSA®**—Available on October 1 and filed without charge for financial aid consideration in the next school year:
  - ▪ Create a Federal Student Aid ID
  - ▪ File your FAFSA® at: www.fafsa.ed.gov
- ◆ **CSS/Financial Aid PROFILE®**—Available on October 1 and filed for a fee for financial aid consideration in the next school year
  - ▪ Create a Student Account on the College Board website.
  - ▪ File at: https://student.collegeboard.org/css-financial-aid-profile
- Check with the college to ensure that there aren't any other requirements or forms.

Project Savings

- Continue contributing to a college savings account if you have one. If not, open one immediately.
  - ◆ It's nearly impossible for you begin saving for the entire cost of college now. However, you may still have a four- or five-year investment horizon: your student will have expenses in the junior and senior years, so saving now still makes great sense.
- Look for opportunities for your student to contribute to increase the college savings account, such as birthday and holiday gifts and/or some portion of an allowance or earnings from jobs.
- Encourage relatives to use a gifting program to add to the college account.
- Evaluate your college savings plan. Are you saving for each child individually or do you have one college savings account for your entire family? How much will be allocated to your high school senior's college tab? You may want to set up a college savings account or segregate these funds for use by your soon-to-be college student.

Student Financial Literacy

Students who do not yet have a bank account will need one for college. Students often open accounts with banks or credit unions near their home.

Some use banks on or near campus to reduce or eliminate ATM and other fees. In addition, technology allows access through desktop and/or mobile banking.

- A savings account will earn some interest and is often used to hold money prior to transferring to a checking account for expected expenses in the coming semester.

- Student checking accounts with both paper checks and debit cards often do not earn interest or earn very low rates of interest. This account should be used for purchases and expected expenses and not as a savings account.

- Students should be very careful to avoid accounts with fees. Banks charge fees for a host of reasons, sometimes including:

  - Monthly or annual maintenance fees if an account is below a certain minimum balance

    - Often these fees can be avoided by maintaining a minimum monthly balance.

    - Some banks waive these fees for minors or student savings and/or checking accounts.

  - Paper statements, which can usually be avoided by choosing an account with online paperless statements

  - Overdraft, which occurs when a check or debit is drawn against an account that does not have sufficient funds to cover the withdrawal

    - Students with savings and checking accounts with the same financial institution should ensure that they have Overdraft Protection, which is an electronic link between the savings and checking account that automatically transfers money from savings to checking if there is a shortfall. This may also be called Cash Reserve Checking.

    - Sometimes, overdraft protection is linked to credit cards. Be careful if this is the case because some banks consider these to be cash advances and will charge a fee for the cash advance.

  - ATM fees

- For replacement cards (and some charge an additional fee for rush service)

- Transactions with cards that are not issued by the bank

  - Other fees, such as using a teller, ordering checks, bounced checks, stop payments, and wire transfers

- Reinforce the importance of protecting identity and credit information. Sites such as the federal government's OnGuardOnline (www.onguardonline.gov) provide great tips to keep your online transactions as safe as possible.

What You and Your Senior Need to Know and Do to Manage the College Application Process

Managing deadlines is ultimately important and can become an issue as your student is balancing the demands of senior year with those of applying to college. Your senior should do the following:

- Check in with a guidance counselor very early in the new school year to finalize the college list and application strategy. Is an Early Decision or Early Action application likely?

- Finalize the college list and application strategy. Is an early decision or early action application likely?

- Get feedback on the college essay

- Determine who will provide the strongest letters of recommendation and contact them.

- Agree on the final testing strategy: Retake the SAT® or ACT®? Is it necessary to take any SAT Subject Tests™

- Make final campus visits and arrange for college interviews, if required or for information.

- Know which applications are required by the colleges:

  - Common Application. Open an account at: https://apply.commonapp.org/createaccount

- ◆ Universal Application. Open an account at: https://uca.applywithus.com/users/sign_up
- ◆ The college's own application
- ◆ The new Coalition for Access, Affordability, and Success application that's being used by more than ninety U.S. colleges and universities

Once the college decisions have arrived, here's what to do if your student has been accepted, deferred or wait-listed, or rejected:

Accepted. Congratulations! You have successfully guided your child through the college admissions process.

- If it was an Early Decision acceptance, you can relax and follow the school's direction to enroll.

- If it was an Early Action or regular decision, the tables have turned, and now it's your family's turn to decide.

  - ◆ Which school offers the best academic and social fit? Was your student accepted into a special program? You may want to make another visit during an accepted students' day to get a better feel for the culture and fit.

  - ◆ Compare financial aid packages. Colleges may be able to increase their aid packages in light of competition but be careful not to appear to be "negotiating" aid packages. If your student is absolutely convinced a school with a lesser aid package is the right school, you may inquire if there might be an opportunity to increase the aid package. It is nearly impossible to handicap how effective this may be.

Wait-listed or deferred. This "no-man's land" can be very frustrating as many students have little real chance of moving onto the accepted list at most colleges. If your student wants to pursue the school, he or she (NOT YOU) should do the following:

- Contact someone he or she corresponded with or spoke to during the admission process—an admissions officer, alumni interviewer, or regional representative—to express a genuine passion to attend.

- Try to find out where he or she stands on the list and if there is something specific to do to be admitted. Colleges often rank students on the list and offer admission in order. It's ok for the student to ask where his or her name is on the list so there is some indication if admission is even a remote possibility.

- Ask the guidance counselor to follow up to reinforce why your student is a great fit for the college.

- Avoid being a pest. Your student should periodically inform the school of new achievements or academic success to show that the school is a great match and that he or she will contribute to the make-up of the class.

Rejected. The unfortunate reality is that colleges reject many well-qualified students.

- Appealing a rejection is possible, but few colleges overturn these decisions unless there are some extenuating circumstances missed in the original decision. It may make your child feel better to make the appeal, but the odds of overturning the decision are low.

Three important things you can do for your high school senior:

1. Help your student keep track of college application, scholarship application, and financial aid application deadlines. There is zero tolerance for missing deadlines.

2. Get the finances straight. Talk to your senior realistically about the plan to pay for college. Prior to filing the applications, discuss what will be necessary to pay for each school. Does it look like he or she will need to incur debt?

3. Do not eliminate a college from consideration simply because it is very expensive and you do not have enough savings to cover the cost or the amount of debt necessary to pay is very large. Your student may unexpectedly receive a great merit-aid award. You won't know until you receive the financial aid package, so don't assume anything.

Congratulations!

You did it. Your senior has now been accepted by a college and will soon transition to young adulthood as a college student! You and your family successfully navigated a process that may have started more than fifteen years ago. Be sure to acknowledge and celebrate this tremendous achievement.

Acknowledgments

This book, and Invite Education, is the product of decades of our own experience and the insightful work of many, many others. We are grateful to each and every contributor.

Special thanks and a debt of gratitude to our families for their insight, patience, and advice as Invite Education was launched and this book was written. Our collective experiences and passion for education shaped all that is written here.

We are particularly grateful for Ken O'Connor's work. His on-the-ground experience in a financial aid office, expertise in the college admissions process, and knowledge of the challenges facing college-bound families makes this a better book. Many thanks to David Bader, who helped us set the the voice and structure of the book. We are also indebted to the fantastic business, creative, editorial, and marketing teams at Peterson's, particularly Robyn Thurman, Lori Gloer, Bernadette Webster, Jill Schwartz, Julie Ammermuller, Tamara Cribley, Stephanie Benyo, Jeffrey Lee, and Rachel Warrington.

Without the Invite Education platform and methodology, there would be no book. Mark Soper led our initial platform development team that included John Pierce, Isaac Cambron, and Daisy Laflamme. Christi Mazareas and Joe Wrinn worked tirelessly to develop the first content.

A special thanks to two 529 Industry leaders—Marcos Cordero and his team at SavingForCollege and Kathy Hamor, Executive Director of the College Savings Foundation—for their personal and professional encouragement and support of Invite Education.

In the early days, Tim Sichler served as our volunteer jack-of-all-trades who helped shape Invite Education's conceptual framework. He introduced us to Tunde Agboola, a marvelously talented software engineer who took a great leap of faith to join Invite Education as our first employee. His contributions to the Invite Education platform and this work are incalculable. Rick Blaisdell, our Chief Technology Officer, brought us into the big time with his experience and wisdom.

The book is substantially better because of the reading, editing, and technical expertise shared by Barbara Tornow, a good friend for many years and the retired Senior Advisor to the Vice President for Enrollment at Boston University; Jeff Jackson of White Pine Advisors; Matt Carpenter and Bill Rabbitt from College Funding Services; and Wayne Weber from Gift of College.

Others have made or are making significant contributions to the development of Invite Education, including Stephen Dow, Vince Sullivan, Peter Quinn, Judy Flynn, and Joe Grillo, as well as, our summer interns Emelio Teran, Matthew Kennedy, and Brady Mokrzycki.

Hopefully the efforts of all of these talented people will help families be better prepared to plan and pay for college.

Many thanks to all of you for your friendship, support, and contributions to this book and to Invite Education.

John & Peter

Appendixes

Appendix A

529 Programs by State

	MANAGER	TYPE	IN-STATE TAX DEDUCTIBLE?
ALABAMA			
CollegeCounts 529 Fund	Union Bank & Trust Company	Direct Sold	Yes
CollegeCounts 529 Fund Advisor Plan		Advisor Sold	Yes
ALASKA			
John Hancock Freedom 529		Advisor Sold	No
T. Rowe Price College Savings Plan	T. Rowe Price Associates, Inc.	Direct Sold	No
University of Alaska Savings Plan		Direct Sold	No
ARIZONA			
Arizona Family College Savings Program	College Savings Bank	Direct Sold	Yes
Fidelity Arizona College Savings Plan	Fidelity Investments	Direct Sold	Yes
Ivy Funds InvestEd Plan	Waddell & Reed, Inc.	Advisor Sold	Yes
ARKANSAS			
The Gift College Investing Plan	Ascensus College Savings	Direct Sold	Yes
iShares 529 Plan		Advisor Sold	Yes
CALIFORNIA			
ScholarShare College Savings Plan	TIAA-CREF	Direct Sold	No

	MANAGER	TYPE	IN-STATE TAX DEDUCTIBLE?
COLORADO			
CollegeInvest Direct Portfolio College Savings Plan	Ascensus College Savings	Direct Sold	Yes
CollegeInvest Smart Choice College Savings Plan	FirstBank	Direct Sold	Yes
CollegeInvest Stable Value Plus College Savings Program	MetLife	Direct Sold	Yes
Scholars Choice College Savings Program	Legg Mason, Inc.	Advisor Sold	Yes
CONNECTICUT			
Connecticut Higher Education Trust (CHET)	TIAA-CREF	Direct Sold	Yes
CHET Advisor	Hartford Life Insurance Company	Advisor Sold	Yes
DELAWARE			
Delaware College Investment Plan	Fidelity Investments	Direct Sold	No
DISTRICT OF COLUMBIA			
529 Savings Plan	Calvert Investment Management, Inc.	Direct Sold and Advisor Sold	Yes
FLORIDA			
Florida 529 Savings Plan	Florida Prepaid College Board	Direct Sold	No
Florida Prepaid College Plans		Prepaid Plan	No
GEORGIA			
Path2College 529 Plan	TIAA-CREF	Direct Sold	Yes
HAWAII			
HI529—Hawaii's College Savings Program	Ascensus College Savings	Direct Sold	No
IDAHO			
Idaho College Savings Program (IDeal)	Ascensus College Savings	Direct Sold	Yes

	MANAGER	TYPE	IN-STATE TAX DEDUCTIBLE?
ILLINOIS			
Bright Directions College Savings Program	Union Bank & Trust Company	Advisor Sold	Yes
Bright Start College Savings Program - Advisor	OppenheimerFunds, Inc.	Advisor Sold	Yes
Bright Start College Savings Program - Direct		Direct Sold	Yes
College Illinois! 529 Prepaid Tuition Program	Illinois Student Assistance Commission	Prepaid Plan	Yes
INDIANA			
CollegeChoice 529 Direct Savings Plan	Ascensus College Savings	Direct Sold	Yes
CollegeChoice Advisor 529 Savings Plan		Advisor Sold	Yes
CollegeChoice CD 529 Savings Plan	College Savings Bank	Direct Sold and Advisor Sold	Yes
IOWA			
College Savings Iowa	The Vanguard Group and Ascensus Investments, Inc.	Direct Sold	Yes
Iowa Advisor 529 Plan	Voya Investment Management	Advisor Sold	Yes
KANSAS			
Learning Quest	American Century Investment Services, Inc.	Direct Sold	Yes
Learning Quest Advisor		Advisor Sold	Yes
Schwab 529 College Savings Plan	American Century Investment Services, Inc.	Direct Sold	Yes
KENTUCKY			
Kentucky Education Savings Plan Trust (KESPT)	TIAA-CREF	Direct Sold	No
Kentucky's Affordable Prepaid Tuition	Kentucky Higher Education Assistance Authority	Prepaid Plan	No
LOUISIANA			
Student Tuition Assistance and Revenue Trust (START) Saving Program	State Treasury	Direct Sold	Yes

	MANAGER	TYPE	IN-STATE TAX DEDUCTIBLE?
MAINE			
NextGen College Investing Plan – Direct Series	Merrill Lynch	Direct Sold	Yes
NextGen College Investing Plan - Select Series		Advisor Sold	Yes
MARYLAND			
Maryland College Investment Plan	T. Rowe Price	Direct Sold	Yes
Maryland Prepaid College Trust	College Savings Plan of Maryland Board	Prepaid Plan	Yes
MASSACHUSETTS			
U. Fund College Investing Plan	Fidelity Investments	Direct Sold	No
U. Plan Prepaid Tuition Program	Massachusetts Educational Financing Authority	Prepaid Plan	No
MICHIGAN			
MI 529 Advisor Plan	TIAA-CREF	Advisor Sold	Yes
Michigan Education Trust	Michigan Education Trust	Prepaid Plan	Yes
Michigan Education Savings Program	TIAA-CREF Tuition Financing, Inc.	Direct Sold	Yes
MINNESOTA			
Minnesota College Savings Plan	TIAA-CREF Tuition Financing, Inc.	Direct Sold	No
MISSISSIPPI			
Mississippi Affordable College Savings	TIAA-CREF Tuition Financing, Inc.	Prepaid Plan	Yes
Mississippi Prepaid Affordable College Tuition Program	State Treasurer's Office	Direct Sold	Yes
MISSOURI			
MOST—Missouri's 529 College Savings Plan – Direct Sold	Ascensus College Savings	Direct Sold	Yes
MONTANA			
Achieve Montana	Ascensus College Savings	Direct Sold	Yes

	MANAGER	TYPE	IN-STATE TAX DEDUCTIBLE?
NEBRASKA			
Nebraska Educational Savings Trust "NEST" Advisor College Savings Plan	First National Bank of Omaha	Advisor Sold	Yes
Nebraska Educational Savings Trust "NEST" Direct College Savings Plan		Direct Sold	Yes
TD Ameritrade 529 College Savings Plan		Advisor Sold	Yes
The State Farm College Savings Plan		Advisor Sold	Yes
NEVADA			
Nevada Prepaid Tuition Program	Nevada Higher Education Tuition Trust Fund	Prepaid Plan	No
Putnam 529 for America	Putnam Investment	Advisor Sold	No
SSgA Upromise 529 Plan	Ascensus College Savings	Advisor Sold and Direct Sold	No
The Vanguard 529 Savings Plan		Direct Sold	No
USAA 529 College Savings Plan		Direct Sold	No
NEW HAMPSHIRE			
Fidelity Advisor 529 Plan	Fidelity Investments	Advisor Sold	No
UNIQUE College Investing Plan		Direct Sold	No
NEW JERSEY			
NJBEST 529 College Savings Plan	Franklin Templeton Investments	Direct Sold	No
Franklin Templeton 529 College Savings Plan		Advisor Sold	No
NEW MEXICO			
The Education Plan	OppenheimerFunds, Inc.	Direct Sold	Yes
Scholar'sEdge		Advisor Sold	Yes
NEW YORK			
New York's 529 Advisor-Guided College Savings Program	Ascensus College Savings	Advisor Sold	Yes
New York's 529 College Savings Program Direct Plan		Direct Sold	Yes
NORTH CAROLINA			
North Carolina's National College Savings Program	College Foundation, Inc.	Direct Sold	No

	MANAGER	TYPE	IN-STATE TAX DEDUCTIBLE?
NORTH DAKOTA			
College SAVE	Ascensus College Savings	Direct Sold	Yes
OHIO			
BlackRock CollegeAdvantage Advisor 529 Savings Plan	BlackRock Advisors	Advisor Sold	Yes
CollegeAdvantage Direct 529 Savings Plan	Ohio Tuition Trust Authority	Direct Sold	Yes
OKLAHOMA			
Oklahoma College Savings Plan	TIAA-CREF	Direct Sold	Yes
OklahomaDream 529 Plan	TIAA-CREF and Allianz Global Investors Distributors, LLC	Advisor Sold	Yes
OREGON			
Oregon College Savings Plan	TIAA-CREF	Direct Sold	Yes
MFS 529 Savings Plan	MFS Fund Distributors, Inc.	Advisor Sold	Yes
PENNSYLVANIA			
Pennsylvania 529 Guaranteed Savings Plan	Pennsylvania Treasury Department	Prepaid Plan	Yes
Pennsylvania 529 Investment Plan		Direct Sold	Yes
RHODE ISLAND			
CollegeBoundfund—Advisor-Sold Plan	Alliance Bernstein L.P. (through June 30, 2016)	Advisor Sold	Yes
CollegeBoundfund—Direct-Sold Plan	Ascensus College Savings/Invesco	Direct Sold	Yes
SOUTH CAROLINA			
Future Scholar 529 College Savings Plan - Advisor Program	Columbia Management Group, LLC	Advisor Sold	Yes
Future Scholar 529 College Savings Plan - Direct Investment Program		Direct Sold	Yes
South Carolina Tuition Repayment Program (SCTPP)	South Carolina State Treasurer's Office	Prepaid Plan	Yes
SOUTH DAKOTA			
CollegeAccess 529	Allianz Global Investors Distributors LLC	Direct Sold and Advisor Sold	No

	MANAGER	TYPE	IN-STATE TAX DEDUCTIBLE?
TENNESSEE			
TNStars College Savings 529 Program	Tennessee Department of Treasury	Direct Sold	No
Tennessee Baccalaureate Education System Trust Prepaid Plan		Prepaid Plan	No
TEXAS			
Lonestar 529 Plan	NorthStar Financial Services Group, LLC	Advisor Sold	No
Texas College Savings Plan		Direct Sold	No
Texas Guaranteed Tuition Plan	Texas Prepaid Higher Education Tuition Board	Prepaid Plan	No
Texas Tuition Promise Fund	NorthStar Financial Services Group, LLC	Prepaid Plan	No
UTAH			
Utah Educational Savings Plan	Utah Higher Education Assistance Authority	Direct Sold	Yes
VERMONT			
Vermont Higher Education Investment Plan	Intuition College Savings Solutions, LLC	Direct Sold	Yes
VIRGINIA			
CollegeAmerica	American Funds Service Company	Advisor Sold	Yes
CollegeWealth	Virginia College Savings Plan Board	Direct Sold	Yes
Virginia 529 inVEST		Direct Sold	Yes
Virginia 529 prePAID		Prepaid Plan	Yes
WASHINGTON			
Guaranteed Education Tuition (GET)	GET Committee	Prepaid Plan	No
WEST VIRGINIA			
The Hartford SMART529	Hartford Life Insurance Company	Advisor Sold	Yes
SMART529 Select		Direct Sold	Yes
Smart529 WV Direct		Direct Sold	Yes

	MANAGER	TYPE	IN-STATE TAX DEDUCTIBLE?
WISCONSIN			
Edvest College Savings Plan	TIAA-CREF Tuition Financing, Inc.	Direct Sold	Yes
Tomorrow's Scholar College Savings Plan	TIAA-CREF/ Voya Investment Management	Advisor Sold	Yes
PRIVATE PRE-PAID PLAN			
Private College 529 Plan	Tuition Plan Consortium, LLC.	Direct Sold	No

Appendix B

Invite Education: College Planning Center

This book is a complement to www.InviteEducation.com—an online age- and grade-appropriate resource for parents and students to use in planning and paying for college. We created this innovative and comprehensive website to help families navigate the stressful, emotional, and complex college process and maximize their chances of fulfilling their family's college dream.

www.InviteEducation.com is a tablet- and mobile-friendly site that offers all of the information, tools, and services discussed in this book. In addition, you can personalize your College Planning Center account with a file for each child to track financial and academic progress and update it as the college years approach.

WHAT YOU WILL FIND AT WWW.INVITEEDUCATION.COM

www.InviteEducation.com offers free information, tools, and services that are meant for single use, as well as an opportunity to open a permanent College Planning Center account, which stores information and can be modified as your children progress to and through high school.

- Free Information, Tools, and Services:
  - College Cost Calculator
  - Cost of Delaying Calculator
  - 529 Comparison Calculator

- ◆ Articles and a Blog

- ◆ Links to Resources

- Link to Purchase a Personalized College Planning Center Account for Your Family

  - ◆ Use discount code **3Free** to get the first three months free.

Why Open a College Planning Center Account?

The College Planning Center is a one-stop, comprehensive experience to help you understand how to save and finance a college education, select a college that is a great fit, and prepare your child for the college admission process. Your College Planning Center account will guide you through the entire process from saving for college all the way to filing the applications, and you can start no matter the age of your child.

Monitor Each Child Individually and See the Impact on Your Family

- Planning and paying for college is a family affair. This program permits you to get grade-specific information for each child AND see how possible college choices will affect your family financially. You can easily do scenario testing by the projecting the costs of specific colleges and your savings to determine the ultimate financial impact of various college choices and assumptions on your family.

- Gauge your child's likelihood of admission for each college being considered and update your child's profile as standardized test scores come in and GPAs change. This information can help motivate your child early in high school and manage expectations as your child progresses through the high school years.

- Update your savings and estimates of financial aid to adjust your expected financing plan for each college. Will you be dependent on financial aid or college loans? The Financial Center helps identify funding gaps and offers suggestions to close the shortfalls so there are no surprises when the first bill arrives.

Spend a Little Time—Get a lot of Information!

The piles of information on all aspects of the college process are boiled down to what's most relevant for the age or grade of your child. Get the information you need quickly and in a form that's easily readable.

- Information is presented in a "snackable" and easily readable format.

- You will have access to "Helpful Resources" to help navigate the process.

Focus on What's Important to You

The College Planning Center offers you flexibility to follow the grade-specific "Passport for Success," explore specific topics, or use one of the search engines:

- **College Search:** Search over 7,000 colleges, save and update those of interest, and get a view of the cost of each along with personalized affordability and admissibility indicators.

- **Scholarship Search:** Sort and save results to get free money.

- **529 Savings Plan Search:** Compare and learn about Plans in your state and other states to select one that best meets your needs.

See How to Afford Future College Costs with the Family Financial Center

- Enter or update current and on-going savings amounts to project how much may be available when each child is ready for college.

- Receive an estimate of your Expected Family Contribution.

- See if financial aid and your savings will cover the cost or if there is a shortfall. If there is a shortfall, you will get tips on how to close the shortfall. You'll also see the projected monthly student loan payment compared to a projected salary, based on the college major, to see if a particular college might be affordable for your student.

Use the Calendar Alert System: Never Miss Deadlines

- **Savings:** Receive periodic reminders to refresh your analysis to determine how much your current savings plan will contribute to your overall financing plan for a specific college.

- **College Admissions Deadlines:** You and your student will get alerts of approaching deadlines for colleges your student chooses, upload the most important to your e-calendar, and get alerts of approaching deadlines.

- **Scholarship Deadlines:** Track important scholarship deadlines and upload and get alerts of approaching deadlines.

- **Standardized Tests:** You and your student will get alerts to register for the ACT® and SAT® and when the test date is approaching.

Leverage the Resource Center: One Place for All the Resources and Links You Need

- Links to the SAT®, ACT®, Common Application, Universal Application, FAFSA®, CSS/PROFILE®, and more

- Articles and searchable information

- Resources—some free and others discounted—to address the many aspects of planning and paying for college.

MORE ABOUT WWW.INVITEEDUCATION.COM

You may invite anyone—your spouse, children, a financial or academic advisor, guidance counselors, or any other third party—to your account, and you can restrict their access to ensure they are able to see only what you want them to see: perhaps the tab for just one child or all of them. You can also easily restrict who sees the financial assumptions and savings information.

The Invite Education website is designed to provide the college planning tools and comprehensive information needed to help you intelligently and properly plan and pay for college for children of all ages. Simply put, our goal is to ensure that parents can help their children make sound decisions, prepare well for college, and increase their chances of success in college and beyond.

Whether or not you keep your College Planning Center Account beyond the three-month free trial, we encourage you to utilize the site for the free tools and information that will certainly help you achieve your family's college dream.

Go to www.InviteEducation.com. Enter the code **3Free** for a free three-month trial.

Index

C

D

G

H

I

N

O

P

Q

R

S